"Thomas interviews athletes, coaches, and sports personalities as he covers topics related to activism from the sporting realm and how it is perceived in America. A necessary read." —*Library Journal*, a Best Book of 2018

"In *We Matter*, Thomas strives to show the influence professional athletes can have when they join the conversation on race, politics, and civil rights. Thomas conducted fifty interviews, which included Kareem Abdul-Jabbar, Bill Russell, Laila Ali, Michael Bennett, and Eric Reid, among many other athletes, as well as journalists, television personalities, and family members of unarmed Black men who were shot and killed. Thomas also explored his ties with the Wizards and spoke with John Wall, Bradley Beal, and current majority team owner Ted Leonsis." —*Washington Post*

"Former NBA player Etan Thomas releases the timely and necessary *We Matter: Athletes and Activism*, in order to add useful, relevant words to the conversation on athletes and their activism." —*The Root*

"In his new book, *We Matter: Athletes and Activism*, Thomas tirelessly interviews a range of people from NBA icons to the families of crime victims to illustrate the importance of athletes using their voice for more than just sports." —*Athletes Quarterly*

"Thomas has spent his life examining inequities in America particularly as it relates to race and poverty. He's spoken out against war, helped Oklahoma prisoners write poetry, and rallied against police brutality . . . Thomas says he's not alone: that social issues dominate what athletes talk about behind closed doors." —*Tulsa World*

"Thomas's book focuses on the intersection of race and politics in sports. It features interviews with several Basketball Hall of Famers including Bill Russell, Kareem Abdul-Jabbar, and Oscar Robertson, countless NBA all-stars, and the Suns' Jamal Crawford. Beyond basketball, the book also addresses the NFL's collusion case of embattled players Colin Kaepernick and Eric Reid, as well as discussions with family members of police brutality casualties including Eric Garner, Philando Castile, and Terence Crutcher." —*Arizona Republic*

"The honest conversations, published in transcript form and often accompanied by black-and-white photos, serve as a primer on recent police violence cases, a history lesson on the first athletes who stood up for racial justice, an examination of the experience of being young and Black in the United States, and an insightful look at how it feels to lose a loved one to tragedy, from contributors such as Jemele Hill, Kareem Abdul-Jabbar, and Carmelo Anthony . . . An important read, executed uniquely."

—*School Library Journal*, starred review

"Etan confronts our collective challenges and reminds us that life is not just a game, but demands a constant struggle for justice."

—Amy Goodman, *Democracy Now!*

"[A]n accessible collection of interviews and essays addressing racial profiling, the power and relevance of athletes' voices, gender inequality, and mental health stigmas . . . In appealing and intelligent writing, Thomas encourages fans and athletes to share their voices and inspires thoughtful action through this well-timed and significant collection . . . An excellent resource to spark discussions and motivate positive community expression and involvement."   —*Library Journal*

"A former NBA player and current activist . . . returns with a collection of dozens of interviews on the subject of race in America—all supporting the efforts of athletes to speak out and up . . . Voices of pain, anger, and hope resound through these pages—and through the reader's heart."

—*Kirkus Reviews*

"Former Marquette University basketball player and twelve-time NBA All-Star Dwyane Wade, along with Basketball Hall-of-Famer Kareem Abdul-Jabbar . . . are among more than fifty athletes, coaches, executives, and media personalities featured in a timely new book exploring the intersection of sports and politics."   —*Isthmus*

"Thought-provoking and often intensely moving reading."   —*Booklist*

ETAN THOMAS, a former eleven-year NBA player, was born in Harlem and raised in Tulsa, Oklahoma. He has published multiple books including: *We Matter: Athletes and Activism* (voted a top ten best activism book of all time by BookAuthority), *More than an Athlete, Fatherhood: Rising to the Ultimate Challenge,* and *Voices of the Future.* Thomas received the 2010 National Basketball Players Association Community Contribution Award as well as the 2009 Dr. Martin Luther King Jr. Foundation Legacy Award—both honoring his advocacy for social justice. He is a senior writer for BasketballNews.com and a regular contributor to the *Guardian* and The Undefeated. He can frequently be seen on MSNBC as a special correspondent and cohosts a weekly show with Dave Zirin called, *The Collision: Where Sports and Politics Collide.*

POLICE BRUTALITY

AND WHITE SUPREMACY
THE FIGHT AGAINST AMERICAN TRADITIONS

ETAN THOMAS

EDGE
of SPORTS

Police Brutality and White Supremacy: The Fight against American Traditions is the latest title in Dave Zirin's **Edge of Sports** imprint. Addressing issues across many different sports at both the professional and nonprofessional/collegiate level, Edge of Sports aims to provide an even deeper articulation about the daily collision between sports and politics, giving cutting-edge writers the opportunity to fully explore their areas of expertise in book form.

Published by Akashic Books
©2022 Etan Thomas

Hardcover ISBN: 978-1-63614-057-5
Paperback ISBN: 978-1-63614-056-8
Library of Congress Control Number: 2021948587

Cover design: Sohrab Habibion
Back cover photo: Koshu Kunii/Unsplash

Edge of Sports
c/o Akashic Books
Brooklyn, New York, USA
Instagram: AkashicBooks
Twitter: AkashicBooks
Facebook: AkashicBooks
E-mail: info@akashicbooks.com
Website: www.akashicbooks.com

TABLE OF CONTENTS

 *Introduction*

In this book, I have taken a deep dive into the topics of police brutality and white supremacy. Many chapters begin with a personal perspective—how I have been affected currently with my family or while growing up.

I have interviewed NBA superstars Isiah Thomas and Craig Hodges about Rodney King; Abiodun Oyewole from the legendary Last Poets about the Central Park Five; Jemele Hill and CNN's Jake Tapper about the US Capitol invasion; and former NBA player Stephen Jackson about his close friend George Floyd.

I have interviewed people directly involved with or affected by those terrible events—such as Rodney King's daughter Lora Dene King, and Raymond Santana of the Central Park Five—hearing their perspectives, thoughts, feelings, and how they are currently functioning in society. I have included the voices of retired police officers Carlton Berkley, Sonia Pruitt, and Joe Ested, to get their thoughts on practical, realistic solutions to the multitude of problems with the way we police in America. They all had interesting suggestions and explained the ways they are actively trying to make these changes become reality. I interviewed police officers for this book because I'm not antipolice, just anti–police brutality.

I have also interviewed a number of white people. It is important to hear white voices speak to these topics because their influence on other white people can be tremendous. Furthermore, there is a segment of the population that will only be able to hear something if it comes from another white voice. That's just reality. So it can resonate powerfully to hear WNBA legends Sue Bird and Breanna Stewart discuss white privilege, Rex Chapman examine racism and white supremacy, and Rick Strom explain why it's crucial to highlight the various ways in which white privilege is manifested.

I spoke to the Sisters of the Movement, a collective of women who share a tragic bond: they all have loved ones who have died at the hands of police. They are the faces and families behind the hashtags, working together to protect Black lives from police violence. I interviewed Alissa Findley, sister of Botham Jean and cofounder of Sisters of the Movement, as well as Amber and Ashley Carr, sisters of Atatiana Jefferson, and Michelle and Ashley Monterrosa, sisters of Sean Monterrosa.

On April 28, 2021, Senator Tim Scott, the only Black Republican in the Senate, said in a televised GOP rebuttal to a speech by President Joe Biden, "Hear me clearly, America is not a racist country." Bishop Talbert Swan tweeted in response: *George Zimmerman got ZERO yrs for murdering Trayvon Martin. Police got a combined ZERO yrs for murdering Tamir Rice, Sandra Bland, Breonna Taylor, and Eric Garner. Delontre Barefield, a Black man, got 34 yrs for killing Jethro, a police dog. But America's not a racist country?*

I love dogs. Our dog Marley has brought much joy to my family. And yet there is historic relevance to the way Black people in this country are valued, as compared with the lives of dogs. Michael Vick's dogs received more justice than most Black and Brown people murdered by the police. But this is not a new phenomenon—America has a tradition of this very dynamic, and it goes back centuries.

Racism and white supremacy have been quite prominent in this country, both historically and presently. In addressing this problem, we have to be honest about their origins. They didn't begin with Donald Trump, although he did provide a leader for white supremacists to rally behind. The origins of white supremacy go back to the very beginning of this country we call America. In this volume, I explore how it became interwoven into Christianity, in this "Christian nation," despite standing in direct opposition to the actual teachings of Christ. I spoke to fellow Christians, including NBA analyst Chris Broussard and Bishop Talbert Swan, who discuss how Christianity has been twisted, contorted, and used to justify and implement white supremacy. We tackled the fact that white evangelicals supported Trump at an alarming rate, in sharp contrast to NBA superstar Steph Curry. Curry spoke passionately to me about his dedication to Jesus Christ and his opposition to Donald Trump, not just on a personal level, but as a Christian.

I have arranged the chapters by topic, to make it easier to digest. I want this book to be utilized in different ways. I feel the leaders of this push for police reform and accountability should include family members of the victims of police brutality. I want this to serve as a reference for practical solutions to the issue of policing in America. I also envision this book providing a history lesson on white supremacy, its origins, and the promotion of it both past and present. Additionally, my aim is to stress the importance of white allyship in eradicating white supremacy and racism, not just in words but in deeds. It's not a matter of blame or white guilt, it's a matter of changing what has historically been woven into the fabric of American society.

From as far back as I can remember, I have taken my kids with me to speaking engagements, panel discussions, keynote speeches, and other public events. This began with my oldest, Malcolm. At first I would have him say a prayer to start the event, and before long I had him opening or closing events with poems. So I have closed this book with a poem that Malcolm wrote after an early draft of this book.

Rodney King

In a racist society, it is not enough to be nonracist, we must be antiracist.
—Angela Davis

My introduction to police brutality was the Rodney King case. I was at Carver Middle School in Tulsa, Oklahoma. I remember seeing the video on the news. I couldn't believe what I was seeing. My middle school mind was desperately trying to comprehend why I was looking at five white cops beat a Black man worse than a dog. I was shocked, horrified, disgusted, and any other adjective you can think of.

I had of course heard and read about police brutality, but I had never seen it like this. This was back in the early nineties when we didn't have social media. Young people today can see police brutality on their cell phones every other week, but for me this was a complete shock.

I remember hearing the verdict. Something like, "The jury finds the defendants Stacey Koon, Laurence Powell, Timothy Wind, and Theodore Briseno not guilty in the beating of motorist Rodney King." And my heart dropped. I was angry. How could this be happening? We all saw the tape. I didn't follow the trial completely, but I saw the tape. They beat him like an animal and we had a verdict that told us that we couldn't trust our lying eyes. That what we all thought was going to be an open-and-shut case somehow resulted in them telling us that they did absolutely nothing wrong legally? They can just do that and get away with it? What possible justification could there be for them to get away with this?

My middle school became a powder keg that was about to erupt. Temperatures were boiling over. I remember some of the girls were crying, and Sheldon, who was a Blood, was talking to Clarence, who was a Crip, and they weren't beefing at all, because they were both upset about the verdict.

I remember Ms. Holmes, a gym teacher, walking into the hallway to tell everyone the bell had rung and fussing at everyone to clear the hall like she did every day, but this day she looked at everyone's faces and turned around and walked back into the gym.

The entire school was really mad. Then I remember word spread about a white student named Kevin making a terrible joke about Rodney King and a piñata, and the entire school turned our anger toward him. He had picked the wrong time to make a joke. It was the match that was needed to light a fire that was burning in all of us.

We searched for him with the intensity of Nate Parker in *The Birth of a Nation*. Nobody said a word. It was understood what was about to happen. We were going to seek justice and make him pay for his words about Rodney King.

Once we found him, our classmate Mia Jackson had already handled the situation, cussed him out thoroughly, and slapped him so hard her handprint was on his face. He ended up apologizing to us and remaining apologetic all through high school.

But everything for me changed that day. The way I looked at the police—I no longer trusted them. I no longer viewed them as "the good guys."

Back in the nineties, we had this program called D.A.R.E. where a cop would come into the school and tell us about the law, and staying out of trouble, etc. The cop who spoke to my class was white. I don't even remember his name, but I do remember that from that point on, I didn't want to hear anything that he had to say. I would protest the session every time he came and would stand in the hall. My teacher didn't even object, she just allowed me the space to peacefully protest, as she knew there were definitely other forms of protest that were readily at my disposal.

I also remember Ice Cube's *The Predator* tape coming out shortly after that and him encompassing everything I was feeling. All of the anger and frustration and loss of trust in the system.

Kickin' up dust is a must
I can't trust
A cracker in a blue uniform
Stick a brotha like a unicorn . . .

There has always been this great debate about music having an influence on young people. Well, for me, Cube's words definitely spoke to the anger that was already there.

My entire world was shattered after that Rodney King verdict. I remember asking my mother, "What happens to Rodney King now? How does someone move on with their life after something like that happens to them? What happens to his family? What happens to his children?" That's why it was such an honor to begin this book with the interview of Mrs. Lora Dene King.

Interview with Lora Dene King
(Daughter of Rodney King)

Etan: Can you describe who Rodney King was before the incident and who he was after the incident? Because a lot of times, people don't understand the aftereffects of police brutality.

Ms. King: My father loved for everyone around him to have a good time. He was a people-pleaser. He would give you the shirt off his back. Really a giving person all around. After that night, a part of him died. And that's something that as a child, I don't wish that upon *any* child. I don't wish that on anybody's family, period. He was very nervous. Very paranoid. He was in constant pain. He was a very proud person so he would never admit it, but I could tell when he was in pain. He had over fifty broken bones. His eye socket was completely busted; he had to reconstruct everything. And to deal with that kind of pain, that's something that doesn't go away. He had permanent brain damage. The news would say all of these things about him later on, not taking into consideration the trauma he was dealing with.

Etan: A lot of times, people look at the settlement as being payback for what the person went through. How did you look at that?

Ms. King: There was a $3.8 million settlement, but half of that went to attorneys. And that's not really a lot of money considering the fact that you have to go your whole life after that. You can't get a job, you have your family, there's three of us, I'm the middle child, you're dealing with the trauma, and at the end of the day that money is really nothing. You're completely damaged for life.

Etan: A lot of people don't understand that every time they see a lawyer on TV speaking on the victim's behalf, those are billable hours, and over many months those bills really accumulate.

Ms. King: Yes, any interaction and phone call, any meeting, is considered billable. And in addition, my father had to pay for all of his own medical needs. He had to pay for complete reconstruction of his entire face and body, so that settlement money dried up so quick just for his immediate needs.

Etan: How old were you when this happened?

Ms. King: I was seven at the time of the beating.

Etan: Talk about the change in your relationship with your father after that.

Ms. King: The first thing that comes to mind is he was very paranoid after the beating. We never had intimate moments. When we would go out to dinner there would always be someone coming up to him, and it could be negative interaction or positive interaction, but we got a lot of both. I remember some of the things that people would say to my father even as a kid—it affected me because I wanted to defend my father, and he would just smile and answer the question. And now that I'm an adult thinking back on it, everything changed.

Etan: What could people possibly have to say negative about your father? He was the victim.

Ms. King: Well, my dad made the news a lot after this. DUIs, he struggled with drug addiction and alcoholism. People were so quick to judge him without taking the time to understand the level of trauma that he experienced and the aftereffects of that trauma.

Etan: I saw an interview where Rodney King was discussing the alcohol addiction and he said he was self-medicating and trying to heal internally. And he kept saying that he had to forgive the officers because the anger he felt inside was eating away at him he used the word "tormenting." A lot of people had strong reactions to him saying he had to forgive the officers, but when he explained it in that context, it just made a lot of sense. People don't understand what your father was going through.

Ms. King: The night of the beating, they were yelling racial slurs, cussing, swearing, etc., at him while they were beating him, and my father was re-living that nightmare literally every single day and night. I think to myself often, I don't think I'm strong enough to recover from that in any way. You thinking you could realistically die and living through it, and that's why I just think they should've gotten him help after that, mental-health help, dealing-with-trauma help.

Etan: How do you personally move forward from that? I see what you're doing with the Rodney King Foundation and you established the I Am a King scholarship and the Walk in Love and the sock racism tags, so you are keeping his legacy alive and you're doing amazing work.

Ms. King: Wow, it's interesting, people never ask me that. I'm still going through it. You know, my father saw my passion to feed the homeless and do workshops with people in prison, and he kept telling me start a foundation and I never wanted to. So after he passed, I was thinking, *How can I honor him? What can I do?* So I started the foundation. He passed in June and I started it in August. And I realized that I was depressed. I stopped every-thing and just worked and went home, worked and went home, that was my routine to busy myself through depression. The last two years, and I'm still going through it, and this year will be nine years since my father passed and I still can't look at his picture for longer than five minutes. Last month was the first time I was able to watch an actual physical interview. I haven't had the strength. I would just break down completely.

Etan: How do you have the strength to do what you're doing now with the foundation?

Ms. King: My dad had all girls but he would talk to us like we were boys. And his thing would be, "Are you gonna sit here and cry about it or are you gonna get up and do something?" So that's what I do now. It would be self-ish of me to sit here and mope about it in my tears when I could be helping somebody with their pain. So the I Am a King scholarship I started because I wanted to uplift and help our Black men. The media has a certain way they portray Black men and demonize Black men like they did my father. The media will literally justify the police slaughtering Black men, so that's my focus, offsetting that. The father is the foundation of where the love starts from—that's a daughter's first love, that's a son's example, and if we lift up our Black men, they can change the world and it will have a domino effect.

Etan: It always amazes me when survivors of police brutality have a passion to help others and to pay it forward. Someone should be helping *you*. But you all want to help others. Talk to me about that.

Ms. King: It would be selfish of me to sit here and not use my pain to help others. That's another way I honor my dad. My pain can help someone else. It wasn't by choice, but now I can make a difference. I often think, *What about the Eric Garners or Rodney Kings or Tamir Rices that were before them who weren't taped, that nobody knew about or ever heard about, and there is nobody to tell their stories or fight for their justice?* So I say yes to fighting for them and no to myself, because I am still dealing with pain, but God gives us the strength to help other people.

Interview with Isiah Thomas

Isiah Thomas is a true basketball legend. He's a twelve-time NBA All-Star, is considered one of the fifty greatest players in NBA history, and was inducted into the Naismith Memorial Basketball Hall of Fame. I talked to him about the Rodney King beating and the history of police abuse. As Isiah Thomas explains, this problem is definitely not new.

Etan: You have been unafraid to speak on issues of race and police brutality for a long time, even when it wasn't a popular subject. Where did that come from? Because in your era, the eighties into the nineties, it was kind of quiet.

Thomas: There was definitely a change in the nineties as far as activism. But for me, I grew up on the West Side of Chicago, and my mom worked closely with Fred Hampton, so activism was always a part of what we did. There is actually a street named after my mom in Chicago on the West Side. Mary Thomas Way. But I was also one of the kids who benefited from the [Panthers's] free breakfast program, and then, after he was assassinated, I had to walk by his house that had the bullets still visibly remaining.

Etan: What was your response to seeing the Rodney King beating and verdict?

Thomas: Unfortunately, I had seen that before in my neighborhood. My brother had his two front teeth knocked out by the police. There were riots in Chicago in '66, '67, '68, and '69. So my first ten years of existence, these were the types of things I was seeing on the West Side of Chicago in terms of police brutality. Growing up and seeing it when everything is burned down, it's not like they came back and fixed everything up, so you had to walk to school through that carnage and every day I had to look at my brother and see the physical scars and the wounds and the emotional scars that was left on him. So watching what happened with Rodney King in '92 was only a reminder of what was going on throughout my childhood. It was a continuation of our fight to be recognized as human. There's only one race of people and that's the human race, and we were put into these subcategories or racialized colors.

Etan: So the Rodney King beating wasn't shocking or a surprise to you at all?

Thomas: No, those riots happened in Chicago for four consecutive years. That was the response to be heard. The voiceless crying out saying, "This is wrong!!! Look what's happening to us as human beings." We just didn't have cell phones to record everything. So what was happening to the victims of police brutality on a daily basis was deemed to not be believable, because we didn't have it on video to show everyone.

Etan: I remember at Carver Middle School in Tulsa, my math teacher, Ms.

Stewart, was asking the class, "Why are they doing this? Why are they burning up their own neighborhoods?" And I remember us Black students telling her, "Because they're not getting justice. You don't understand how they're not treating us as human beings? And people feel like they have no other way for their voice to be heard." And her response was simply, "No, it's wrong, and that's why I can't support them." And it's interesting hearing the same rationale today.

Thomas: I remember when Rodney King happened, I unfortunately heard a lot of the same rationale that your teacher had. We as a society have been miseducated on this concept of race and how we view other human beings, so everything is looked at through racialized lenses and stereotypes. And going back to my growing up in Chicago, this is what I was being taught by Drew Ali, reading John Henrik Clarke, W.E.B. Du Bois, Frederick Douglass, and they were talking about how we have been declassified and taken out of the human race so everything is viewed through eyes of white supremacy. So trying to fight for your humanity in America has always been our fight. So your teacher only viewed what was happening in racialized terms and not human terms, and unfortunately that's the problem with our society as a whole.

Etan: I was in middle school saying to myself, *They wouldn't have treated a white person that way no matter what, because he would be a human.* So how do you navigate through that?

Thomas: We all have to stop believing in this concept of color and race. This system is no different than what Nelson Mandela went through with apartheid in South Africa. You're taken out of your classification as human, and you're placed into color boxes. And they govern, rule, and legislate based on these colors. And that's why Dr. King had conversations with Gandhi and Malcolm X went to Mecca to see what the rest of the world was doing and how people were being treated, acting, behaving, and existing in relation to the color classifications. Now, there have always been religious differences, nationality differences, etc., but to govern and to legislate based solely on skin color, that's where America and democracy has failed and why we are in the position we are in today as a country.

Etan: Rodney King's daughter, Lora Dene King, told me how traumatized her father was afterwards and how he was never the same, and it really hurt my heart to hear it because people don't understand the aftereffects and the impact on the family. She was just a little girl at the time.

Thomas: It's heartbreaking indeed. When you talk about post-traumatic syndrome, I can speak from experience with how it affected my family and how it affected our neighborhood. And I'm sure Rodney King, his daughter, and his entire family was traumatized for years after. Those sirens going off in the neighborhood, anytime you see flashing lights or the uniform, there's an emotional response to that. To this day, I still tell my wife and my kids, "If something is going on with me, don't call the police." And by the way, my brother is a police officer, I have two nephews on the police force, so I know there are some good and some bad. But at the same time, I myself am still traumatized.

Etan: My family and I watched the movie *One Night in Miami*. The part where Jim Brown is talking to this white man on his porch who is talking about how great and amazing Jim Brown is, the records he's broken, and how big a fan he is, then Jim Brown asks to use his bathroom and the white man says, "You know we don't allow N-words in the house." My kids' mouths were wide open, they were shocked he said that after he had been praising Jim Brown. It displayed the dynamic of loving you as an athlete but not seeing you as a human.

Thomas: That's a very unfortunate reality, and yes, I have felt that as well my entire college, professional career, and in life. And yes, it's a reflection on the bigger issue of not being seen as human and not treated as human, and that's what has to change.

Interview with Craig Hodges

Craig Hodges played ten seasons in the NBA (1982–1992), led the league in three-point shooting three times, and was white-balled from the league for his outspoken views and how he utilized his platform. This was a much different NBA than what we have now.

Etan: What were your thoughts after you first saw the Rodney King beating?

Hodges: The biggest part was just the shock. Seeing four or five policemen pummeling the brother mercilessly with their nightsticks. And the manner in which they did it just left me speechless. It was beyond brutality. I looked at it and said regardless of what the brother did, no human being deserves to be beaten like that. There are measures you can take to subdue him without beating him like that. But unfortunately, this has been the mentality of policing in America for generations and nothing has changed, but with Rodney King, that was one of the first times everyone could see it happening in real time. And the fact that someone was smart enough to tape it brought it to America.

Etan: I remember being in middle school and the first thing I thought was, *They wouldn't treat a dog like this.*

Hodges: Exactly, and this happened right at the beginning of the NBA Finals and some athletes were speaking about it, others weren't, but I was like, *Any and everybody should be able to speak to this because this could be your brother, this could be your father or your uncle.* And it was just too obvious and blatant what was going on as far as the racism and the evil of police brutality right there for all of America to see.

Etan: It's interesting going back and watching the media coverage. The person who was the victim was being put on trial. Then they started bringing up his past, almost to justify the beating.

Hodges: So many times in their justification of their actions, they look into the background of people. Whether it be Jacob Blake or George Floyd, and they cherry-pick what they want, and what they are basically saying is, "He deserved to be beaten like that because ten years ago he ran a stop sign and got a ticket." And people are now seeing through the garbage—well, *some* people are seeing through the garbage, but back then, I watched them demonize Rodney King and literally make the case that he deserved exactly what he got.

Etan: Malcolm X once said that the media portrays the Black community as one large criminal element, and they use certain language. I correlated that to what I was seeing with Rodney King and the language they used to justify anything the police did.

Hodges: Absolutely, and seeing things like this is what made me feel the need to have to be vocal while I was playing in the league. I was an athlete, but this goes for everyone no matter what your occupation is. You have to be able to stand on truth and for what is right and to call out what's wrong. We, as a society, have been collectively letting so much slide and we just can't allow it anymore. And we have left a lot on the table for the next generation to fight for, and they are fighting for now.

Etan: The frustrating part is the bar is set so low. We're starting the discussion just fighting for our humanity.

Hodges: We get caught up so much in our differences, whether we're Republican, Democrat, Christian, Muslim, all of these different labels that divide us. We are all humans, and that's the basis that we should be unified on. Kwame Ture told us it's all about organization and we have to all bring what we can to the table and we all have different strengths and attributes and we have to use all of them for this fight.

Etan: In the movie *One Night in Miami*, Malcolm X and Sam Cooke are talking and Malcolm X is challenging him, and you're the first person I thought of when I saw this. He's telling Sam Cooke, "Listen, you're the most talented brotha on earth, your voice can captivate audiences both Black and white, you have all this power, you can play in white venues and be accepted, other musicians can't do that." And then he told him something like, "You're not using the power for good. You're not challenging what is going on with us in society. Black people are dying in the streets and we cannot afford to straddle the fence anymore. We have to pick a side: either you're on the side with us or you're on the side with them." Did you ever feel that level of frustration in relation to what we're talking about now with Rodney King and everything that was happening to us at that time?

Hodges: Yes, I did. And trying to get someone to see it is one hurdle, but to get someone to *feel* it is a whole 'nother mountain to climb. We're at that point now where there is enough information out for people to be able to easily educate themselves as to what's going on. There's really no excuse now. You can't say, "I didn't know about this," because it's everywhere. During the nineties when Rodney King happened, we had great athletes who were similar to Sam Cooke as far as their leverage in white communities, and not nationwide but worldwide, and the option was, do I make a stand or do I get paid? People were hesitant because they were afraid that it would hamper their ability to earn. And that has been the common denominator in us coming up short. Those who have been in position to really make a difference don't. And what I saw from a lot of athletes was, "I'll play my career and then come back after and revisit Black people and Black issues." And from my standpoint, during the time where you are making the wealth and you have the bully pulpit to speak from, utilize that. You may not be able to be all-out Malcolm X with it, but you can definitely have an impact. The Rodney King incident really brought to life what Black people have been facing for centuries, and that's something that not just athletes but *everyone* should be able to speak on.

Etan: By the end of the movie, Malcolm's impact on Sam Cooke showed. Cooke was on this program, and was singing the songs that they liked, and then he said he wanted to sing a song that hadn't been released yet, and it was "A Change Is Gonna Come." And it was passionate and moving and Sam Cooke dropped a tear at the end and they showed Malcolm X smiling. Now, I want to make this correlation to you and Michael Jordan, because people portray it as Craig Hodges was talking bad about Michael Jordan. But it wasn't personal—you saw MJ and the impact he could have had in particular after Rodney King happened, the same way Malcolm X saw the impact Sam Cooke could have had.

Hodges: When Rodney King happened, it was a galvanizing time. Right before the '91 NBA Finals with Michael and Magic, we have the whole world watching, all eyes are on us, and we can have an impact. And to think about how my mom was organizing in the early sixties, she was having this tremendous impact with no resources, and here we are with all of the resources of the NBA Finals, with the two biggest athletes in the game, and the impact you can make just from your voice would be amazing. And that's what I was trying to talk to Magic and MJ about, especially after Rodney King. And here's the thing: in private, we all were having discussions about what was going on, but then in public, we went quiet And now we're at the point where people outside of our community are feeling our pain and we simply can't be private anymore. And that's what Malcolm was telling Sam Cooke: "Hey, talk to them white folks at their clubs," and that was my position with MJ on a lot of things. I would say, "Hey, you have the ear of a lot of people that I can't reach." So yeah, that's a very good comparison.

Etan: One last correlation: I mentioned how Malcolm X watched Sam Cooke on the program singing "A Change Is Gonna Come" and he was smiling. Did you ever feel that after watching Michael Jordan in the last five years or so? MJ has become more vocal, and spoken out against police brutality.

Hodges: Oh yes. I love it. People have to understand that everyone grows at different points in their lives, and I definitely feel like that every time I see not only MJ and Magic but all the young athletes, like LeBron and the current generation of athletes. It's great to see.

The Central Park Five

We have to acknowledge that there are massive problems if we want to fa-
cilitate change. There has been no effort to change the design of this country.
—Elaine Brown

I recently sat down and watched Ava DuVernay's *When They See Us* with
my kids Malcolm, fifteen, and Imani, twelve. The four-part series followed
the infamous NYC Central Park jogger case of five young Black teenagers
falsely accused of raping and beating a white woman in Central Park. It
depicted the NYPD's illegal interrogation and eventual coerced confessions.

During the movie, Imani paused it and said, "Wait a minute, Daddy,
you always tell us that you spent all of your summers in Harlem. Were you
actually there when all of this was happening?" My plan was to talk about
that after the movie was over, but my smart little daughter put the pieces
together before I got the chance.

I explained to Malcolm and Imani that watching this movie was trig-
gering because I remember it happening in real time. Public Enemy had
just come out with the song "Fight the Power," which started, "*1989, a*
number, another summer . . ." My maternal grandparents lived in Harlem
while my paternal grandparents lived in Mount Vernon. During the summers I split my time between them. Grandpa Freddy would take me to the
parks around Harlem to watch the older guys play ball. After they finished,
they let the younger guys get on the court. When we were about to leave,
Grandpa Freddy would run over to a nearby bodega and get something
cold to drink.

On this particular day, the NYPD (as depicted in the movie) were
rounding up young Black and Hispanic teenagers in Harlem as they looked
for suspects. After my grandfather left to get the drinks, I saw the police pull

up. My grandfather always taught me to be aware of my surroundings, so I saw them approaching and said to myself, *This doesn't look right,* and quickly exited stage left. I was semilost for a brief minute, and by the time I got to the bodega, my grandfather had left. The store owner saw us there all the time and knew us. He told me that I had just missed my grandfather, so I should stay put and he'd probably return soon.

I can only imagine the panic that must have been going through Grandpa Freddy's mind. I was eleven years old in 1989, but tall for my age, and I could've surely been mistaken for a teenager the police were looking for. Which was *every* Black and Brown teenager in Harlem. I didn't have any ID because it was not a requirement for kids in Tulsa.

I remember the store owner looking out the window and spotting my grandfather arguing with a few of the police, then asking the person who was sweeping up to watch the register while telling me to stay there. I saw him cross the street and whisper to Grandpa Freddy, who immediately turned around and walked back toward the store. As soon as they came through the door, my grandfather grabbed me and hugged me tighter than he had ever hugged me before. I could literally feel his heart beating through his shirt. He had tears in his eyes and was breathing heavy. The store owner told us to go to the back and sit down for a few. I had no idea what was going on but would soon find out.

For the next few days, the New York media seized on the "Five" and kept a stream of articles coming about the "gang attack," "beasts," "wilding," and the dangers posed by Black and Brown teens in particular. It was disgusting to see, and even at a young age I could comprehend the demonization and generalizations they were making.

A few days later, Grandpa Freddy and I were watching wrestling in the back room when we both heard a scream from my grandmother, whom I called Ning (long story). My grandfather told me to wait there and rushed to go see what was wrong.

Donald Trump was on the TV talking about the Central Park Five case. Ning was furious and crying. She kept saying that he was going to put targets on the backs of every Black and Puerto Rican kid in New York. To this day I still can't remember her ever being this mad. She was screaming, "He's trying to get our kids in the neighborhood killed! They're talking about these kids like they're animals or monsters! Why do they talk about us like that!!! Who is going to protect our kids from the police? That's why we need the Panthers and the Young Lords—who is going to keep our kids safe?"

She was hysterical and all Grandpa Freddy could do was hold her, rock her, and cry with her. They were both terrified for me.

That same night, Ning came to me and hugged me and talked to me for hours. She must've run down every scenario of encounters with the police, telling me what to do and what not to do. I remember her saying, "I know you like to stand with your hands in your pockets when you are nervous or uncomfortable, but you can *never* do that if the police stop you because that will make them nervous and jumpy, and the last thing you wanna do is make them more scared of you than they already are."

That really stuck with me. The police were scared of *me*? They had the guns, they had the power, why would they be scared? And Ning said, "That's exactly right. They have all that and they're still scared and will be quick to pull out their guns, so don't ever forget that."

Ning worked as a counselor at Spofford, which was the main juvenile detention center in New York City at that time. She'd had her share of run-ins with the NYPD and knew how they treated kids who were both innocent and guilty. She told me how the police would take advantage of people who didn't know the law and were unaware of what the police were legally permitted to do.

Some of the other lessons included:

"If you see trouble or a commotion, don't be nosy—you mind your business, grab your little brother, and go the other way."

"Always be aware of what's going on around you, especially in the city."

"Don't ever run. It might be your first instinct if a cop approaches you, but don't do it. Bad things happen when you run."

"Know your rights and study them because people perish for lack of knowledge."

I remember one of Ning's main points was to never, ever speak to the police if they picked me up without her or Grandpa Freddy being present; or, if I was back home in Tulsa, without my parents being present. She stressed it over and over: "Don't say anything. Tell them to call your grandparents or your parents, and you don't have to say a word beyond that no matter what. Don't admit to anything, don't fall for the good cop/bad cop routine, where one cop tries to act nice to you as if they are on your side. Or they send a female cop in to act as if she only wants to help you or bring you a soda or a burger." Ning implored me not to fall for any of that because they are all police tricks to get a confession.

My grandparents actually sent me back to Tulsa early that summer. They were literally afraid for my life.

And as I was sitting there watching *When They See Us* with my kids, I saw exactly what my grandmother told me being depicted.

Interview with Raymond Santana

Raymond Santana, Korey Wise, Kevin Richardson, Antron McCray, and Yusef Salaam each spent a range of five to eleven years in prison for a crime they did not commit. The group had become known as the Central Park Five, but have since adopted the title the Exonerated Five. It was an honor to be able to talk with Raymond Santana.

Etan: First, I want to ask you how you're doing now. I see the pictures on Instagram of you with your wife and you're smiling and you look like you're enjoying life.

Santana: That's what it is. It's about joy and life, right? It's about the little things, the little moments, things that we take for granted on a daily basis. So for me now, that's what life is about. To see where my life has come from 1989 to now, it's a total blessing, so I'm just happy to know that it's here and to be living.

Etan: Who was Raymond Santana before this happened?

Santana: Raymond Santana was this fourteen-year-old kid who was energetic, loved to go to school and hang out with his friends because they were funny to be around. He loved to be goofy, and at fourteen Ray loved hip-hop music. He loved to sketch, one of his passions was that he loved to draw and it started with comic book figures and stuff like that. I was just this carefree kid who never had any dealings with the law, who never had any encounters with police.

Etan: So let's go back to the night when everything happened. You didn't know any of the other Central Park Five, right?

Santana: That's correct. I didn't know any of the other guys. Korey and Yusef are the only actual friends in this story. Kevin lived in the building, he knew them, but it wasn't like they hung out every day. Antron lived maybe two or three blocks down from them. I didn't know them, I lived on the east side of Harlem.

Etan: They made a big thing in the movie about "wilding in the park," and really, it was just young people having fun, right? Is that an accurate description?

Santana: One hundred percent. We went over to the Schomburg houses. I went with a group of guys over to Schomburg because there was to be a party, plus there were these young girls back then that I liked. That's what put me on the west side at that time, because I'm from the east side. When you get to Schomburg, in front of those two towers, all the boys hung out in front of those buildings.

That 110th Street entrance is right there. So back in '89, they hung out there all the time, and that's what happened that night.

Etan: You mentioned that you had never had any dealings with police, never had any encounters or interrogation. I'm guessing that you didn't know not to say anything to the police at all whatsoever, without your lawyer or parent present—nobody broke that down for you?

Santana: No, nobody. I never knew that. Now we know what Miranda is, but back then we definitely didn't know that. Like I said, I never had no dealings, no experiences. You hear that police is bad, because this is the hood, word of mouth, but you have to learn from your own experience. I never had an encounter. So no matter what people can tell you, for a fourteen-year-old boy, when you put him under that extreme amount of pressure, all that stuff goes out the window, it doesn't make sense.

Etan: Each of you had a different experience and I'm trying to think of exactly how it went with you going down to the police station.

Santana: At the gate when I'm arrested, the police officer hit me in the back of the head with the walkie-talkie and so I didn't say anything, I was quiet. They took us to the precinct and they processed us, they had to call our parents, and so they charged us initially with trespassing, menacing. All those misdemeanor charges that said that we had to appear in Family Court. So now our parents had to come and pick us up and then take us home. We waited until the wee hours of the night for our parents to get there, because all of our parents work.

We come from middle-class families. So your parents had to wake in the middle of the night, eleven or twelve at night, to come pick you up from the precinct. So we were sitting there literally with no food, no drink, just waiting, and according to the documents, at two or three in the morning the detectives were saying that they wanted to come in to talk to the boys. But we didn't know about this woman until we were actually put in the interrogation rooms, that's when we found out.

Etan: *When They See Us* showed them talking to your grandmother who didn't speak English, and they had a cop come over and speak to her in Spanish and then took her away from you. Then they started interrogating you a little bit more. Is that pretty much how it happened?

Santana: One hundred percent. We find out now that there's a technique, seven steps that can get somebody to confess. These are tactics against the people of color in these interrogation rooms, and so when you go in, I tell people that you have to look at the playing field. We are fourteen- and fifteen-year-old kids, who never had no dealings with the law. we're under the impression that we're going to be questioned about events that happened that night, you know, which is like, assault charges, running from the police, trespassing, right?

We're not thinking of crimes of rape and murder. Listen, when the detectives want to talk to you, it starts out calm. It starts, "Hey, Raymond, what were you doing that night? Who were you with and what happened?" And you give them a story, then it's, "Okay, but what about this or what about that?" And I'm like, "No, I didn't see none of that. A police car pulled up and they flash a spotlight at the boys and everybody runs, we just did that sometimes. We just didn't do anything, but everybody runs and the crowd is scattered."

I don't know my way in Central Park, so for me, I'm lost. All I'm trying to do is listen for the voice of somebody I know and so it takes me awhile to meet other guys. But we find out that a man gets assaulted in the park, a woman and a man on a bike encountered a group of kids who took them off their bike—this happens while I'm looking for the people I came with. I finally meet some guys who I don't know, but at this point, because I'm not familiar with the park like that, I stay stuck to these guys until I can find my guys.

In the police mind, they go, "Okay, so you didn't see any of that?" and I'm like, "No," which is a perfect explanation of why I didn't see it, but in their mind, I'm not telling the truth. Then they go, "Well, what about the woman?" At that moment, I'm like, "What the . . . ? What woman are you talking about?" And they go, "Yeah, the woman that was raped in the park."

And at that moment, as a fourteen-year-old kid, I'm like, whoa, whoa, whoa, stop, because as kids we do dumb stuff, but rape and murder, robbery, now you have gone too far. The pressure starts to mount, it's a Spanish-speaking detective who's asking me the questions, and then he has to interpret it. The process became long because you have to keep stopping. These were seasoned veteran detectives, this was the elite of the police force.

There's a knock, a short detective comes in and he says, "Ms. Colon," in Spanish, "can I talk to you in the hallway?" And this is the authority figure, the police, detectives, she gets up and she walks into the next room, and at that moment is when it starts, but it starts subtle. A tall detective comes in and he's talking to the detectives about me, and at that moment, I'm like damn, they are just talking about me in my face.

He's like, "Well, who's this guy?" and he's like, "Yeah, this kid, he's withholding information, he's not telling us everything we want to know." At that moment, I'm wanting to say, *You're lying,* but I'm so scared. I'm afraid, and when I look at this tall detective, he gives me this look. He looks me in my eyes and he says, "What the f**k are you looking at?"

At that moment, I'm shook, but then the knock comes back and my grandmother comes back in the room and then we start to proceed with the questions. And it happens a second time, and the second time a different detective comes in, he's more loud, he's more funny. Again, they're shooting the breeze and he tells me that I'm not telling the story and I'm withholding information. So this detective pulls up a stool, pulls it right next to me, he sits really close to me and he just starts talking very forcefully in my ear and it's more like, "You know what the f**k you did, you know you f**king did it. You f**king stuck your d**k in her, right?" and I'm just frozen scared.

At that moment he starts to scream at me, and the detective who's interrogating me starts to scream at me. So now I'm getting it from both angles and I'm like, *I don't know what to do*, but the knock comes and it stops because the detective brings my grandmother back in the room. So at this point, my grandma, she sits down and she sees that I'm physically shaking, I was crying. She says, "Wait a minute, what's going on here? This isn't right, this don't look right, why is he crying?" And the detective is saying, "Well, because he doesn't want to tell us everything and he's withholding what happened to this woman."

And it's at that point that I go, "I don't know what you're talking about." So now I'm starting to talk back a little bit, because my grandmother's sitting there with me and so I'm starting to say, "I didn't see no woman. I don't know about no woman. You got the wrong guy," and we go through the line of questioning again from the top to the bottom, but before we get to the woman, the knock comes again and the detective comes back and he talks to my grandmother. Now, my grandmother was saying, "Look, this don't look right." So the detective said, "Well, let me just explain what's going on. He's going to be okay." She gets up and she walks out.

It's at this point that I focus on the detective and we get to this woman part again, and now I'm drained. It's estimated that we are in these interrogations for fifteen to thirty hours and so this is torture, I'm like, "Look, man, I don't know what to say." I don't, because I'm a fourteen-year-old kid, I can't make a rape up, and so this detective, Detective Arroyo, he bangs on the desk. He gets upset and he's like, "I'm tired of this sh*t, you are going to give me what I want." At this moment he reaches out like he's going to grab me. I'm so scared that I'm thinking, *I am going to die in here, I'm not going to make it out of this precinct and my grandma's in the next room. Nobody's here to help me.*

In the same instance, somebody's voice in the back just starts yelling. He's like, "What the f**k are you doing? Are you crazy? What the, get the f**k out!" and so I looked and there's another detective who comes in and he's balking on this guy who was about to kill me. And I'm listening to him balking on him, screaming, "What the F**k! You don't do this sh*t, get the F**k out of the room!" The detective gets up and leaves and he walks him out through the door, screams on him, then slams the door and I'm like, *Wow, this dude just saved me* . . . Then, here comes the pitch, but I don't know this as a fourteen-year-old kid.

Etan: So they're doing the good cop/bad cop thing.

Santana: Yes, to a T. So when he closed the door, he goes, "Raymond, man, I'm sorry about that." I'm like, "All right," and then he starts shooting this pitch. It's like, "Listen, I know you know these other kids," and he starts giving me names because that night I was arrested, Kevin Richardson was arrested, but what people don't know is that we were arrested with a guy named Steven Lopez, Lamont McCall, and another kid by the name of Clarence Thomas. So this is a whole different five, this isn't Korey, Yusef, and Antron, and what happens is that he's saying, "Well, do you know these kids?" And I say no, and he says, "Well, do you know Antron McCray?" The only reason why Antron McCray's name comes up is because one of those kids whose name is Clarence was Antron's best friend. Clarence gets arrested and they interrogate him. I say, "No, I don't know Antron," and he says, "Well, this kid is in the precinct and he's saying you did it."

I go, "Okay, well, I don't know who Antron is," and at that moment he pulls out this picture, right. He pulls out a picture of Kevin Richardson and he says, "Well, do you know who this guy is?" And I said, "I know him because he's arrested with me, but I don't know him." Then he says, "This is Kevin Richardson," and he says, "Now look at this picture, do you see the scratch under his eyes?"

He had this scratch that came from the police hitting him with the helmet, but we didn't know that at the time. I say, "No, I don't know him," and he says, "That scratch came from the woman fighting him off. Now we know he's going to jail, that's without a fact, but I don't want you to go to jail. I need your help," and then he just left the picture there and he just sat back and everything was silent. And for me as a fourteen-year-old kid, not knowing what to do, where to turn, nobody there to talk to. I said, well, what is a fourteen-year-old boy going to do in this situation? Lie his ass off, because that's all he got left. But I can't lie because I don't know what the facts are. I don't know what happened. So the only thing I can say is, "All right, he did it," and he says, "Who?" I say, "That guy right there, Kevin," and he says, "Okay, well, how did he do it?" I don't know how the fuck he did it. So I've got to lie, I've got to say things, I'm so stupid. Like why I saw him struggling with the woman. "Well, how was he struggling with her?" "He was fighting with her and he took her down with his leg."

Etan: But they can tell that you're making this up. I'm sure they can see that.

Santana: So, he's feeding me info and he gives me the names. It was Kevin Richardson who I used, Antron McCray who I used. I used a guy named Steven Lopez, and Steven Lopez in my statement would have been the actual guy who committed the rape. At this point there was no Korey Wise, there was no Yusef Salaam, because they got arrested maybe a day or two after. So they're not even in my statement. You see how this looks crazy now?

Etan: The scene where they had you all in the room and talking to each other, realizing that the police were running game on all of you—is that kind of how it happened?

Santana: That happens later on. Really, eleven guys went through the system that night. Everybody wasn't charged with the jogging case.

There was Korey and there was a guy named Michael Briscoe, he got charged with assault or something like that. Both of them go to Rikers Island and they get jumped by the inmates at Rikers Island. So everybody's in this room and it isn't until we get to the booking, when we get to the booking they separate us now and they say, "You're going to Rikers Island, and you guys are going to Spofford." So three of them went to Rikers Island and the rest of us all went to Spofford. So at this point it was Yusef, Antron, Steven Lopez, Lamont McCall, and Clarence Thomas. It was seven of us that went to Spofford initially and then the rest went to Rikers Island.

Oh, they did us so dirty, because now, what happens is that we go through arraignment. We have these half-a-million-dollar bails, $250,000 cash, you hear all the charges. We were charged with, I think it was thirteen charges. You have to process all that and then now you're being taken to a jail. When you get to intake, a counselor comes downstairs and he tells us, he says, "Yo, the whole jail wants to kill you all."

Etan: I don't understand. Why did they want to kill you?

Santana: Because at this point the articles were being written and we've been charged with a brutal rape of a white woman in Central Park and now the public outcry starts early. People were already calling for our deaths.

Etan: These are the white inmates?

Santana: No, this is *all* inmates. You become public enemy number one for a rape charge. The only thing that trumps a rape charge in jail is child molestation. So, if you have any of those, you better be ready, you know what I'm saying? Well, this counselor, he came downstairs and he kicked it with us and he just kept it real, and he was like, "Yo, listen, I don't believe everything that I'm reading. I just want to put you on your game, the whole jail wants to kill you." And then they put us through intake and then they separated us again, nobody went together.

Etan: I'm flashing back, because my grandmother worked at Spofford, her name was Constance Bodger, and I remember her coming back, because I'm in New York that very summer. She never believed that you all were the ones who did it. She was like, "Yeah, this whole case doesn't sound right." I remember them all talking and they were like, "No, this doesn't sound right." Not saying that they were legal experts, but I'm just trying to understand how if so many people saw that something didn't sound right, how did they push it through, because they didn't have any evidence. They didn't have any DNA, they didn't have any eyewitnesses, they didn't have anything but coerced confessions.

Santana: When you go back to Spofford, you talk about Ms. B and she's saying—

Etan: Wait, you said Ms. B? That's what they called her. You knew my grandmother?

Santana: I spent seventeen months in Spofford. There was nobody I didn't know. People who worked there, they did band together and say, "Nah, this don't sound right," and so the treatment that you got from them was totally different. They treated us like humans. I remember talking to Ms. B, and her looking me in the eye and telling me, "I believe you." Nobody else had said that to me, not even my own lawyer. So yes, I definitely remember your grandmother, and I was thankful for her.

Etan: Oh, wow, okay, I really didn't expect you to say that.

Santana: People really started to see there was no evidence, because the DNA evidence came back, maybe two months later when Donald Trump took out the ad. Now these counselors are seeing that for themselves and I believe that they protected me in a lot of situations, because it could have been crazy, but it was because they knew, like, "Nah, this kid don't belong here." The night that I was convicted and I came back to Spofford, I went through intake and a lot of the counselors was there waiting for me. When I came back up to the housing unit, that night was like the only night that all the inmates didn't sleep in their beds in my housing unit. I had the back room of the dorm in Spofford and when I got back to my room, all the inmates were either in my room or they were outside my room and they were just showing me support and there was that solidarity. They all understood that I was innocent, that *we* were innocent, and so Spofford, to see it close, was like, wow, you know what I'm saying?

Etan: But then also Spofford changed to just being like a little Rikers Island. But before that, they had actual things to try to help you and give you support and things of that nature. Do you remember Abiodun Oyewole from the Last Poets? I interviewed him for this book as well.

Santana: I remember Abiodun, I loved the workshops he used to do. He used to perform his poetry, "Martin, Martin, Martin." He had another one about Malcolm X and I remember him coming in and back then, even though it was a jail, even though it was a detention center, it still ran on rehabilitation, going to school. Actually, you *had* to go to school, and so what happened with the change was that, even when you go to the division for youth and you go to maximum juvenile facility, because I went to Goshen Secure Center in New York, even that facility changed. All of it changed after Governor Pataki came. He took the college program, he started messing with the budget, and he started putting up more prisons in New York, that's when everything changed and everything became more about correction, more about punishment than rehabilitation.

Etan: That's terrible. Talk about Linda Fairstein, she was actually upset at the way she was portrayed in the movie. If anything, they did her a favor by not making her as evil as she really was. Is that a correct assessment?

Santana: One hundred percent. This is the woman who they bring in to consult on episodes of *Law & Order*. This was the woman who came off a big case when she locked up Robert Chambers and so here it is, she gets our case and she's a villain, she's a straight villain. I mean, here it is that the DNA evidence comes back and so you test the five of us with the sample and you take hair samples, footprints, handprints, blood, all of our clothes, and you test it.

And none of it comes back [as a match]. Then we find out later on in the deposition, that you tested over forty kids and none of them match. So you knew you had the wrong group of people, period. There's a book by this guy named Harlan Levy, who worked at the DA's office at the time, it's called *And the Blood Cried Out*. He writes a chapter when the DNA evidence comes back in and Elizabeth Lederer called him to the office and she says, "I feel like I've been kicked in my stomach because the stuff came back and none of it matches, nothing."

And at that point she's formulating a plan on "How do I still get a conviction?" because she has to go to Linda Fairstein and this is the prosecutor and the head of the sex crimes unit. These are the people who can make the ultimate decision to say, "Nah, let's go back and reinvestigate, because this just doesn't sound right." But instead they played chess with us and our statements. So you see that Yusef is not in my statement, Antron is, so they made Antron connected to me, but in Antron's statement he'll say a tall Black kid with a flattop that was Yusef. Even though Antron never said his name, and so that's how they played chess with us to get a conviction.

We also found out that a lot of information being leaked to the news media early on during the case came from her. We also found that a whole box of files showed up missing, that's on her, and we also know that within the first two weeks of this case, there were over four hundred articles written about us [with] all those outrageous headlines where you got wilding, urban terrorists, super-predator. "Super-predator" was the terminology given to us, that became the terminology used for mass incarceration for the 1994 crime bill. We became the poster children.

And she was spearheading all that. So this is how much of a villain she was. With Ken Burns she sends a cease-and-desist to them. She tries to sue them, nothing works, then she said, "When we can get to trial, everything's going to come out." Okay. We've been waiting for the trial seven years ago.

People don't know this, but our civil case lasted eleven years. She would show up at some of those federal court dates and she would come in there with twenty interns, flooding the whole spot, and just be looking at us like she's trying to intimidate us. It was crazy, because the DA's office is so powerful and she was very powerful at the time.

This was a no-pay case. Mayor Bloomberg, he was the mayor for three terms, and he said, "We're not settling this case. Go to trial, do what you have to do." Look at the legal bill that those city attorneys racked up in the process, well over six or seven million dollars for their legal fees to fight against a case that they knew they were going to lose from the beginning. So they dragged it on and everybody got paid and kept it moving, and then when it came [to] our point, they were like, "Well, here's some hush money and you all can just go."

Etan: Matias Reyes, he's the inmate who confessed. Explain to me what happened with that, because he had to fight for them to accept his confession, that he was the one who did it?

Santana: What happened was that he saw Korey in the yard, spinning in the yard at Auburn Correctional Facility. At this point, Korey's been locked up thirteen and a half years for a crime he didn't commit. So he sees Korey and he goes over and he talked. Now what people don't know is that back in 1989, 1990, him and Korey had a fight over the TV.

And so this was Reyes seeing him eleven, twelve years later, and knowing that Korey is here for a crime [that] he committed, but he never told Korey.

In that conversation he started to tell Korey about going to church and trying to put his life in perspective and be better. He talked to his boys and he
told people before he actually told the chaplain.

And so they said, "Well, you know, you've got to do the right thing."
Matias Reyes, he has another inmate that he's cool with. And so this inmate
is a confidential informant for the district attorney's office. So Reyes is telling
this dude, this dude tells his lawyer.

So his lawyer, her husband calls my lawyer, says, you know, "They got
this dude in jail who was saying that he committed this crime and he's going
to the DA's office." The district attorney's office is saying, "Don't contact us
again. We don't want to talk about that." So they're not even trying to look
out for the confidential informant. But the lawyer's husband tells my lawyer.
And then my lawyer winds up getting with some people that we know. And
then they're the ones that find out that Matias Reyes exists.

So they hired a private investigator. He goes up to the jail. He talks to
Matias Reyes. They get the affidavit. He tells the whole story. And so at that
point, now the DA's office is forced. They have to listen because this kid is
talking and now we have this whole document of the whole story of what
he did. And so now the district attorney's office, they do an eight-month
investigation. Even with us, they tried to come back and talk to us and they
tried to trick our, you know, do the same. But it's different now. We're grown
men. That's not going to happen.

We ain't commit this crime. Y'all know what y'all did to us. And that's all
we going to say, but we don't know that Matias Reyes exist. We don't know
and so, all we know, we don't even know that there's a story because it's all behind the scenes. My lawyer ain't saying nothing. And their people definitely
not saying nothing, and at that time, I'm in, I'm in prison, you know, me
and Korey, we were the last two in jail. And so what happens is that it isn't
until they take the DNA sample [from Reyes] and then they match it. So
once they match it, they go, "Oh sh*t, all right. He *did* do it." And then they
find out that he's the east side rapist, the east side slasher who went on a spree
that summer, right? Where he commits like seven rapes and the murder of a
pregnant woman in 1989. That's why he has thirty-three-and-a-third-to-life.

They also know that two days before the jogger, he tried to rape another
woman in Central Park. The reason why the lady ID'd him, she said that he
had stitches on his chin. Now the detective goes to the hospital and he finds

out that a guy named Matias Reyes has fresh stitches on his chin. So they're looking for Reyes, they don't find him. Now, this is the crazy part. Matias Reyes worked in a bodega on 102nd Street and Third Avenue. All the police knew him when [they were] going to the bodega.

Matias Reyes says that upon leaving the scene of the crime, after he finished raping this lady and left her for dead, when he's exiting the park, a police car pulls up. It was the plainclothes boys, right? A detective, a police officer he called by name, a blondie who worked at the 23rd Precinct. And they stopped him. And they said, "Yo, you see any kids running around?" And he said, "Nah," but because they knew him, they looked in his face. They didn't look at his clothes. If they had, he had blood all over his jeans.

Etan: Are you serious, man?

Santana: This is Matias Reyes. His words.

Etan: So at that point, after they see who really did it, any decent human being should apologize. They should say, "I was wrong," publicly, just as loud as they said, "Crucify all of these kids." How surprising is it to you that Donald Trump has still to this day not apologized to you all?

Santana: It ain't just him. Linda, all the detectives, they still say we're guilty.

Etan: They still say you're guilty?

Santana: They say they did nothing wrong. It's good old-fashioned police work, it's deposition. We conducted over a hundred depositions. Commissioner Ray Kelly, who was the commissioner at that time, said Matias Reyes is credible for the murder and the four rapes, but he's not credible for the jogger case.

Etan: Why is he not credible for this?

Santana: They believe that we're still guilty. They believe that we had something to do with it. You can look this document up. It's called the Armstrong Report. And it tells you on theories that they think that we're still guilty. And one of those theories is that, like, we cohost this whole thing together, us and Reyes, like we made this whole plan and we went to jail and we're going to sue the city. We're going to split the money later on.

Etan: Are you serious?

Santana: You can't make this up, brother. You cannot. I mean, there's another theory where they say that due to the underground prison network of gangs, the Bloods put so much pressure on Matias Reyes, that's the only reason why he came forward. They still say that we're guilty to this day. And some of them say, "Well, they didn't do the rape, but they did *something*."

Etan: Y'all are kind of bonded for life for people who didn't know each other before this.

Santana: It's like, no matter what, I can't be like, "I won't be your brother, don't call me tomorrow, don't call me ever again." That won't happen. It can't happen, no matter what. And it's crazy because the system of people who still think that we're guilty, you know, we're going to always have to maintain that brotherhood and that war, because there's always going to be a common enemy out there that's against us.

Interview with Abiodun Oyewole

Abiodun Oyewole is part of the legendary music/poetry group the Last Poets, from the late-1960s Black nationalism. In fact, they were formed on May 19, 1968, which is Malcolm X's birthday. I wanted to talk to Abiodun Oyewole about the atmosphere in Harlem at the time of the Central Park jogger case.

Etan: Could you set the scene of what happened with the Central Park Five, and the target that it put on Black and Brown young men? You were there in Harlem living through all of it.

Oyewole: Well, people rushed to judgment as they often do when it comes to Black and Brown kids. These kids were demonized because they thought they raped this white woman, and right away, white America declared them as beasts, and Trump was leading the lynch mob. They called them every name but a child of God. It was horrendous. And consequently, quite a few of the folks that didn't even know went along with it, because when you shout something out in the media, it echoes. And a lot of people believe in what the media says. And so right away, they were already judged as guilty before the facts were brought out.

But I had a chance to talk with Raymond Santana. I used to do workshops for youth communication, to get the kids to write some poetry. And he was in one of my workshops. And I remember he stayed after the workshop was over a little longer 'cause he wanted to talk to me because I knew who he was. And I was totally hurt behind the fact that he was caught up in this whole incident. And he looked at me in my eyes. And you can always tell when somebody is telling you the truth. He said, "Brother Dun, we didn't rape anybody in the park. We were acting out. We were having fun, but we did not rape this woman."

And so I said, "Well, listen, I believe you, but I'm not on the jury, and they're the ones that have got to make that final decision." And that was where I left it. But I felt so bad because I felt that they were going to be railroaded straight to prison, which they were. And there was so many people who had just decided that they were just bad kids. And unfortunately the atmosphere at that time was not much different than it is now.

Etan: Race and racism was the driving force in this entire case.

Oyewole: Racism rules this country and has from the moment that we landed here, and these boys were subjects of that. They were victims of racism, absolutely. And I felt really bad that I didn't have any power to change whatever the defining situation was in their regard, but I felt they were being wronged. And of course, so many years later, it was sad to think that the youth of their lives were totally destroyed by that circumstance.

No one really came to their defense, and I felt very bad because they were out there by themselves. I'm grateful that the truth is now known. But during that particular period, they did not have too much support other than the people who knew them closely, who knew them well. Maybe some of them came out and spoke on their behalf, but I don't even remember that because it was an overwhelming discussion of how horrible these kids were to be running into the park, harassing people, and attacking people.

Etan: Trump took out an ad calling for the death penalty. Talk about how that not only demonized them, but *all* Black and Brown young men.

Oyewole: Anytime you take one person out of a crew and blow them up and make them look like monsters, it does have a strong effect on everybody, on all the other young people. And I believe honestly that they knew what they were doing. I don't believe that this was just by chance that they made a statement about some kids who were convicted for raping a white woman in the park. They were making a statement about *all* Black kids and they were deliberately doing it, because first of all, the prison industrial complex needs bodies. They are trying to recreate slavery. And we have always been the target for that. And if they can fill up the prisons with us, it is putting money in somebody's pocket.

And when you take a Black child or Brown child out of the hood and say that this person has raped or has killed a white person, without any proof, many folks, and unfortunately even people in the community, have begun to buy these lies because the media supports what these folks say. When Trump said what he said, there were many people who did not come to the assistance or to the aid of those young men. It created a nasty atmosphere and for many young men since, there was like a ripple effect. If you were just walking with your friends in the street, the police might just pull you over just because you're Black in a group and you might be up to something. It's like you were actually convicted of doing something before you did anything.

Etan: And that continues to happen even today.

Oyewole: Oh yes, since that time we have seen many young Black men getting shot down easily because there is a certain kind of energy and a vibe that kind of set a precedent for this type of behavior, for the Michael Browns to be killed, and for all the other young men that we've seen get killed. And now, of course, we can't leave sisters out, Breonna Taylor.

This kind of laid the groundwork for cops to just have their fingers on the trigger, if you see a Black man. Trayvon Martin, Eric Garner, Akai Gurley, we have had so many killings, so many deaths that have taken place unnecessarily. And the Central Park Five was almost like a repeat of the Scottsboro Boys incident that took place many years before that. And once again, the Scottsboro Boys were found innocent. They hadn't done anything, but they served a lot of time in prison. So we're repeating these cycles of racist behavior and they're supported by people who have already put in their minds that Black kids are out of control and they need to be locked up, or they need to be shot.

I just recently started working with an organization called Returning Youth. And this brother is trying to set up a program that allows the kids that have been locked up to come out and make some kind of living so that they won't get locked up again, because the recidivism rate is like 85 percent. If you have been put in a prison situation and you get out, chances are you're going to go back to prison. So they set you up for failure for the rest of your life; this is still going on. There needs to be an effort to change that. And people need to recognize that every young man, every young woman, needs an opportunity to live a life that is not being harassed by police and not have to worry about somebody charging them with crimes that they did not commit.

Etan: All stemming from white fear of a Black man harming a white woman in any possible way.

Oyewole: And that energy exists right now. The Central Park Five was just . . . even though before them there were other brothers and sisters, but that was such a sensational situation. Because we're talking about a group of young men supposedly ganging up on a white woman, and just the image of that alone in your mind, just to put that in your head, it kind of sets off a scary scenario for white America that this is going to happen all over the country. But this fear is not new.

Etan: Right, that fear of Black men and white women has been going on since slavery times. They wanted to lynch the Central Park Five in the town square like they did back in slavery days. They didn't even care about the evidence or anything like that. But we've seen that before, a classic example is Black Wall Street where I'm from in Tulsa, Oklahoma.

Oyewole: Exactly. I mean, if a young man is on the elevator and it kind of has a glitch or it jerks, he touches a woman supposedly, and she claimed that he raped her, or tried to rape her, and that's all that was needed for everything that transpired after that in the Black Wall Street massacre.

Etan: That was all that was needed for white people to immediately go into action. Even as little as whistling at a white woman, although Emmett Till actually had a lisp or a way of speaking that made it sound like a whistle, but even if he had whistled, they brutally murder him because they thought he *whistled* at a white woman?

Oyewole: And when you look at the history, it's the other way around, the total opposite. We have had Black women who have been attacked, and raped, and abused in the most savage, barbaric ways by white men with no regard to humankind or human worth. And that's been proven over time. Our very existence in America is proof of that. And the other thing that we need to recognize is that on the slave ships, many of our sisters were raped, and not just the sisters, the young boys as well, and nobody talks about that.

Etan: That's a good point.

Oyewole: And I don't know how this is going to end. The only way it is going to end is that we need to come together. We need to have unity. We talk about this until it's like overtime. I mean, these words just after a while, they lose their power. Because we're always saying, "Unify, unify, unify," but the unity has to come with an understanding that if we don't, we're going to lose our lives, in many ways. We're going to lose our young people. We need to be more concerned, more conscious, about our young people and how to save them. And we need to have programs and there need to be efforts made, because we have a lot of dysfunctional families. We weren't brought over here to be a successfully united family. We were brought over here to serve. And then serving these folks has not served *us.*

And this not serving ourselves has caused us a great misfortune because many of our folks are going to waste, are being kicked to the curb and lost. And really, this is one reason why I spend a lot of my time working with young people, because I believe in us. I know the gifts. I know the magnificence of Black folks. I know our resilience. I know our genius. And I want each one of us to recognize that we have something special for the world, and that we're not here just by chance. We're here with a mission. And the mission is to enlighten people, to give them an understanding of the gifts that we were granted by our ancestors and the gods. To recognize all of that is going to take a bit.

But in the meantime, we're going to see some more suffering and more pain, primarily because the people who are running things right now, *they* are in pain. They're suffering. If the white folks in charge felt better about themselves, we wouldn't see this.

Etan: Were you at all surprised that neither Giuliani nor Trump has apologized or recanted their statements?

Oyewole: I'm not surprised at all, for multiple reasons. Not only are they incapable of apologizing and admitting that they were wrong; also, sometimes you stick your foot in a hole so deep, you can't pull it out. And suddenly your ego gets involved to the point where for you to apologize means that you've got to do something extraordinarily special to maintain your so-called status as a leader. They have a certain cold callousness about themselves that they have used as a shield for all of the nastiest things that they've done. And to apologize for anything is out of their realm. They are incapable of apologizing, mainly because they don't . . . It's like you have to have a certain human vein that they just don't have.

There are quite a few who really do carry a pitchfork. And they do not care and they will crucify, they will hurt you. And primarily it's because there is something missing in them. There is some deep hole of discontent that they have with themselves, something that they can't measure up in terms of their humanness. And because when you attack Black people, you're attacking the very soul of humanity. If Black people were all the nasty things that they like to think or say, or that they've conjured up about us, this country would have been knee-deep in blood a long time. Because if anybody's had a reason to go crazy, to go buck wild, and pull into your house and cut your head off, Black people have had a reason.

Etan: You mentioned how after the Central Park Five there were a lot of cases of police brutality. It's not like it started with the Central Park Five. There's plenty of decades of terrorism, from the NYPD in particular. And specifically with the NYPD, after the Central Park Five, you saw Sean Bell, you saw Akai Gurley. The list goes on. Eric Garner, Eleanor Bumpurs, you could just keep going.

Oyewole: Abner Louima. It started a pattern of demonizing Black boys in particular.

Etan: Abner Louima, right, just sick, twisted, like something out of a horror movie that they did to him. And you look at the facts and you're like, *What is wrong with . . . Why would you even think to do something like that?* And you see this demonization of Black men and Black women, particularly in New York, continue after the Central Park Five demonization.

Oyewole: You're patrolling these areas that you've already listed on your chart as high crime areas. And why are they high crime areas? Because those folks in those communities can't get jobs as easy as folks in other places, so they're going to sell drugs. They're going to do something. I mean, God, Eric Garner was selling loose cigarettes. How horrible is that? I mean, he did not deserve to die for selling some loose cigarettes.

Etan: Still unbelievable that's what started it all with Eric Garner.

Oyewole: I remember when years ago, there was a brother named Clifford Glover in Queens. And he was a kid and he was killed by a cop running down the street. And then they said they found a toy gun on him. And the cop, he got off by simply saying, "I thought it was a real gun." And then about a year or two later, his partner in the precinct said that toy gun was Shea's gun. Shea was the name of the officer. And he used to keep that gun in his locker. And what he had done is planted the gun on the brother.

Etan: It's terrible that they keep getting away with this.

Oyewole: Well, when you have it in the Constitution that Black folks are three-fifths human, how much are we worth? They may have taken it out but you don't think that's not how many of these police officers who are supposed to protect and serve us feel about us? Which translates to, *Well, this person is not really human, so if we kill them it's okay. It's not a real problem.*

Etan: You're absolutely right, because if they viewed us as humans, they wouldn't treat us this way.

Oyewole: Exactly. When the truth of the matter is there's only one race on the planet, and it's the human race. And we need to recognize that. But people have cut us up, put us in boxes, put labels, and tried to make us less human. And yet we have shown a tremendous capacity to be more human than they will ever be. But there's a lot of hatred just because we have managed to find a way to struggle and be okay.

Interview with Officer Carlton Berkley

Retired New York City detective Carlton Berkley has a program educating youth and parents about their rights, similar to Colin Kaepernick's Know Your Rights Camp. I'm a big fan of Berkley's work and we've done projects together. At different events he has pointed out that the NYPD don't always do everything by the book. He speaks out on it, challenges and holds them accountable in a way that most police officers, whether retired or active, do not.

Etan: Why do you take it upon yourself to challenge the NYPD in the way that you do?

Berkley: Well, first of all, Etan, we are children of God, right? And I'm a deacon in my church. And we are supposed to look out for others. And when I became a police officer, I raised my right hand and I gave an oath to uphold the law and the Constitution of the United States for everyone. And that meant that no one would be above the law. If anyone, whether police, nonpolice, was to break the law, I had an oath to bring them to justice. And that includes the NYPD.

Etan: I've sat at some of your seminars. You're very direct. You use your book and give them the steps of what to do and what not to do when stopped by the police. I'm encouraging everyone to watch the docudrama from Ava DuVernay, *When They See Us*. I want to be able to utilize that story with young people. With that in mind, can you go through the steps that you tell young people of what to do and what not to do or say in that situation.

Berkley: When I do the seminars, Etan, I want parents to be there too. There was a time, if the police officer brought you home, your parents always believed the police officer. And what we are trying to tell all Black and Brown parents especially is: that time is over. You have to believe your child. And in that Central Park jogger case, all those young men were innocent from day one, and the police knew it. Right? But they went on and prosecuted them anyway, because of the pressure that was put on NYPD and the district attorney's office.

I was personally involved in the Central Park Five case, because we had a councilman, Charles Barron, who brought me down to City Hall to testify as to most of those detectives, which is not in the docudrama, who responded to the Central Park jogger case, were out in a bar. They were intoxicated when they responded to that scene.

What I tell young folks is that whenever stopped by the police, whenever, first of all, you don't resist. You stay calm. Whatever questions they ask you, what you should say to them is this: "Officer, am I under arrest?" Just ask them, "Officer, am I under arrest?" Make sure that they answer that question because the minute they say, "No, you're not," then you should say, "Well, then I must be free to leave." And then you step off. Now, if they force you to stay there, now they're holding you against your will.

Etan: So you don't have to stay there if they don't say you're under arrest?

Berkley: No, and most people don't know this. That's why I'm breaking it down. So when they tell you, "Oh no, you can't go"—now you're holding me against my will. Police like to use semantics, "Oh no, I was temporarily detaining them." But detaining can turn into an apprehension, you know? And you don't know when the apprehension starts, because when you are fed up and you say, "No, I'm not staying here, I am leaving," now, all of a sudden, you are arrested. But when the conversation started off, you were not arrested. You were being detained against your will because you did nothing wrong. So then I tell people, you should not answer any questions that the police ask you, because now you are under investigation, but you don't know you're under investigation. So anything you say can and will be used against you.

Etan: At what point should you ask for your attorney or your parent?

Berkley: Great question. So what I teach young folks is, when confronted with the police, first thing you ask them, "Officer, am I under arrest?" After they say no, then you say, "Well, then I must be free to leave." And then as you start to leave, if they stop you at that point, you should say right then, "Well, officer, I feel that you're arresting me or you're detaining me or I'm not free to leave. So since I'm not free to leave, then I don't want to answer any questions, and I would like to have my attorney or my parents." And this is if they're young folks, you know, under sixteen you're considered a minor. The NYPD is not supposed to interrogate a minor without their parent or lawyer sitting right next to the minor. And it has to be sort of like a two-prong, meaning that the young person has to agree to talk to you and their parent [agrees]. It can't be, the young person wants to talk and the parent doesn't want them to talk. They both have to be in accord.

Etan: I didn't know that.

Berkley: And this is why, in my seminars, this is a part of me educating the community. Now, getting back to that Central Park jogger case, I just implore all parents to look at that because those parents were lied to, Etan, they were lied to by the cops saying, "Look, we just want to talk to your son and we just want to get a statement from him." And if you notice, the cops said, "And then they will be free to leave." They were never free to leave. And with the parents not knowing their rights, those parents played a significant part in their kids being arrested.

Etan: Most parents would think, *Just answer their questions and they'll let you go*, right?

Berkley: Right, but unfortunately, that's not always the case and this is what I teach in my seminars. I always tell parents, never allow the police to talk to your children without you being there. Because—and this is something else parents don't know—even if a parent does give the permission for the child to talk to the police, at any given time, that parent can say, "Hey, I want to stop this. I want to end this interview."

Etan: I didn't know this either.

Berkley: A lot of people don't. I have spoken to so many parents that have gone through my seminar and read my book and they said, "When I tried to end it, the officer said, 'No, you can't.'" And then the officer escorted the parent out of the interview room, leaving the child in there, getting additional statements. And then the officer lied later on and said no, they saw something where the child wanted to speak, but the officer saw where the child didn't want the parent to know something, so then what the officer said was, "Listen, your son wants to say something to me, but could you just step out of the room?" These are the tricks they use.

A parent should say, "No, I'm never leaving the room. I want to hear each and every thing my son has to say." Because once you remove yourself from that room, you can't testify as to what's going on. Those are tricks that the police use. And when parents don't know, they'll go along with it, thinking, *My child didn't do anything wrong, so my child could speak with the police.* No, no, parent, your child cannot speak with the police. And you should not be out of that room.

Etan: And this is just with minors? What's considered a minor?

Berkley: Yes, I'm talking about minors. Now, once a child is over sixteen, seventeen, they are considered adults. Now, even if [a minor] has requested their parent, the police can say, "Well, you have to talk to *me* first." Or, "If you don't talk to me, I'm just going to arrest you and you won't see your parent," They're not supposed to do that either.

Etan: You explained what the police are not supposed to do, but when they tell the child, "I'm just going to ask you the questions without your parents," and the child says, "I would like my parent or lawyer here," and the cop says no, what can the child or the parent do at that point?

Berkley: What the child should do, if they're in the room with the officer, just cease talking. Just say, "I'm not saying any more. I want my lawyer or my parents here." And don't say anything. But there's tactics that are used—an officer can keep you in an interview room for two, three hours. They've already been in custody six or seven hours. They haven't eaten. They haven't used the bathroom. They ask the officer, "Can I use the bathroom?" "No, you won't use the bathroom until you talk to me." "Can I call my parents?" "No." "Well, you already have me in custody for seven, eight hours. My parents don't even know where I am." "Well, you talk to me and we'll call." See, these are the tactics that officers use.

Etan: How does a child or a parent go about bringing up charges or complaints about the officer to hold them accountable when they use these tactics?

Berkley: You get the officer's name, shield number, and if the officer removes the parent from the room and the child is still there, the parents should say to the child, "Don't say anything else." Then, the parent should get in touch with a lawyer, reach out to the community, let everyone know what's going on, and bring a stop to it. Every parent should have a number of a lawyer or someone in the neighborhood that they trust.

In our cases . . . people would call me two, three o'clock in the morning. I have to go from the Bronx to Brooklyn or to Queens. And mind you, I didn't know this parent, all I did was get a phone call saying, "I need your help. My child is in the such and such precinct. And they haven't been advised of their rights. The police are framing them." And as an organization, we have members in every borough, but starting off, we ourselves would travel to whatever precinct it is. Then we would walk in the precinct with that parent and stand next to that parent, letting the police know that I am a current New York City detective. This parent has called me; their loved one is inside. And I'm saying to you, "If there's any questioning going on, it must stop."

Now I'm getting the names of the sergeant, the lieutenant, whoever else was there, and I'm letting them know that as of this time, anything that has gotten asked at this point, I'm going to testify against you in court. I came here and I said to you to stop the questioning, that the parent here wants an attorney for their child. And nine times out of ten, the police wouldn't want to go through that because now they have one of their own who's going to testify, and I'm going to bring out names and I'm naming supervisors. Supervisors get very nervous when their names are brought up because of what cops are doing.

Etan: The first instinct for all young Black men is to run. But once they have you and they're questioning you, how do you avoid being arrested if they have their mind set that they're going to bring you downtown?

Berkley: Okay, Etan, that's very hard, but that's why in my book, the first thing I say is never, never resist. If you are running in the street and the police are running after you, everybody has this preconceived notion that you did something wrong. And then people are less likely to help you while you are running from the police. All the police got to say is, "No, he know what he did wrong. That's why he was running from us." And most people just walk away.

But if you stand your ground and say, "No, officer, I don't want to leave," and you start talking to the community, not resisting, but talking to the community, "This officer's taking me down to the precinct. I did nothing wrong. I do not want to go" . . . See, the police don't want a crowd. I always tell people to take out their cell phones and start filming what's going on. Because now you're putting a police officer on the spot because when a person's saying, "No, why do I have to go downtown?" Or, "Why do I have to go to the precinct? I did nothing wrong," and the police saying, "But we want to talk to you. We just want to talk to you," that goes back to what I said originally, "Officer, am I under arrest? If I'm not under arrest, then I must be free to leave." Force the officer's hand. Again, never put up any resistance. When you put up resistance, it looks bad for you even in court.

Etan: But what's considered resistance? If you say, "No, I don't want to go," is that resistance?

Berkley: No.

Etan: You're just using your mouth and saying, "I don't want to go with you. I have done nothing wrong and I don't want to get in the car." That's not considered resistance?

Berkley: No, what's considered resistance is you running or you're fighting not to go down with them. Because let me tell you something: cops can make up just about anything, right? Disorderly conduct, which is a violation. Disorderly conduct means that technically just you're disagreeing with what a cop is telling you to do. Meaning like, you're jaywalking and the cop says, "Hey, you were supposed to cross the street at the corner. You did it in the middle of the block." And the person says, "Yeah, okay." And shrugs the cop off. That's disorderly conduct. You can be arrested for that.

So with a cop saying, "Look, I'm arresting you," the first thing a person will do when a cop grabs him is to shrug him off, and that motion technically is resisting arrest. You don't resist arrest with your mouth. You resist arrest with your actions. Whether that means running, whether that means pushing a cop, preventing a cop from putting their hands on you when they have already said you're under arrest, that's resisting. Resisting is not your mouth, because your mouth doesn't put up any physical force to an officer.

Etan: So they can put their hands on you. They can do whatever they want to, and you have to basically go limp and not do anything or else they call it resisting arrest.

Berkley: Exactly.

Etan: That is such a messed-up system. Now, there's a lot of places where the police will come up and say, "You cannot film me." And you said earlier that you advise people to stay twenty feet away. So can you clear up any misconception? Because a lot of policemen will quickly say, "You cannot film me, turn it off."

Berkley: They're 100 percent wrong. And they know it. There's a patrol guide that every New York City police officer has, and it tells the police officer everyone has the right. When the news media is out there, do you ever see the police going to the news media, telling them that they can't film them? Do you ever see officers trying to grab the camera of the media? No. The reason why they tell people in the street not to do it is because they are doing something that they know they are not supposed to do. And if you can get it on camera, then you got them. But yes, you can definitely legally film them.

Etan: I think everybody needs to go to your seminars, including parents, because you're providing them with information that will help them when the police lie to them.

Berkley: I hate to be looked at as an enemy, because 90 percent of all the officers on that force are good, hardworking men and women. But there are some that are bad apples. And when the good officers stand by and watch the bad officers do something, I tell the good officers, "You're worse than that bad officer, because you're allowing him or her to violate."

Etan: Much respect to you, and keep doing the very important work that you're doing.

Berkley: Thanks a lot. And God bless you, and you keep doing what you're doing too, because, you know, I look up to you, brother. I watched you at Syracuse, with the Wizards, and you were a beast, but the work you are doing now will benefit our people in ways far more tangible.

George Floyd

Trust me, you can't change anything without causing some degree of disruption. It's impossible, that is exactly what change is. Some people are uncomfortable with the disruption that change causes, but the disruption is necessary if anything is going to change.

—Afeni Shakur

I was sitting in my office when my nine-year-old daughter, who I call Baby Sierra, ran into the room and asked me if I'd heard about the story where the policeman put his knee on a Black man until he died. She was terrified. I could hear it in her voice and see it in her eyes. It was like déjà vu because I'd had a similar situation happen when my son Malcolm was about six and he saw the news coverage of the murder of Trayvon Martin.

Baby Sierra asked why he would do that. And why wouldn't anyone help him? And why were all of the other police officers just watching? She was literally shaking.

I hugged her and tried to calm her down as she was crying, and that was my daughter's introduction to police brutality. And just as I can easily recall the first time I saw the Rodney King beating, I'm sure this image will be etched into Baby Sierra's mind for the rest of her life.

On May 25, 2020, George Floyd, a forty-six-year-old Black man, was murdered in Minneapolis, Minnesota, while being arrested on suspicion of using a counterfeit twenty-dollar bill. During the arrest, Officer Derek Chauvin, a white police officer with the Minneapolis Police Department, knelt on Floyd's neck for nine minutes and twenty-nine seconds after he was handcuffed and lying facedown. Two other police officers, J. Alexander Kueng and Thomas Lane, assisted Chauvin in restraining Floyd. A fourth police officer, Tou Thao, prevented bystanders from interfering.

On June 25, 2021, a jury sentenced Officer Derek Chauvin to 22.5 years in prison. It's a tragedy the bar is set so low that anything feels like justice. 22.5 years is one of the longest sentences a cop has ever been given for murder, and that's the problem.

The same exact system that allowed Derek Chauvin to murder George Floyd and almost get away with it remains fully intact today. In fact, there have been more than a thousand murders at the hands of the police since George Floyd's death, and countless other cases of police abuse and brutality of Black men, women, and children.

In addition, when you examine the fact that there are Black men serving longer sentences for marijuana than murdering George Floyd, and that Chauvin had eighteen previous complaints of excessive force officially filed against him with the Minneapolis Police Department Internal Affairs, 22.5 years doesn't seem as much of a victory.

I interviewed former NBA player Stephen Jackson about his relationship with George Floyd and how Floyd's murder set him on a path of activism, prompting him to use his voice and platform like never before. During the interview I asked him a question my twelve-year-old daughter Imani asked me while we were discussing the George Floyd murder. "Daddy, if the person wasn't there to record Officer Derek Chauvin murdering George Floyd, do you feel that we would've ever heard of this case?"

Stephen Jackson's reply was, "No, because I would have never seen it, I would've never gotten involved, and the world's outrage wouldn't have been the same if the world never saw it. It was all on TV everywhere, all day. If she didn't record it, it would've been just like the millions of other murders that we never hear about."

The she-ro my daughter was referring to was then-seventeen-year-old Darnella Frazier. And Stephen Jackson was absolutely correct: if she didn't wisely and fearlessly take out her camera and record, Derek Chauvin would've continued terrorizing the streets of Minneapolis as if nothing ever happened.

The official police report showed what Minneapolis police originally said happened to George Floyd. The heading read, *Man dies after medical incident during police interaction.* It also says, *At no time were weapons of any type used by anyone involved in this incident.*

As reflected in this report, the Minneapolis police were ready to close the case, and the world would have never known what really happened. None of it would've ever been seen if it weren't for Darnella Frazier, who kept the camera rolling as she watched George Floyd breathe his last breath.

"I heard George Floyd saying, 'I can't breathe, please, get off of me' . . . and [crying] for his mom," Frazier testified in court. "He was in pain. It seemed like he knew it was over for him."

And thanks to Darnella Frazier, an entire movement started. People from all across the country got involved. Stephen Jackson, who knew George Floyd personally, thrust himself into a movement that resonated with the entire world. He flew down to Minneapolis and spoke at rallies, and went on every media outlet he possibly could, including CNN, ESPN, *Inside the NBA*, The Undefeated, *Undisputed*, BasketballNews.com, always calling for justice for his friend, who he called Twin.

Interview with Stephen Jackson

Etan: The media loves to demonize us after we are murdered by the police. They did it with Trayvon Martin, Eric Garner, Mike Brown. We get murdered and somehow we are the ones on trial instead of the police officer who committed the murder. Malcolm X actually spoke about this back in the sixties and it's still happening today. So I want to start by you painting the correct picture of George Floyd and who he was.

Jackson: Georgie was every Black man in America that comes up in the ghetto that's trying to make a life for his family. You make mistakes, you try to figure it out, and you learn from experience. He struggled to find his way at times, but he did make a change in his life. He moved away from that Houston third ward area and moved to Minnesota, and changed his life for his daughter Gianna. That's all we talked about. Our daughters are the same age and all he wanted to do was do better for Gianna. And that's what hurt the family so much—when he finally got to that point where he was actively taking steps to change his life, he gets murdered by the police.

Etan: He did some work in the church too, right?

Jackson: Yeah, he always spoke about his faith. When he wanted to change his life, he knew that the only way he could get there was to have a relationship with a higher power. And he dedicated himself to it. There were times I saw him actually preaching at different places. He had really changed his entire life.

Etan: How did y'all meet?

Jackson: Funny story. So I'm from Port Arthur, Texas, which is about an hour away, and rest in peace to one of our friends, his name is Telly, he came down to Port Arthur and said, "Hey, Steve, I got someone who looks like you, y'all may be related." I was like, "Yeah, right, bro," and he said, "When I bring him down here, you're gonna see." So I'm on the court a couple days later and he pulls up with him and as soon as he walked on the court, the first thing we say to each other is, "Who your daddy?" We looked that much alike. We just became close friends from that point on. And we called each other Twin. And our relationship just jelled from that point on.

Etan: And this was before you got to the NBA?

Jackson: I was sixteen at the time. When I made it to the NBA, he was proud to tell people, "That's my twin." He was just as happy for me as my own family. Everywhere we went, he wanted to be my protector. We were close, like brothers.

Etan: What happened when you got the call and found out about George Floyd's death? Where were you, who broke it to you, and what was your immediate reaction?

Jackson: It was probably ten thirty in the morning. Something made me get up and come get on the couch. Me and my girlfriend's mom talk about police brutality and all the nonsense that's done to Black people all the time, and she sends me videos.

So my phone is ringing, vibrating. I look at it and I see the video from her, but I don't even correlate that this is my brother. I'm not even thinking about George when she sent me the video. I look at it, not even putting two and two together. I'm just like, *Oh man, they done killed another brother.* My phone vibrates again. And I pick up the phone and I look at it and it's a message from my friend Mike Dean, and it says, *You see what they did to your twin in Minnesota?*

I went back to the video from my girlfriend's mother. And I see the video and I look closely and see that's him on the ground and I lose it, E. I was actually hurt because I saw myself in him, and this is somebody who I consider my twin getting murdered by the police for the world to see. I never thought that I would see that with my own eyes—somebody that I loved, that I consider *me.* I've never dealt with nothing like that, E. And so to see that, it knocked the wind out of me, honestly. It knocked the wind out of me and I just cried. I couldn't even get myself together for a while.

Etan: When I watched, I was looking at the evil in the officer, Derek Chauvin, as he was kneeling on his neck and putting his hand in his pocket. The facial expression that he had. I looked at it with my kids and I'm breaking down too. We talk about Black Lives Matter and that showed us that, to that officer and all those officers around him, our lives didn't matter at all. You don't even treat an animal like that. I mean, if everybody saw a dog being murdered like that . . .

Jackson: They would go crazy.

Etan: They would go absolutely crazy. And that's the part that was so tough to me. You think that we've made some kind of progress and then you see something like that, and it just knocks us all the way back. I'm feeling like, *Wow, so what do we do now?* And you went into work mode after that. You had your moment of grieving and feeling upset, and then you went to work. Talk about that switch.

Jackson: You never know what God has for you in your life. I was really upset. In the past, I had been upset that I didn't make All-Star games I should have made, for being judged for the ["Malice at the Palace"] brawl for having my teammates' back, and it messed up my career and accolades I should've gotten. But God works in mysterious ways. What I'm doing now, I want to be known for that. I don't even want to be known for basketball at all. Me going to Minnesota . . . I wanted to go down there so they wouldn't demean my brother's name. Like you said, the first thing they do when they murder one of us is try to make it look valid—they demean our character.

Etan: Yeah, that's what they always do. With Eric Garner, Philando Castile, Terence Crutcher, Alton Sterling, Ahmaud Arbery, and so on. They literally do it every time.

Jackson: Yup, and I wanted to go down there to let the world know who he really was. Nine times out of ten, when this happens, none of these people that get killed by the police have a celebrity to speak up for them. That's one thing that messed up Minnesota and the world: nobody expected Stephen Jackson to be considered George Floyd's twin. And nobody expected Stephen Jackson to put everything he had on the line and fight for justice for him. While I was in Minnesota, not only did he have a celebrity speaking up for him, but at the time my podcast was one of the bigger podcasts in the world. I was all over ESPN and doing all of these shows.

When I went down there, seeing how the city of Minneapolis got behind me and supported me let me know that this has been going on for a long time. I walked to the corner [and saw a woman holding a sign that said], *His name was Hardel Sherrell*. His mom was standing on the corner, crying and holding signs, trying to get justice for her son just by herself. I stopped, I put the cameras and the mics in front of her, and she tells her whole story. I ended up being the voice for her [too]. So I inherited being the voice for so many people who have been brutalized by police or by racism and never got justice. The fact that I was a celebrity basketball player that everybody knew, that a lot of people respected and loved, all eighteen countries and fifty states got behind me. And it became one of the biggest protests all at one time ever in the history of protests.

Etan: It was really amazing. That was for me, in my lifetime, the most white people I have ever seen protest the murder of a Black man at the hands of the police.

Jackson: Right, me too. So the fact that that happened, I just dropped on my knees because I never knew God would make my life that important. It's way more important than basketball because I'm changing lives. And it sparked me to want to go to all fifty states and to let people know—in the areas we come from—that we care about them, that we hear them, that we have money to give and resources to help you out to try to get to a better life. Like I said, you never know what God has for you. It was meant for me to be in this position. It was meant for me to have a domino effect of helping people after going out there and standing up for my brother, and to fight for change, and I would rather be known for what I'm doing now than anything else.

I've been a member of First Baptist Church of Glenarden since I first came to DC with the Wizards, over twenty years ago. One of the many things I respect about Pastor John K. Jenkins Sr. is that he doesn't stay silent on these issues. He spoke about George Floyd right after it happened. He calls out racism, police brutality, white supremacy.

Interview with Pastor John K. Jenkins Sr.

Etan: There's so much going on in the world right now and you're not afraid to discuss it, you take it head-on. You take on these issues of racism, of police brutality, of injustice, at a time where, honestly, a lot of pastors are quiet on these topics. Maybe they're reluctant, or a little afraid, but for whatever reason, they are quiet. What makes you different? What makes you want to take on these topics?

Jenkins: Well, when I see what's going on in our country and around our communities, it produces a strong response, internally. I just see these things, and it drives me to have to say something. If I'm feeling it and I'm frustrated or angry or whatever, I know other people are feeling the same way.

I try to be a ministry that speaks to and addresses the needs of the community on a consistent basis. You meet people where they are, you meet people where they're hurting, where they're frustrated, and you speak to it. I'm trying to speak to those needs of the community that I serve.

Etan: Let's talk specifically about the George Floyd case. Last summer, you dedicated an entire message one Sunday to it, and you didn't hold back one bit. You called out racism, called out police brutality, white supremacy. Walk me through how you got to that point.

Jenkins: I was out of town, so I wasn't at church that Sunday. I wish I had not been traveling and had been able to actually respond [the day Floyd was killed]. I did the following Sunday, and the inability for me to speak to it just caused, what I felt on the inside, to rise even more. By the way this George Floyd response wasn't just a United States issue. There was protests around the world. I mean, people all over the world saw what happened and the anger and the frustration.

The reality is, the steps that have led me is watching this go on repeatedly in our country, where police officers have unjustly and wrongly killed Black men, in particular. That could have been my son, that could have been my brother. I just felt the need to speak to it and address it. It's a call. I don't even know how to respond to answer that, Etan, other than what I felt was rage, anger, frustration, and I just needed to call it out.

Etan: We just got the guilty verdict for Chauvin. It says a lot that I was surprised. A lot of people shared that same sentiment. Were you surprised that there was a guilty verdict?

Jenkins: I thought it might be mixed. I thought that the manslaughter might be guilty, but the other two might not be, because the other two, I think, implied some level of intent. It's kind of hard to look into a person's heart and know what their intents are, but I was glad when they added the manslaughter charge to it, because I felt strongly that that would be a guilty verdict. I wasn't sure about the first two that they charged him for. I was surprised that all three was guilty, because I thought he might get away with just the one manslaughter charge.

Etan: It's interesting that after the verdict, I felt relief. It wasn't happy, it wasn't joy, it was like relief.

Jenkins: Right, absolutely.

Etan: I was relieved for about five minutes, and then I started thinking, *If Darnella Frazier, hadn't whipped out her phone and recorded this, then we would have never even heard of George Floyd?* Then I saw that this was the first case in Minnesota history where a white police officer is actually found guilty of murdering a Black man. How many Black men were murdered by Minnesota cops? Hard to be happy about that.

Jenkins: Yeah, you're right. Matter of fact, when it happened, I was so full of emotions that I couldn't even teach the churchwide Bible study. I had to just spend the whole Bible study addressing this issue. Why did it take a video recorded by a civilian for this to happen? Why didn't any of the other police officers report what their partner, their coworker did? That was irresponsible and unhealthy and ungodly and wicked. None of that was in the police report.

Why did it take outrage around the world? Why did there have to be protests in other countries, thousands of people in other countries protesting? That was a level of frustration for me, that it took all of that. Think about all of the times that things have been reported by a person versus a police officer, and people are expected to put trust in police officers?

I don't doubt that most of them are wholesome people. Most police officers are. My son was a police officer for seven years, and he always, I know, tried to do his work in a wholesome, godly, righteous way. But this Officer Chauvin, he went too far. I can't speak of his heart or his intentions or his motives, but what he did, his actions, that's what we hold people accountable for.

Etan: We always have to give the caveat that we're not against *all* police. I've actually sat on a panel with your son Joshua and we had to speak to this, but not so much about the "bad apple" theory, because we know all cops aren't bad. But as far as the system, that's what is bad, to be honest. Case in point, looking at the official report the Minneapolis Police Department first put out, before the video, it was a closed case. They had really tied a bow on it. They said no weapons were used. He died of a medical condition, and that was it.

That's a system issue. How many other times were there when there was no video, when they only had the police report stating the person just died by accident, and they just went on about their business? That's why it's tough for me to rejoice in this guilty verdict.

Jenkins: Well, now there's a move afoot, across the country, to rein in this freewheeling posture and attitude of police departments to put better accountability in place. The reality is the autopsy report listed that he died by homicide, that he was killed. Even though the police report said something different, the fact that it said he died by homicide should have, and I hope it would have, called forth a deeper investigation of what happened, even without the video.

The police officers over time have been empowered by this police officers' bill of rights that a lot of states have, and it gives them the freedom to just treat people however they want to treat them, with no accountability, but that's finally changing across the country. The State of Maryland that you and I live in just recently passed a law that puts some accountability on police officers, and this is happening in many, many other states across the country. That gives me a sense of hope, that they can't just continue to behave wildly and treat people just any kind of way, without any regard or accountability.

It's going to take awhile to get it countrywide. There actually are some federal laws trying to get passed now, and hopefully those federal laws will be passed. It's a challenge, because there are still components of our Congress that are opposed to it, but if we let our voices be heard, and I would encourage people to call their congressmen, call their senators, because there are some laws—matter of fact, there's the George Floyd law that they're trying to get passed. It holds police officers accountable for their behavior.

Etan: Talk a little about what's going on in Maryland, because you're actually involved in that.

Jenkins: The Maryland state congress passed a law that puts better accountability, and in terms for police officers, and it was sent up to the governor. He vetoed it, didn't sign it, and sent it back, and they overrode his veto. I salute the state legislators for recognizing that some kind of accountability needs to be put in place. It's expansive. The main deal is it keeps a level of accountability with police officers, so I'm thrilled about that.

Etan: Governor Hogan originally vetoed it?

Jenkins: He did, he didn't sign it. He vetoed it and sent it back, and they overrode it.

Etan: That's interesting. We don't have to go too deep into Governor Hogan, but it's interesting when you're looking at things being passed or held up, and the specific people who do veto it and vote against. There are a lot of politicians who are against these bills, and I have to wonder, why would you not be in full support of police accountability? It's not about being anti–all police, but something in the system needs to change as far as checks and balances. Even if you love the police, you would want them to have a system where they're held accountable, right?

Jenkins: Absolutely. Everybody has to have accountability. And I can't stress this point enough: you can't have police in charge of their own accountability. That's not what accountability is. You don't hold *yourself* accountable. Somebody else holds you accountable.

And you mentioned it earlier, but yes, I did talk to some of our legislators, and they actually sent me the bill, and I'm happy that we have something in place in the State of Maryland. Hopefully it'll spread to other states, to hold police behavior accountable.

Etan: Qualified immunity is something they definitely have to get rid of. Last summer, you talked about the silence from the evangelical church in particular, and you called them out.

Jenkins: The white evangelical church.

Etan: Yes, the white evangelical church. Sorry. Gotta make that clear because sometimes they lump us in with them. Talk about why you called them out the way that you did, because I was so frustrated seeing their silence.

Jenkins: Yeah, well, it is painful to me. It's another point of anger and frustration for me, the silence, the deathly silence of white evangelical leaders to speak to injustice. Injustice anywhere is a potential threat to justice everywhere. The church is called and anointed and gifted and [charged] by the Scripture to challenge injustice. It's our responsibility. Time after time after time, of event after event after event, of police doing things unjustly, and to never hear them say anything about it, it was more than I could bear.

Most Christian churches, I should say, are evangelical in their convictions. Our church is an evangelical church, but we speak to injustice. We speak to behavior that's unrighteous and wicked and needs to change. That's our call, that's our assignment. It is the appeal of God for us to speak to it, so I had to speak out about it, not just about what has happened, but also about the failure of influential white evangelical leaders to speak to it.

It was appalling, and it still is appalling to me, because even with the guilty verdict on this police officer who murdered George Floyd, they still are silent. The reason they don't say anything is fear and the white supremacist attitude across our country—they won't raise their hand and say, "I'm a white supremacist," but they'll hide behind beliefs and convictions and rejection of certain things.

They'll try to label everything as liberal or far left. Standing up for righteousness and what's righteous is not far left, nor is it far right. It's truth and what is right. I make an appeal to my white brothers and sisters: they must do the same thing too. You can't just remain silent and act like it's not going on.

Etan: I'm watching the Frederick Price series on racism in Christianity, with my family. He was my wife Nichole's pastor growing up. Racism in Christianity runs deep, and it would take a long time for us to even start to peel back all the layers of how deep it runs.

I think it's difficult for white evangelicals to even accept the historical facts of the way that white supremacy and racism were interwoven into the white church, and the white man's distortion of Christianity. So when I see the silence now, and I don't expect them to speak on every single incident that happens, but an incident like George Floyd, where the entire world is watching, in an uproar, that's a little different.

Jenkins: Oh, absolutely. I remember when Fred Price did that series some years ago, and this was awhile back, but it was powerful. He stirred up a lot of anger and resentment, and he lost members in his church because of it. They thought he had gone too far, but I thought he was right on target. He shared biblical truth. He shared his experiences and experiences of others.

He was profound. I salute him for that. I would urge anybody who really wants to examine the depths of white supremacy as it relates to the church to watch this series and how he breaks everything down.

But racism is not new and it's not an American problem. I'm a student, Etan, of World War II. I watch a lot of documentaries about World War II and the Nazis' roles from the Germans being infiltrated with a mindset that they were superior to everyone else. That's what the whole world war that got started around, that centered around Nazi Germany, feeling they were superior to others, and that's what racism is. You think your race is better than or smarter than or superior to someone else, and it's ungodly.

Etan: There is silence in a lot of the Black churches as well. And a lot of young people are not seeing their pastors speak to these issues and they're losing faith. They're like, "Why is my pastor not talking about this at all?" Then they're seeing the white evangelicals standing for the opposite. They're standing with the other side. They're standing with Trump. They're standing with white supremacy, and the young people are like, "Okay, well, if this is what Christianity is all about, I don't really want any part of it."

That's why it's so important for Black pastors in particular to do what you do. To talk about these issues, to talk about the roots of white supremacy, racism, police brutality, call out injustice, to understand and speak to the anger and frustration that an entire generation is feeling, looking at the situation that we have with police terrorism in this country.

Jenkins: I spend a lot of time equipping and training pastors how to be effective leaders in their community. A lot of these pastors just don't know what to say. They don't know how to lead. The mantle on me, Etan, is to do my best, to take the things that the law has taught me and that I've learned from Scripture and mentor other pastors. To teach them how to provide strong, godly, anointed leadership to their communities.

I would say to the young people: be patient with some of our leaders. A lot of them have never seen it modeled before them. They don't know how to do it. We try to get them trained and equipped to be able to speak to these issues, and how to speak to it. I would just ask them, don't lose faith in the church. The great thing is, if your pastor's not speaking to it, there's enough pastors on the Internet speaking to it, and pray that your pastor will get to a place where he can be equipped and trained and knowledgeable on how to speak to it.

Etan: That's very well said. Pastor Jenkins, I really appreciate you, and I appreciate your willingness to stand for what's right. You share in the people's frustration about this. You stand for justice as a biblical principle. I have a lot of respect for that.

Jenkins: Thank you, Etan. Let me say one more thing, very quickly. You mentioned young people who are frustrated. I'm not a social media person, and I don't follow all that stuff. I want to say to young people to continue to tweet and post these things, because older folks like me may not know how to stay plugged in to everything. Of course everyone saw George Floyd, but there is a lot I would've missed if I wasn't following your Instagram page, to be honest. You do a great job. You know, sometimes I call you: "Etan, tell me about this. What's going on?"

Etan: Right, we've had quite a few of those conversations.

Jenkins: And they have kept me informed. I would say to the young people, be a resource for your pastor to make him aware and share with him, "Hey, here's what's going on. I don't know if you know about this, Pastor, but you might want to check into this. Let me advise you and tell you what's going on." I appreciate that you provide that level of help for me, and I want to tell the young people to do the same. Please alert your pastor, because a lot of them, again especially the older generation, are not as social media savvy as you are. We watch the news, but not everything is always covered in the news, and it's important that we all continue to push for change and accountability. I'm glad this officer who killed George Floyd was found guilty, but we definitely still have a long way to go.

Defunding the Police

People get used to anything. The less you think about your oppression, the more your tolerance for it grows. After a while, people just think oppression is the normal state of things.

—Assata Shakur

In the aftermath of the murder of George Floyd, various protests detonated around the world declaring Black Lives Matter and calling for cities across the US to defund the police.

This was met with much resistance from a large portion of society. For decades, we have been taught to equate policing with public safety and can't imagine alternatives to a punitive law enforcement model. Politicians called on Americans to "restore faith in the police," but how are we going to do that without anything changing? Have faith in the same system that murdered George Floyd and regularly terrorizes Black and Brown communities?

Police forces have become more militarized every year. Since 1990, the federal government has transferred $7.4 billion of excess military equipment to local law enforcement agencies under its 1033 Program, giving police access to mine-resistant vehicles, assault rifles, and grenade launchers. For years police have also undergone "warrior training" that teaches them to see every encounter as potentially life-threatening, especially when those encounters involve people of color. Every year, on-duty police kill an estimated one thousand people.

Despite the billions of dollars spent every year on policing, more than fifteen thousand people were killed by gun violence in 2019 alone—disproportionately young Black and Brown people. So if policing and imprisonment had any actual correlation to stopping violence, the US would be the most peaceful country in the world. But decades of evidence show us this is not the case.

US cities collectively spend $100 billion a year on policing, while needed investments in education, health care, housing, and other critical programs go unfulfilled, particularly in poor communities and communities of color. New York City, in particular, spends more on policing than it does on the Departments of Health, Homeless Services, Housing Preservation and Development, and Youth and Community Development combined.

So the question is, what sense does it make to keep spending more money on a system that produces these results?

Two summers ago (pre-COVID), I was part of a powerful event at the Alexandria Police Department with Valerie Castile (mother of Philando Castile). She is promoting a "not-reaching pouch" to save Black lives—so you don't have to reach for your license and registration when stopped by the police. They would be in your driver's-side air vent, in a pouch.

Ms. Castile is an amazing woman, as is her daughter, Allysza Castile. I interviewed them both in my book *We Matter: Athletes and Activism,* and told them I would try to support their efforts in any way I could. It was heartbreaking to hear Valerie speak about the murder of her son Philando by Officer Jeronimo Yanez. I learned that Philando Castile had been racially profiled almost fifty times by the police.

At the Alexandria event, there were Black policemen in attendance, but not one white policeman. I asked an event organizer, Jacquelyn Carter, if they had invited any white policemen. She said yes, but unfortunately they declined.

I spoke with one of the higher-ranking Black police officers, who requested anonymity, but agreed that it made no logical sense for the police to be in charge of situations they weren't trained to handle. When asked if it would make the job easier to focus on the situations they are trained to do, he explained in detail that nobody wants their funding cut. That said, he agreed with the transfer of responsibility to social workers, EMS, etc., to handle nonviolent mental-health calls.

However, after months of talks headed by Senators Cory Booker (D-NJ) and Tim Scott (R-SC), and Representative Karen Bass (D-CA), the country's expectation that there would be a landmark legislation bill passed on police reform after a short span of time that saw the deaths of both George Floyd and Breonna Taylor, marches and rallies and protests and demonstrations and nationwide calls for tangible changes to actually happen, a bipartisan police reform deal failed.

"After months of exhausting every possible pathway to a bipartisan deal, it remains out of reach right now," Cory Booker lamented. "The time has come to explore all other options to achieve meaningful and common sense policing reform."

President Biden echoed Booker's sentiments: "I still hope to sign into law a comprehensive and meaningful police reform bill that honors the name and memory of George Floyd, because we need legislation to ensure lasting and meaningful change. But this moment demands action, and we cannot allow those who stand in the way of progress to prevent us from answering the call."

Senator Tim Scott blamed the Democrats' push to cut funding to law enforcement for the collapse of bipartisan police reform negotiations on Capitol Hill. In September 2021, President Biden blamed the failure of the deal on Republicans in Congress and claimed they had "rejected enacting modest reforms, which even the previous president had supported."

According to Senator Scott, "We said simply this: 'I'm not going to participate in reducing funding for the police after we saw major city after major city defund the police.' Many provisions in this bill that he wanted me to agree to limited or reduced funding for the police."

I want to address a particular case where defunding the police could have actually saved the life of an unarmed man named Willie McCoy.

Kori McCoy is the brother of Willie, a twenty-year-old who was asleep in his car in a Taco Bell parking lot when police in Vallejo, California, fired fifty-five bullets at him in 3.5 seconds. The killing, which McCoy's family has called an "execution by a firing squad," was deemed "reasonable" by the city of Vallejo's hired consultant. The murder sparked national outrage and led to intense scrutiny of the Vallejo Police Department's frequent use of deadly force, and a history of misconduct and abuse.

Interview with Kori McCoy

Etan: Let's first talk about your brother's case.

McCoy: Okay. So we're going back to February 9 of 2019. It was a rainy night, I remember that, and I received a phone call from my older brother Saturday night, and he was in shock, not really knowing exactly what had happened. He had got a phone call that something had happened to our youngest brother, Willie.

And my older brother and some other family members immediately went to the scene and it was hard to get information. The police were stand-offish, and trying to control the scene. My oldest brother was trying to find out just what had happened, and the police officer was like, "Well, I'm only going to talk to one of you guys. I'm not explaining this over and over," real nasty-like, and when he went over there, the officer told my brother, "All I can tell you is that I can't tell you anything." Basically, just to kind of piss off and let us do our job. So we see the body on the ground, but we're at a distance.

Etan: That's what they said to you?

McCoy: Yes—crazy, right? So my brother and the rest of my family members, they're out there trying to figure out what's going on, but they're not having any success. The police are trying to clear the scene. And so they left a few hours later, and that's when I get the call from my older brother telling me that what they had surmised was that Willie was dead and, apparently, that the police had killed him. But we didn't know the scenario or any of the details as to what had led up to it, or the aftermath, or anything. And so over the next couple of days, information started coming out because there was a bystander that had taken cell phone video. He was in the parking lot, and he sees this enormous amount of police presence standing around this car that's not moving in the Taco Bell lot.

Etan: So nothing from the police?

McCoy: No, they told us absolutely nothing. And ironically, this person that's taking this cell phone video actually went to high school with Willie. He didn't know that at the time, obviously, but he's video recording and he's talking, saying, "God, these police are standing around the car." And then all of the sudden, he captures the police unleashing what is just open fire. It sounds like just dozens of bullets ringing out. So this bystander posts this video, and it was something that the police immediately kind of had to account for. "Well, damn, you guys just opened fired on this car. What happened?"

We retained the services of an attorney, who was familiar with cases that had been going on in Vallejo relating to police misconduct, so I might be bouncing around just a little bit here. In Willie's case, the police immediately put out a press release and reports that when they were called to the scene, they discovered Willie had a gun in his lap. He moved and they gave him instructions to put his hands up. They all claim he reached for the gun and they felt their lives were in danger, and so they opened fire.

Etan: So basically the police lied.

McCoy: Yes, and our family disputed this from jump. I don't know if they were thinking that our family was just going to go with the police narrative of things, because as a society we are somewhat conditioned that when it's coming from an authority figure or an official figure such as the police department, we tend to just automatically believe that it must be the truth. And knowing now what I do know after becoming a student of the history of Vallejo policing problems, it makes more sense to me than it would the average person.

Etan: What's the history of police in Vallejo?

McCoy: Vallejo, California, has a history of problematic policing. We're talking about nineteen police officer kills in the last decade. We're talking about over thirty in the last two decades. Recently, there was a story broken by a reporting agency called Open Vallejo exposing that Vallejo police have been celebrating their kills of citizens by bending one of the six tips of their badge. Captain Whitney, former SWAT commander, tried to whistleblow on what was going on with this ritual within the police department. He was ultimately fired for speaking up.

Etan: Yeah, I read about the badge bending—it's like they wore it as a badge of honor.

McCoy: Exactly, and he actually has a case against the police department that's being litigated. But he shined a lot of light on what was taking place within the Vallejo Police Department, the support they have from their police union as well as the city government, manager, and attorney. So what we're trying to do now is take some of this solid reporting to continue to shine light and confirm things that many of the impacted families have known to be the truth for several years, but many of these cases have been swept under the rug. And the narrative of the officials is kind of what has been bought by the press and by the layman person out there.

And so getting back to Willie's case, there was a council member, Hakeem Brown, the only African American member of the city council. He was giving a Saturday city talk, where they welcomed the community. Now, I don't know if he slipped up or if he said this on purpose—this was maybe a couple weeks after my brother had been killed. Someone asked him what he thought about what had happened to Willie. And he actually said that he had been personally shown the body cam video by the police. And him saying that, it kicked a law into effect where because the Vallejo Police Department had shown this to him, they now were obligated to share this with the public.

Etan: Wait, so they didn't allow it to be seen before that slip-up?

McCoy: No, so my older brother, myself, and my cousin, David Harrison, who I love dearly, the three of us were allowed to go into the police department. Our attorneys were kept outside. But we were allowed to view the body cam video with the police chief at the time, some high-ranking officials of his staff, a lead detective, and, for whatever reason, there was a chaplain in the room. And we were shown the video, but we were not allowed just to sit back and watch it as it went.

Etan: What do you mean?

McCoy: They kept pausing it and talking to us directly as if they were trying to kind of tell us how to interpret what it was that we were seeing. And what it was that we were hearing. And they would have subtitles under some of the video at the bottom, trying to explain. And we now know there have been people that have done studies on the video since it's been released, that many of the subtitles that they put at the bottom did not match up or correspond to what was being said on camera by some of the officers. So it was very disingenuous from the beginning, but we got to a point where we told them they could stop it, that we had seen enough because in our eyes, we just saw an execution.

Etan: So they were trying to convince you that you were seeing something other than what you were actually looking at?

McCoy: Yes, it was ridiculous and insulting. It was to the point of, "Well, what you're seeing right here might be kind of fuzzy, but actually, he's reaching for a gun." At no point did we see a gun, ever. And so we left. This was maybe just a month after Willie had been killed. Shortly after, the video was released to the public with a lot of police spin and narrative. Fast-forward to where we are today, a lot has come out since then.

Etan: That's just criminal.

McCoy: And the badge-bending scandal that I indicated has come out. We had another young man by the name of Sean Monterrosa who also lost his life a few months ago. Officer Jarrett Tonn shot an AR-15 from the backseat of an unmarked police truck, [shooting] between two officers that were sitting in the two front seats. He shot an AR-15 through the front window to kill Sean Monterrosa, who was on his knees with his hands up. Later, after he was searched, they found that he had a hammer in his pocket. Of course, they tried to put a spin on that—we've heard some of the audio, and you can hear them like, "God, he had a gun, right? He had a gun, right?" And the officer that shot him, Jarrett Tonn, this was his fourth shooting.

Etan: Terrible story.

McCoy: It really is. You can hear on the audio, one of their staff command consoling Officer Tonn, telling him, "You've been through this before." Like I say, Vallejo police have multiple officers with multiple kills. I want to make it clear that I'm not antipolice. I'm anti–bad police. My oldest son will be thirty years old next month. And he for a short time was a police officer himself.

Etan: I actually interviewed Sean Monterrosa's sisters for this book.

McCoy: Oh, that's great they will be included in this project. So I have a perspective from both sides. My son, because of certain conscious reasons, he decided very quickly that policing was not for him based on his upbringing and the things that he believed in. There were certain things that he was being asked to do that he personally couldn't get on board with. And so where he thought he possibly could make a difference, he now uses that experience to try to share and give other people a perspective on [how] he is someone, a Black man, that did try to go make a difference. So when I speak on this police misconduct, I just want to give you my full background that I'm not someone that has just been impacted, and I'm just out to rail against the police.

What I need people to understand is when we're talking about Vallejo police, we're not talking about a few bad apples. We're talking about an entire orchard. This is a corrupt police department that has been getting away with not only brutalizing people and taking life, but abusing people. Terrifying people, terrorizing people. They have been supported by a city government that has been compromised with a lot of articles coming out now about backdoor shady dealings within Vallejo regarding money and land deals and all these things connected to the Vallejo police union.

Vallejo is a city where the police department is given 49 percent of the city budget. So we're talking about a police department that is getting nearly half of the budget to run a city. This is an ongoing problem.

Etan: I want to go all the way back to the first initial call to the police from the person at Taco Bell. Correct me if I'm wrong, but there was no mention of a gun?

McCoy: No.

Etan: They just said there was a person who is sleeping in the parking lot, and they're nonresponsive, and that's all, right?

McCoy: Thank you for bringing that up because there is so much, yes. What had happened was my brother had fallen asleep behind the wheel of his car in the Taco Bell drive-through. He was incoherent, unconscious. Before the police were called, we know that there were three different people that went to the side window of where he was asleep on the driver's side, trying to get his attention. And they couldn't.

The last person that went out was a person that delivers food. So they were behind him, and they were trying to pick up their food order so they could go do their job. And he actually got out of his car, and he went to the side of the window and he went into Taco Bell and told them, the gentleman, "People are honking their horns, and I went, and he looked like he's unconscious. He's not moving." No one ever said, "I see a gun in his lap," or anything like that.

So when Taco Bell made the call to 911, you can go back and listen to the audiotape, the mention was for a wellness check. When the 911 operator called, dispatched it to the police, it was for a wellness check. There was no mention of sight of a gun, and there are so many layers to this thing. Because each officer has stated in their police report that there was a gun.

People need to understand that officers are not obligated by law to tell the truth when they give their statements in these police reports. They have a representative from their union by their side, and in most cases, the person asking the questions is a coworker, and even if they're listed as Internal Affairs, they are actually a friend of this officer that's being questioned.

Etan: I understand. So going to a broader level, we hear about defunding the police, and we know what it actually means. We know what they've tried to turn it into, and we know what it actually means. But I want to ask specifically, you said that almost 50 percent of the budget in Vallejo is given to the police department?

McCoy: Yes, that's correct.

Etan: And this is my issue: they are not even trained to handle mental health calls. In this case, when they called them, there was no gun mentioned, there was not an immediate threat. It was for a mental health check.

McCoy: Specifically called by the operator herself a wellness check.

Etan: A lot of people who don't believe or who are against defunding the police need to examine this case in particular. No, defund doesn't mean *abol-*

ish, defund means to redirect some of the funding that is given to the police department, to give to other places that are more equipped and have been trained to deal in this stuff. There should have been another organization called who deal with this type of a situation. Police are trained to deal as if there is an immediate threat, even though there was no immediate threat.

McCoy: Right. There are many cases of impacted families who have lost a loved one to police violence, and they all vary in circumstance. In Willie's case, some people may be like, "Wow, that's a little bit conspiracy sounding for me to believe that these police would actually go out of their way to murder." Well, in my brother's case, that's what happened. These police created the circumstances that they then used to justify murdering Willie.

Policing in Vallejo has been so bad that back in 2008, because of so many civil lawsuits that they were having to pay out for their police brutalizing and taking the lives of people, Vallejo had to go into bankruptcy. They came out of bankruptcy, I want to say in 2014. But what people need to understand, in essence, when the city went into bankruptcy, that defunded the police department in many ways. And what the city saw was more murders by police and more kills by police than it had ever seen. In 2012, Vallejo police killed six people.

You had one officer, Sean Kenney, killed three people in a five-month period. Vallejo's response was to promote him to detective. So, when you talk about defunding the police department, I'm not really someone that is gung ho about that. I want to get to how do we discourage police officers from killing people, and from taking advantage of their badge and brutalizing people? And I think how you do that is you have to set an example by prosecuting.

You put these police officers in jail, the same way you would you or I if we stood around Willie's car and we talked for six to seven minutes, and we're getting ready, and we're setting up our cameras and the angles, and then we go ahead and we murder this kid. You and I are going to jail for life, if not the death penalty.

And I think that once you start sending some of these police officers to jail, not to make an example, but to give them the sentence that justifies the crime . . . We've got to get rid of these protections for police officers, because they're taking advantage of these protections. And they're not worried about any consequences.

The cities, the insurance pool, is paying for their misdeeds and their lawless behavior. And once again, Vallejo, they're on their second insurance pool. They were kicked out of their previous insurance pool because the other police departments in their areas that were in this pool with them were like, "No, you're making it go sky-high for everyone, because you guys are brutalizing and killing people at a rate that for a city with only 120,000 people, it's per capita some of the highest in our nation."

Etan: I agree with your point 100 percent. My counterpoint is: would it be beneficial to have both? To actually have police being held accountable and being prosecuted, and given actual prison time so that they don't have the license to kill—there's one. And then also, wouldn't it make more sense to be able to call an entity who are trained to deal with nonviolent, nonthreatening situations where there's mental health involved or wellness checks?

So the police are not even called in that situation. A totally different entity, because what you described before was them losing funds because of bankruptcy. That's a little bit different than defunding. Specifically, you have the funding geared toward an entity who is specifically trained to deal with wellness and mental health issues, as well as having the police officers and the police departments be held accountable. So I think both of them, not like an either/or.

McCoy: I definitely agree with that, because the statistics even show that one out of every four people that police officers kill is someone going through a mental health crisis. There is an inordinate amount of people going through mental health episodes, so do we really need to call our police to deal with those things?

Etan: So tell me about the work you're doing now. I've done a lot of work with survivors of police brutality and family members of police brutality, and all of you have this in common, you are advocating for laws to be changed.

McCoy: I'm a shy, quiet person. At least that's what I've always considered myself. And for me, two months after my brother was killed, to be speaking at the state capitol in Sacramento is something that I would have never thought I'd be doing. And so it's almost like I'm having an out-of-body experience. I really feel God is pushing my buttons, and pushing me to do right by Willie.

And in doing that, I'm trying to bring attention to the other lost sons of Vallejo that I've come to know—their families and their stories—and so many of them were swept under the rug. We have a new police chief in Vallejo, and he talks a lot about moving forward. And my thing is, no, no. We have to recognize what's been taking place, and what's been going on. And so we're trying to use the platform to leave a memory for Willie

Etan: Talk about how the Vallejo newspapers wrote about your brother.

McCoy: You read hurtful things, like he was a thug with a gun in a car, and he deserved what he got. He was just a rapper, which is something that he did, but it was not who he was. And I think that if you knew Willie's story, to know that he spent time living in group homes, and he spent time in juvenile hall, and he came out of that a better person. And he was a leader and when he started having success with music, he was trying to pull as many young people up with him as he could.

Willie would ride up in the neighborhoods, man, and he would give to the young people, even buying them something to eat. He might look down and be like, "Damn, man, this kid needs a pair of shoes." And he was that dude. And that's why to this day, you see nine-, ten-year-old kids speaking for Willie, out at these youth events. Because that's the Willie that they knew, and so Willie was a person that had dreams of wanting to establish group homes, and do it the right way.

Etan: So you're also in a fight to protect your brother's good name.

McCoy: You hit the nail on the head. We've established the Willie McCoy Foundation. If people go to TheWillieMcCoyFoundation.com, they can see our goals and what we want to do and bring back to the community, a community where we're caring about each other, where we get a sense of values back about how we treat each other and how we respect each other. Where we're listening to our elders, who can provide knowledge and experience. How we treat our women. It's a long list of things that we want to do in the name of Willie. Outside of our foundation, we've started a media network called the Secrets of the Rabbit Hole Media Network. We have a podcast and a YouTube channel.

We've got a few episodes up. And we're trying to provide a platform for impacted families to come on and speak freely, and speak their truth. Because we felt that it was something missing, where the police and the city officials, they're always putting out these narratives. There's a redacted eighty-eight-page police report that was released on Willie. And to then start matching some of the inconsistencies to the press releases that were released in the days after he was murdered, and to hear the same script being followed on other impacted families, I have to do what I can to help them.

Etan: That's amazing.

McCoy: No, it's amazing when you see what's going on. Listen, since my brother was killed, the police chief has retired. The city attorney has retired. The chief lieutenant of Internal Affairs has retired. They brought in an officer who is African American, from San Jose, California, to be the police chief in Vallejo. I'm not bashful about saying that it was a move of, "Bring a Black face in," to try to subdue the Black voices and the uprising of the impacted families, and he's really in over his head. You have a good old boys' network that's just been established within the Vallejo Police Department through their union and they don't listen to him. I mentioned Sean Monterrosa earlier; he was the most recent person to be murdered.

The president of the Vallejo Police Officers' Association, their union, is Michael Nichelini. He is the head of anything relating to automotive within the police department. He got rid of the windshield that was shot through in the Sean Monterrosa case. So Sean's attorneys and no one else would get to see the windshield, and have their investigators look at angles and the certain things that their forensic people would get an opportunity to look at. So this is the president of the Vallejo police union, who had to get suspended by the new chief because of destroying evidence.

Etan: For real?

McCoy: So this runs really deep in the city of Vallejo, and we're just trying to shine light. I have met some great people, not only in my own Bay Area where we live, but across the country. The families, it's a special thing because it seems like only the families can really understand these truths. People, either they don't want to know or it just sounds too much conspiracy theory for people to buy into. But we hope to open up the eyes of people, to let them know that things like police officers shooting someone so they literally can get a paid vacation really take place in this society that we live in.

Interview with Marc Lamont Hill

Marc Lamont Hill is an academic, author, activist, and television personality. He is a professor of media studies and urban education at Temple University in Philadelphia, Pennsylvania. He is also a correspondent for *BET News* and the host of *Black News Tonight*.

Etan: One thing I really respect about you is that you're not afraid to take unpopular positions.

Hill: Yeah, well, you do the same, so the respect is definitely mutual.

Etan: So, President Obama came under fire a little while ago for criticizing what has become, and I don't even like saying this, because it shouldn't be a controversial phrase or a controversial slogan, but he was coming under fire for criticizing defunding the police.

President Obama did explain that the criminal justice system needs reform and should be unbiased and fair. But then he said something along the lines of, "A snappy slogan like 'defund the police' risks doing more harm than good." I'm paraphrasing. What was your response to that?

Hill: Well, first, snappy slogans work. Part of how he became president was because there was a snappy slogan, "Yes we can." That's not exactly a sophisticated policy, right? But it's a way of inspiring people and galvanizing people around an idea, which is what "defund the police" is. Sometimes those slogans are easy and compelling. Sometimes those slogans are hard, and they force people to move in a different direction. I mean, abolishing slavery, women's suffrage now. These were slogans as well as political movements, and they made people uneasy. And abolition now could have been softened to workers' rights for Black people, better working conditions, make plantations nicer, reform the plantation. I mean, we could've come up with different ideas, but at some point, if we reform it too much, or rather if we shape the language too much, then we lose the fundamental substance.

Etan: That's a good point.

Hill: Obama's argument is, if you want criminal justice reform, cool, but this ain't the way to get there, because you lose so many people along way. I don't disagree with that analysis. I think where the president is wrong is that we don't want reform. And so, the premise is wrong. If we wanted reform, yeah, this probably wouldn't be a way to get it. But when you're calling for more radical and durable solutions, then you need a different language to get you there. And that language will be jarring to people. The language will make people uncomfortable. But let's be honest here. We didn't start there.

Etan: What do you mean?

Hill: When you and I were growing up, we saw Rodney King beaten on camera. We just wanted the police officers fired. We just wanted them prosecuted for beating him on tape. I mean, think about how low our bar was. We were happy to have a Black police commissioner. Then it was, well, let's integrate the police force. Let's make the police have to live in the neighborhood. Let's have community-based policing. Let's have civilian review boards. The asks got bigger. And many times, the smaller asks were dismissed too.

Etan: Oh, I see.

Hill: At the time that Rodney King was beaten, LAPD had a clearance rate in the high nineties for officers who were investigated, meaning almost no one, no police officer, was actually punished for beating us. So that's the backdrop to this. So let's not act like if you all were just a little nicer, you would've got it, because we've been there. It's just the same thing with Black Lives Matter, right? "You don't have to tear the city up. If you just ask nicely, we'd give it to you." We've been marching, sitting, protesting, singing, for centuries. That's not the answer.

And so, for me, the call to defund is the right call, but it's not just a call born out of frustration. It's a call born out of a deep analysis that shows that policing as an institution doesn't work. And that the way to get us here, the abolitionist vision that I hold onto says, forces me to ask the question: what could the world look like if all of our needs were met? And if all of our investment is on containment and blame, rather than investment in love, then we never can create the world where our needs are met. And that's why defunding the police is an important start, because it forces us to reimagine where we put our resources. It reinforces us to reimagine what we value and, particularly in a capitalist context, how we mark what we value, which is where we are spending the money. What our priorities are.

Etan: Right. Hearing the people who are fully dedicated to misrepresenting what this means. Then we have to go into explaining that "defund" and "abolish" are not synonyms. And it seems like we're always doing it. It's just like with Colin Kaepernick taking a knee during the national anthem, we had to go and explain that he wasn't anti-American. He wasn't antiveteran. Wasn't antipolice.

Just like Black Lives Matter. We say, "No, they're not a terrorist organization." And I just felt that President Obama fell into that narrative when he stated, "We have to say it a different way," or, "It's not going to be productive," or, "It's going to make us feel good amongst our peers." And I was just like, "President Obama, what are you talking about?"

Hill: I had the same reaction. I was very frustrated. And the president rarely misses an opportunity to do that to us. And he has a habit, there's a way that he establishes equivalency of positions, right? Like the whole, "*Everybody's* mad." Oh, when he gave his race speech, "Black people feel like this. White people feel like this." After Ferguson, well, people getting beaten by police. Yeah, I get that, and it's wrong. But other people feel like . . . There's always a way that he establishes equivalency between pain as if there's no power dynamics at play.

If he's saying, "Tactically and strategically, you lose your message, you lose the people, your coalition," if you say it like this, I understand that argument. But he also sort of demeaned us and sort of minimized the significance of what we're doing. People walked away with hurt from his remarks.

They walked away feeling like all this work we're doing on the ground is being dismissed into snappy slogans and unrealistic politics. And again, from a centrist, liberal perspective and from a reform perspective on policing, he has an argument. But the point is, reform doesn't work.

Etan: Well at least reform up until this point hasn't worked because they haven't held police accountable. You can't have one without the other, right?

Hill: Absolutely not. And I happen to believe in abolishing the police. And you're right, "defund" and "abolish" aren't the same thing. And a lot of people who are calling for defunding don't want to abolish. They're not there yet. And I'm okay with that. I respect that. But I don't want people to run from these terms, even "abolishing." Why is it a venial sin to want to have a world without police? I think it's more important for people to unpack what that means and to set that as a goal and a vision than it is to just sort of say, "Oh my God, who's going to stop the killers and the rapists and murderers?" These are all legitimate questions, but let's not presume that those of us who have been doing this work for decades have never considered those questions, or that we've considered them and are indifferent to the outcome.

Etan: What's your vision in terms of defunding and abolishing?

Hill: My vision of defunding and ultimately my vision of abolition is one where harm is reduced, where people are made whole again, where violence is contained. It's not that I'm saying the world will look like it is right now, or let's just fire all the police and they're all going to go work somewhere else, and now we don't have anybody to deal with our problems. Abolition is a long-term vision that rests upon investment. It rests upon reimagining our relationship to one another. I'll give you one quick example. Walter Wallace in Philadelphia was killed right before the election of 2020. He had a knife, and the police shot him. He was mentally ill. And there were debates. People were saying, "Well, see, this is why we need police. Guy's running around with a knife. What else are you going to do?"

Etan: Yes, that was the case where he had a knife and the family said he was having a mental health crisis and the police shot him like fourteen times.

Hill: Yes, and people were saying, "Well, the police shouldn't have shot him." People say, "The police *had* to shoot him. What else are you going to do?" And so, all of our debate was within the context of a world that keeps police at the center. For me, the question wasn't whether or not the police should have shot him, because in this context, yeah, if you ran at me with a knife, and I've got a gun, I might do the same thing. The question isn't that. The question is, how can we create a world where this mother, when her son is having a mental health episode, can get support without calling an armed police force? Right? The question is, how can we create a world where Walter Wallace's needs are met? His mental health needs are met in such a way that he doesn't get to the point of having a mental health episode, and he's pulling a knife out.

Etan: I see what you're saying.

Hill: That mom didn't call for the police. She called from medical support and got a militarized response. Now, I'm not blaming the particular officers. Again, you're running at me with a knife, and I've got a gun, I don't know what I would do, but that's one of the many reasons why I'm not a police officer. But we have to come up with solutions and strategies, so that that's not the only option. If all I have in my toolbox is a hammer, then everything is going to look like a nail.

And so, the idea is we take the money out of policing, and we put it in institutions that could help Walter Wallace before he ever gets to the point where I have to call the police to stop you from stabbing.

Etan: And in addition to that, they're not trained to handle mental health situations. But then the issue comes with funding. It's like, "Wait a minute, so if you're going to give the money to somebody who is trained for that, that means that we're going to get less money." And that's the part that they can't get behind. But if you're not trained for that, then why are you being paid for it?

Hill: Right. And that's the fundamental question. I think one way to frame this that actually is helpful, I think, for bringing people into the debate, is when we frame it as, look, police are overworked. We're asking them to do too many jobs. In a town like Ferguson, where Mike Brown was killed, Mike Brown wasn't even stopped by Darren Wilson for stealing from the store. He was stopped for jaywalking. That's not something that we need to be stopping people for. But then, when you look at the fact that Ferguson doesn't have money, town resources depleted, I talk about this in my book *Nobody*. Part of how the town generates revenue is by these petty tickets and offenses. At the time of Mike Brown's killing, 80 percent of the town of Ferguson had warrants. They weren't for murder. They weren't for kidnapping. They were for jaywalking or parking or whatever.

But you get these petty offenses you can't afford. So, they give you five days to pay the ticket where people get paid every two weeks. All these strategies, to make sure that the fines go up, and then you get a warrant. And so, that's the town business. In that case, the police become tax collectors. Someone has a drug overdose in your city; police aren't trained to handle that. Now they're medical staff. They're violence interrupters. They've become social workers. So, we put all these jobs on police, when as you rightly point out, they're not trained to do it. And they certainly can't do it well. And so, the idea is to say, let's take some responsibility off your plate so that you can concentrate on these other things. I happen to believe those other things also should not exist. I'm an abolitionist.

Etan: Gotcha.

Hill: But if you're just talking about defunding, we're just talking, it's like in sports, right? Sometimes you get somebody who's president, GM, and coach, and they just can't do all those things well.

Etan: Good analogy.

Hill: And you might be a good GM, and a great coach, but the problem is you've got to do *all* of it. And you've got these conflicts that can become troublesome. Same thing with policing, right? So, let them concentrate on *one* of these things. Now, my job on the ground as an activist and as a scholar is to help us reimagine those things too, to figure out how we can create a world where there's less criminalization, so that not only can the police focus on crime, but we can say, "All right, how can we reduce what constitutes a crime?" Because what we've done over the last few decades is widen the net so that more things are crimes. So, what if we shrink that net? What if, as we've done with marijuana, it's a great example, right? What if we say marijuana is not illegal. So now a police officer is not stopping everybody smoking a L on the corner. The world hasn't gone up in flames, there's just fewer people in the jails, right?

Etan: Yeah, but it was a specific strategy, though. And we saw that, especially in New York with stop and frisk. I mean, Black people were stopped for any type of little suspicion. And then it led to something else where white people are walking by smoking weed, whatever. And they're not stopped. We have to look at the actual training as well and hold police officers accountable, because, and you've used the reference before, if somebody is coming at with you with a knife, and you have a gun, then you're going to shoot. But that doesn't happen with white people.

Hill: Right.

Etan: White people come at them with knives, with guns, with axes, with all kinds of stuff. And we see police use discretion. They're calming. They're de-escalating the situation. But then we see us, someone with no weapon, just upset. And then they're firing. And that's an issue. So there has to be something with the entire system of how they're being trained and what is being allowed. If we don't see any police officers being held accountable for things, the conviction rate is really, really low. And right now it seems like they have a license to kill. And they'll just get away with it. So then we have to start addressing that part as well. Would you agree?

Hill: Yeah, I think that we should do all that. We need accountability. We need measures, we need to retrain, we need all of these things. My concern is that within the practical context of a white supremacist world, I don't know how you can *unlearn* white supremacy. And it's not just white cops. It's Black cops too.

So that's why I'm skeptical of the possibility of retraining police in ways that give us justice, but we certainly can do better than we're doing right now. That's where retraining comes in. I think that's where accountability measures come in. And we try. The whole point of body cameras was that maybe if they know we're watching, they won't do it.

Etan: That definitely didn't help.

Hill: Exactly, and civilian review boards is one of the biggest things that police officers have pushed against. They do not want anybody but the police to police the police.

Etan: They want to investigate themselves. Let us know if they did anything wrong.

Hill: Right. That's basically what Internal Affairs for the police is. We've got to reimagine this stuff. We need outside accountability if we're going to have these institutions in place. And again, I'm not naive or idealistic. I don't believe that we're going to have a world without police, probably in our lifetime. But that's the goal. Just like in 1619, a world without slavery wasn't possible for several lifetimes, for multiple generations, but it was still the vision. And we worked toward it. We fought toward it.

I'm not against reforms, to be clear. I'm against reforms that undermine a radical solution. So I don't want reforms that make us believe that this system is savable. But if I can do something that will continue to chip away—for example, getting rid of cash bail is a reform, but it's also a radical solution, because it's still abolitionist.

So getting rid of cash bail de-carcerates people. I'm with that. Decriminalizing drugs is an abolitionist move, because it ex-carcerates. It stops using the prison as the resolution to a social contradiction or a crisis. I'm okay with that. What I'm not okay with is giving people body cameras or making police have to live in the neighborhood, because then it's suggested, "Oh, this is fixable. If they just lived with us, and we could get rid of the bad apple, we'd be fine."

Etan: Well, I grew up with police officers that knew me. And it was a little bit different. Across the railroad tracks, we had police officers that we actually knew. They went to our church. Their kids went to our school. So it's a little bit different than just moving them into the neighborhood. But I think the main thing is to hold them accountable. "If you do *this*, this will be the punishment," and you give them that punishment. Right now, they're doing whatever they want to do, because they get away with it.

Hill: Impunity makes everything more challenging. But those officers knew you. They live in your neighborhood. They knew your family. They loved you. They saw you as a person. And I'm not sure that systemically, we can replicate that large scale. And so, that's my concern about that, but you're right. Accountability is a huge step. If they know they can shoot me, and the worst thing that'll happen is they might get fired, and there's not even a national database of this . . . So that if you get fired for killing me in New York, you can get a job in Camden. You can get a job in Tulsa. You can get a job in Philly. You can get a job in Syracuse.

Etan: And that's absolutely absurd.

Hill: So this becomes part of the problem too. There's just no outrage. There's just no outrage about this that's consistent, because the value of the lives that are getting extinguished in the most unjust fashion are ones that are seen as disposable: poor people, Brown people, Black people, people who are addicted to drugs, mentally ill folks, disabled folks. These are all populations that are overrepresented on police rolls. And we have to do something different.

Interview with Officer Joe Ested

Officer Joe Ested is the author of the book *Police Brutality Matters*. He's a police/legislative/corporate consultant, cultural diversity facilitator, public speaker, and the former vice president of the New York City police union.

Etan: Where do you stand with defunding the police? Is it as much of a trigger for you as it appears to be for many police?

Ested: Honestly, I've heard so many different explanations as to what it means, we would have to deal with every single explanation. If you ask ten people, you will get ten different descriptions, so for that reason, until there is one universal explanation that everybody uses, I don't even like to comment on it.

Etan: Fair enough. Tell me about yourself and what you do with Police Brutality Matters.

Ested: I come from a low-income community which we all know is most affected by police brutality. I grew up antipolice because what I saw growing up was excessive, aggressive, abusive policing. So that was my mindset. And I always wanted to figure out how we can change this. I was challenged by my brother, who was also a police officer, who said, "Why don't you join if you think you can make a difference?" So I did, and once I joined I did see that there were a lot more good cops than there is bad, but I also saw the systemic problems that have in fact existed in law enforcement for many years. And I came to the realization that these problems will always exist because law enforcement hasn't acknowledged that there is in fact a problem. So I spent a large amount of my time trying to make that change from within, and I also discovered that there is definitely a retaliation from within when you try to create change.

Etan: What led you to found Police Brutality Matters?

Ested: Being fed up with the system led me. And what we do here is we talk with high school kids and college kids on how to stay alive when they encounter excessive, aggressive police officers. We're talking police reform—I speak to congressmen to push for reform because what we are seeing as far as discussions is not actual reform at all. It's window dressing. The culture of policing is like a gang. Codes, fear and intimidation, things that you see common with street gangs, you see police using those same tactics, and they only use those tactics on certain communities. I became vice president of the police union, so I got the opportunity to see firsthand how the police union impacts if an officer gets disciplined or not.

Etan: There's a lot to unpack with this. I want to first ask you about a specific case, Willie McCoy. I interviewed his brother Kori for this book and so much went wrong with that case, so much was done incorrectly by the Vallejo police.

Ested: This is a very common call. And just FYI, I wasn't only a beat cop, I also worked in specialized units—we targeted drugs and guns, so we dealt with the real criminal elements of society. So when we talk about responding to armed party calls, I am very familiar with the protocol. So you have a 911 call: "Subject is sleeping inside of a vehicle." And in this case, there was never any mention of a gun in the 911 call, but it was a wellness check, correct?

Etan: Yes sir, that's correct.

Ested: That distinction is important because that determines the level of response from the police according to protocol. They get to the scene, one officer suspects a gun, they draw down, they start yelling, he's not responding, right then and there if they thought in their minds that Mr. McCoy had a gun, they should've immediately taken a cover position. If you notice watching the video, none of the officers took a cover position at any point in this encounter. They remained directly in front of the driver's-side window where if the person did have a gun there is no cover, so now I have to escalate to using deadly force. The training that law enforcement receive is to prevent officer death and prevent officer injury. So anytime you even suspect a gun, you take cover. You see, these guys never took cover. They even started trying to figure out, "I'm gonna reach inside, I'm gonna pull this alleged gun, and if he moves, I'm gonna shoot him." Isn't that what they said?

Etan: Yes, and you can see all of what you describe clearly in the video.

Ested: So that tells me that all protocol was out the window by these officers. Now, there are times when an officer has to use deadly force. To save yourself from being killed or to save someone else's life at that very moment. Neither of those two elements existed. They created a deadly force situation. This is consistent across all departments across America.

Etan: Why weren't any of these cops held accountable? Because after that, they just opened fire like it was an execution, and on top of that, no gun was found.

Ested: Well, one of the major systemic problems we have in law enforcement is that the DA is assigned to investigate officer shootings. So day in and day out, I personally work with DAs, I'm their probable call for their cases. When I make a case, I go and I sit down with the DA and go over the elements of the case. The DA says, "No, you have to make it stronger here, this part needs to be better." I'm building a relationship with them. I've gone to DAs' weddings, Christmas parties, there's a relationship there. Now, I'm in a situation where my friend has to investigate me? So it should come as no surprise when the DA says that there is no indictment given to this officer no matter what the facts are. The DA has the power to give a strong indictment or a weak indictment when they testify in front of a grand jury. They don't even have to present a case to the grand jury. They have huge discretionary powers.

Etan: That's just a bad system. Everything you said proves why there needs to be an outside investigator whenever there is a lethal police shooting. Why is that so hard to put into place?

Ested: You are 100 percent right. Let me illustrate it like this, and I put this in my book *Police Brutality Matters*. Special investigative unit. You know when a plane crashes and they send an NTSB? People who are experts in plane failure, human failure, people who are totally independent from the actual airlines. Delta doesn't send in their own investigators. It's an outside agency, nobody has a connection to the actual airlines. I definitely think any police shooting should be investigated by a special task force who has no relationship with the local law enforcement, and you have prosecutors and state and federal agents of that task force to go investigate shootings. Because once we start knowing each other, there's a human attachment to want to look out for the person you know. A huge conflict of interest. You're taught out the gate this is a family, it's us against them, we take care of each other at all costs, so in a good situation, that's a wonderful thing. If I have to get involved in a shoot-out with a real bad guy, I know my brothers and sisters are coming to help defend me and they will die for me. But on the flip side of that, if I'm a dirty cop and violating, I have that same support coming to defend me. So yes, it allows the bad elements to have the same protection you give good policing, so to answer your question, yes, that's a terrible system.

Etan: What roles do the union play in this problem?

Ested: The union has taken the position that my members, I'm representing all of them and I'm going to fight for all of them good or bad right or wrong. And even as the vice president of the union, I used to have these conversations with the president and say, "You know he was dead wrong, right? Why are we defending someone who is wrong?" We had to be actual representatives for the officers during their process. And I had a hard time defending someone who was blatantly wrong, we're not defense attorneys, don't we have an obligation to what's right? You've never seen a union come out and say, "This officer got it wrong," and that's the problem.

Etan: How do you have a system where nobody is held accountable and everyone is defended, whether right or wrong? That's not even logical.

Ested: Not at all.

Etan: I've heard you tell the story of the brainwashing of Black officers.

Ested: I had an officer send me a video that he recorded recently in class and the chief said, "All my Black officers raise your hand, you're no longer Black, you're blue, and you are now a part of the blue family." And this shows how it's a gang. You know, the Bloods or Crips. When you cross over, you become red, you become blue, and law enforcement has that exact same mentality.

Etan: Talk about the backlash you receive as an officer if you do want to break that protocol and call another officer out for being a bad cop.

Ested: Most officers want to continue to move up in rankings whether it's promotions, specialized units, certain work schedules, and these are all elements law enforcement powers that be use against officers who don't just go along. And any officer will tell you, if they're being honest, that's what happens.

I was in pursuit of a suspect on foot. He was running away from me. I caught him and I cuffed him. As I'm walking him back, other officers who came for backup walked up to me. They showed up and started punching and hitting him. So I pulled the guy who I just ran down and chased away from them and said, "What are you doing?" And they said to me, "He ran, we gotta tune him up"—those were their words. And I was like, "That's not what I was taught in the academy." And this is what they said, "Listen, the academy is one thing, the streets are different. We have to do things differently in the real world than what you were taught in the academy, and you need to wake up and realize that or you won't last as a cop."

Etan: Wow, so that explains why it's not about better training.

Ested: Right, and let me take it a step further. So much of the taxpayers' money has been wasted paying for bad policing. The reason why it's so easy to win civil suits is because nine times out of ten, what the officer did was in fact outside of their training. And I've heard officers time and time again say, "What are you worried about it for? Let the city cut the check. We have to maintain control on the streets."

Etan: Should officers have some type of financial hit instead of the city? Should they maybe lose their pensions or something so they could feel the sting and not, "Oh, just let the city take care of it"?

Ested: I also outlined this in my book: instead of letting the taxpayers pay for bad policing, let each officer get their own insurance. So what happens then is when someone makes a civil suit to an officer, that officer has to represent himself through his own insurance company. And if he is found liable, his premiums go so high and he won't be able to afford it. And that should be a condition of you having your license as a law enforcement officer. So if you're not following protocol, the city no longer protects you financially. This is the only job I know where you can literally do anything you want and there's no accountability.

Etan: That makes a lot of sense.

Ested: Let me throw this one in too, this is something else I would change. That special investigative unit, state and federal, that I spoke about earlier that should investigate all police shootings—they should also investigate if a whistleblower or good cop comes forward and says, "This bad policing is going on," or wants to turn in a bad cop, which so many people are calling to happen and should happen in the right system, but they shouldn't only be able to make the complaint to the same people who are now assigned to actually handle the complaint. If me as a cop sees an officer beating someone up while they're in handcuffs, or any type of corruption, we should be able to contact an outside entity and know that we won't face any repercussions. Stop letting the police investigate themselves. If you do that, you will change the entire culture of policing—I'm 100 percent confident in that.

Black Women and the Police

The Black Woman is not being taken serious, and we have the men in the media, entertainment business, and ourselves to blame. We as Black Women must make the decision to choose how we are seen in the world.
—Kathleen Cleaver

My daughter Imani walked into my office while I was preparing to interview Chikesia Clemons. I was watching YouTube clips from her case as well as the news coverage. Imani asked, "Daddy, what are you watching and why are the police beating this girl like this?" I took a deep breath, told her to sit down and watch with me. I explained that a waitress called the police on Clemons because they had a dispute, and this is what occurred when police arrived at the Waffle House. Imani was angered by what she saw: the image of a white police officer abusing someone who looked just a little older than her. On the video all you could hear was screaming: "Get off her!!!!" "Why are you doing this to her!!!!" Police slammed her to the ground and her top came off, exposing her. One cop looked like he was intentionally trying to break her arm, and you could hear Clemons yell, "What are you doing?" The response was, "I'll break your arm, that's what I'm about to do," while another officer appeared to have his knee in her stomach.

Then we watched the YouTube clip of Clemons speaking for the first time since the event took place, saying, "I can't eat, I can't sleep, I'm constantly crying."

This was followed by attorney Benjamin Crump breaking down what had happened. Imani looked at me with tears in her eyes and asked, "Why would they do that to her?" I told her I didn't know but was preparing to find out. We talked about different cases, from Sandra Bland to Breonna Taylor. I introduced Imani to SayHerName and its mission.

The more we researched, the more frustrated Imani got. We found that Black women are often overlooked when it comes to conversations, media coverage, and outrage about police terrorism. We discovered that most people killed by police get little to no attention from national media outlets; we only hear about a select few. And Black women are far more likely to be killed by police than other women, according to the *Washington Post*'s database of deadly police shootings.

According to FiveThirtyEight: "Women account for less than 4 percent of fatal police shootings, but almost 20 percent of them are Black, even though Black women make up only around 13 percent of women in the US. Since 2015, at least fifty-one Black women have been killed. Half of those women have gotten some national media attention within sixty days of their death." However, the coverage is limited overall.

Cases that did spark national news coverage—like those of Breonna Taylor and Ma'Khia Bryant—are the exception. We also read opinions such as that of Alex Samuels, Dhrumil Mehta, and Anna Wiederkehr, who wrote an article titled, "Why Black Women Are Often Missing from Conversations About Police Violence."

Bryant's death most likely received national media attention only because the news cycle at the time was already focused on police brutality. Derek Chauvin—the officer who murdered George Floyd—was convicted only minutes after Bryant was killed in Columbus, Ohio. Similarly, toward the end of the Chauvin trial, Daunte Wright was fatally shot by Minneapolis police. (As with Bryant, Taylor's death received an uptick in national attention only after Floyd's death, when police brutality was again dominating headlines.)

"Michelle Cusseaux, Tanisha Anderson, Korryn Gaines, India Kager, Natasha McKenna—these are Black women who were killed within weeks, sometimes days, of men whose names we know—sometimes by the same police department," said Kevin Minofu, a senior research and writing fellow with the African American Policy Forum, in an email to FiveThirtyEight. (The African American Policy Forum founded the SayHerName campaign in December 2014; its mission is to publicize how Black women are killed and brutalized by police with alarming regularity.)

I also moderated an all-female panel consisting of WNBA players Angel McCoughtry, Elizabeth Williams, Renee Montgomery, and Tierra Ruffin-Pratt, along with Emerald Garner (daughter of Eric Garner). I sat down with my daughters Imani and Baby Sierra and showed them a recording of the panel—I wanted to see their response.

Imani immediately said, "Hey, I remember Emerald!" I had taken her to a panel with Emerald Garner, her sister Erica Garner, and Trayvon Martin's brother Jahvaris Fulton at Canaan Baptist Church in Harlem a few years back. Imani and my wife Nichole had opened the event with a song, the Faith Evans remake of J. Cole's "Be Free." Imani also sang the song by herself at another event with the Garner family.

Imani and Baby Sierra listened to Emerald talk about her book and everything she is doing to push for justice. They listened to Renee Montgomery (who took a year off from playing in the WNBA to focus on activism after the murders of George Floyd and Breonna Taylor) and Elizabeth Williams (who was at the time the longest-tenured member of the Atlanta Dream).

Montgomery and Williams discussed what prompted their revolt against Kelly Loeffler, a CEO of the Atlanta Dream, and detailed how the team banded together (along with the help of the entire WNBA) to elect Loeffler's opponent, Raphael Warnock, to the US Senate.

A little background: The franchise had been at the center of turmoil since Kelly Loeffler wrote a letter to WNBA commissioner Cathy Engelbert objecting to the league's embrace of the Black Lives Matter movement during the 2020 season. Players around the league initially called on Loeffler to sell her share of the team (49 percent). When she refused, they publicly endorsed her opponent, Reverend Raphael Warnock, in her senatorial race, who was polling at a lowly 9 percent before the Atlanta Dream and the WNBA got involved. Warnock defeated Loeffler in the January 5 runoff in large part to the work of the WNBA.

Baby Sierra was really inspired by the women all standing together in unity. She actually got hyped and said she wanted to do that when she gets older: get her volleyball teammates together and stand for people and causes the way the WNBA players did.

Imani turned to me while we were discussing all this, and I could see the wheels turning in her mind. She asked, "How many more situations have there been like that? Why did they have to create a SayHerName? Why don't more people bring attention to what happens to Black girls?" Then she started breaking down for the whole family what she had learned, and later did more of her own research about Chikesia Clemons. It was like she was giving a book report. She was so affected by it because she obviously saw herself in Chikesia Clemons.

Interview with Chikesia Clemons

Etan: What happened to you is heartbreaking. This all started at a Waffle House because they didn't want to give you plastic utensils for your takeaway food?

Clemons: That's correct. They wanted to charge fifty cents for plasticware. We always ask for plasticware because of the germs. Especially when I go into a restaurant and eat. We asked them for plasticware, and they told us it was fifty cents. We had never heard that before anywhere in America, charging for plasticware when you're eating at a restaurant. So yes, that's what it stemmed from.

Etan: How did they go from that to calling the police?

Clemons: It went from us disputing the fifty cents to the waitress butting into the personal conversation between me and my friend, and spiraled from there. We weren't talking to her nor referring to her. She just took it upon herself to interject herself into our conversation, and her and my friend started going back and forth.

Etan: When the police came, they claimed they were told there was a gun and you all were drunk. Two eyewitnesses completely refuted their claims, with one witness adding that if there had been a gun, she wouldn't have stayed and continued eating. She further said that nobody appeared drunk or anything like that. It was a complete fabrication by police.

Clemons: Absolutely. "The young lady came into this restaurant, and she was loud and belligerent. And then she stated that she was going to shoot us with a gun. That was a threat." So that's how they built their whole case and narrative. But none of that actually happened. I had no weapon. So, completely fabricated story. I wasn't belligerent. Wasn't drunk. None of that.

Etan: And then you were arrested for disorderly conduct and resisting arrest.

Clemons: Correct.

Etan: I watched the video. You were sitting down, not threatening or doing anything, when the officer came in and grabbed you?

Clemons: When the officer first came in, I was standing up. He sat me in the chair. I was sat there physically by the officer. And he made me sit there until the second officer came in.

Etan: I heard you repeating, and you could hear it on the video, "What did I do wrong? Can you tell me what I did wrong?"

Clemons: Right.

Etan: I heard the officer say, "I'm going to break your arm. That's what I'm going to do." It's interesting, because on your local news they're saying you were "involved in a scuffle with the police." That was no scuffle. You were assaulted by the police. But the language the local media intentionally uses gives the perception this was a two-way incident. That just wasn't the case.

Clemons: That's correct. The local news here played a big factor in the narrative and how everything got portrayed and put out in the public. Still to this day, anything with me or my name attached to it, it gets news really quick. No matter what it is. It's always "the girl from the Waffle House incident."

Etan: The police did what they always do: justify their actions. They said you were disrupting other customers, because you asked to speak to the corporate manager when you were treated unfairly, which you are allowed to do. I see white women ask to speak to the manager and create scenes all the time. Nothing happens to them like what happened to you. Not just in Alabama, all over the country. Do you feel if the racial dynamics were different, the waitress would have called the police?

Clemons: Absolutely not. There was no need to even involve police. That was something that could have been handled between us. I don't think police would have been involved if it was a different racial dynamic.

Etan: There were two different trials: One where you were found guilty of disorderly conduct and resisting arrest in a lower court. The other one ended in a split jury. Explain the two trials.

Clemons: Okay, so the first trial was held in Saraland, Alabama, where this situation happened. They automatically found me guilty for disorderly conduct and resisting arrest. We didn't get out of court until about ten thirty, eleven at night from them deciding on what they want to charge me with, disorderly or resisting arrest or not. So they had already had in their mind, "She's guilty. We're going to go ahead and charge her. This is what she's going to have to do after that."

Etan: Wait, so they decided it that day?

Clemons: Yes, and after I was found guilty for disorderly conduct and resisting arrest, we appealed it. After appealing it, it went to our circuit court here in Mobile, Alabama. Mobile is the actual county. So it was our county court. We had a jury, and the jury had three Black people, and about eleven or twelve white people. Half of the people were within law enforcement, have a family member in law enforcement, or worked somewhere in law enforcement. The other half had seen the story on the news. They had already picked out their opinion as to what should have happened and toward me.

We had what's called a Batson challenge, which is when one party objects to the exclusion of potential jurors from the jury on the basis of race, sex, ethnicity, etc., etc. So we ended up winning our Batson challenge and we had to do jury selection all over again.

So we started that process, and there everything came out as far as the lies, what time it was when they called the police, who made the phone call. We had the recording. My lawyers did such a great job. Got all the information out. So after that deliberation, they found that I was actually not guilty of disorderly conduct, but I was still charged for resisting arrest. The law does state that if you had no reason for being arrested, then you can't be arrested for resisting arrest.

Etan: Okay, I didn't know that but it makes sense.

Clemons: Right, so they never had a reason. Disorderly conduct was the reason for me being arrested. Then they took that away. They have to take away resisting arrest. So the courts here in Alabama, they're a little tricky. If they know something is right, they're going to try to find their way to get around it. But they still charged me after we brought the information to them, they still charged me with resisting arrest. So we're actually appealing that now. Due to COVID, everything has been pushed back for court. So we're actually just waiting now for a date for the appeal.

Etan: And your lawyer, Marcus Fox, really did a great job, especially with all the hurdles. Going back to the video, your dress came down, and you were exposed, and they didn't even try to cover you. It was just so heartless. I'm watching with my daughter Imani, and she asked, "Would they have done that to a white lady? Would they have done that to a lady that looks like she could have been one of their daughters?" She also said, "Well, if her friend wasn't there to record everything, nobody would've known what happened to her?"

Clemons: Absolutely not. Your daughter is 100 percent correct.

Etan: Were their body cameras on? Were the Waffle House cameras on? Because I haven't seen any other footage except for what your friend recorded.

Clemons: Right. So they did issue a few of the video footage from that night. It doesn't have any audio on it, so the only thing that you see is me standing by the register, walking back and forth. That's it. But other than that, the police officers didn't issue or offer any body cameras or any body footage that they had recorded on themselves that night. And the only thing that we had to go off of was the video that my friend recorded.

Etan: So, *did* they have body cameras?

Clemons: No. They did not. No.

Etan: In Alabama, are police body cameras supposed to be used?

Clemons: I don't think it's a requirement for them to have them here. You have to remember, we're talking about Alabama. Alabama is one of the most racist states down South here.

Etan: Saraland police officer Chris Ramey argued in the court that everything the police did was justified. That was the first thing he said. What was going through your mind when you heard him say that?

Clemons: I was pissed, of course. When I was younger, I was in this program called Police Explorers and they teach kids their rights. They teach you what police officers can and cannot do to you. They teach you the rules of police policy, enforcement of policy, the way they're supposed to approach you during a dispute.

The entire way the police handled this situation was inconsistent with what I was taught was proper procedure. For example, when he first came in and approached me, he was supposed to separate both parties, take me outside to understand what was going on, and then ask her what her side of the story was. That never happened. When he first came in, he said that he told me that I was under arrest. He never approached me and said, "Hey, you're under arrest for such and such." He never gave me the reason for arrest.

Etan: They didn't follow procedure at all.

Clemons: Not at all. Also, he just had me in full force and his hands on me, and he's not explaining to me what's going on. That was something else that they're supposed to take into consideration, as I'm a female and you're a male police officer. You are already supposed to have a female police officer searching me. No man is supposed to be touching me without my permission.

Etan: That's the protocol everywhere, right?

Clemons: It's supposed to be. But when I asked the second police officer, "Hey, can I please speak with you to let you know what's going on, what the situation is?" he completely stopped me and told me, "No, I don't want to talk to you." That was something else that they could have done correctly. So when they said that in court, I was like, *I'm writing down everything that they're saying, everything.* This is not right. So that's why I'm full force in backing myself up, because I know it's not right.

Etan: Waffle House issued a statement saying that they also supported the officers' actions. They never recanted that?

Clemons: Nope. That was their response then, and to this day that's what they're sticking with. That's their position.

Etan: What would you tell someone like my daughter Imani? Seeing all of this going on, how would you tell younger girls especially how to stand up for their rights in a situation like this?

Clemons: I have an eight-year-old daughter and she's wanting to know why. "Why did this happen to you? Why did this restaurant do that? Why can't you go in there?" So my advice to her is to learn, educate yourself. That's the most important thing that we have to do. Reading is very, very important when you're trying to stand up for yourself. Read, write, understand, ask questions. If you need someone to let you know how something goes, or even if you want to reach out to a police officer, just so they can let you know.

Ever since this situation happened, I have been educating myself. Okay, what kind of law is this? What does this go for? What does this do? Will it help me in this situation? Will it not help me in this situation? Read more. Talk more. Understand and listen more.

Etan: We always refer to the talk that we as Black parents have to have with our children. It's something white parents don't have to worry about. It's not their reality. But as a father, you want to just protect your daughters and put them in this protective bubble, but you have to prepare them for what they're going to face. It's heartbreaking, because that's not the way it's supposed to be.

Clemons: I totally agree. There's no reason why my eight-year-old has to see me go through the things that I went through for the last three years, it's traumatizing for her as well. It was definitely hard for me. And I'm still going through the things that I'm going through now. It's still hard. I'm learning how to ease my way out of it. But I still have a daughter that I have to be strong for at the end of the day. She does not deserve to carry my burden from me being assaulted by police officers.

Etan: Tell me about the support that you received. First, let's talk about attorney Benjamin Crump.

Clemons: As soon as my situation happened, Ben came down. We met, and he's been on the forefront ever since, anything that I need, anything that I have questions about. Just anything, Ben is always there. So he has been one of the biggest supporters that I have. He also reached out to a few of his activists that he worked with, like Tamika Mallory. She's my sister. If I don't have nothing, or if I need anything, I can call. She's always going to answer the phone for me. Along with her came Mysonne "the General." Brittany Packnett, she is my sister as well. She has been in the forefront, helping, supporting, doing everything that she needs to do. And Jamilia Land, of course, that's my heart. She's been full force with helping me as well, so the support has been enormous. It has been very appreciated from then all the way up until now. So I still have these people still here supporting me. Oh, and Al Sharpton, can't forget him. He's been great.

Etan: A lot of people criticize Reverend Al Sharpton, but when I talk to family members or somebody dealing with police brutality, they speak very highly of him.

Clemons: People say a lot of things they don't know anything about. I've heard things about everyone I've mentioned. My experience is something totally different. And I will always back him up and support him, because that's my experience with him.

Etan: You also received an outpour of support from the community. I saw within days, you had petitions with like fourteen thousand signatures calling for the arrest of the officers.

Clemons: From my hometown, from everyone, from all states. There was support from everywhere. When you're going through a situation like that, you don't know what to expect. I was also receiving a lot of backlash, and my life was actually in jeopardy. With the support, it really helped me feel like I can actually do this and do what I need to do. I can stand up for myself, because I have all these people looking at me. They're going to be inspired by me standing up for myself. So the support actually motivated me to inspire more people to stand up for themselves.

Etan: People don't really know all of the stuff that you went through after this. You lost your job. You were forced to move multiple times, and your children were being tormented and bullied. Talk about that aspect.

Clemons: At the time, I was living in Saraland, Alabama. I was headed home once we left the Waffle House. So I stayed in Saraland where it happened, and the police officers are actually from that area. It's a predominantly white community. And so, once it got out, I had all those people threatening me. They were finding me on social media, sending me threatening messages saying what they were going to do to me. I'll never forget, one man told me that he would have raped me. And he would have showed me what a little Black girl is supposed to feel like.

I will never forget that. That hurt so bad to even know people even just think like that or say something like that just to get at you. I had a neighbor who, after seeing me exposed on the news, started sending me explicit messages.

Etan: These are all white people?

Clemons: All white people, yes. They even went so far as to make on social media a private page . . . And they made muffins, pictures of me and my mom on the muffins, and they were brown muffins, and they called them "nigger muffins."

Etan: Wow.

Clemons: Yeah. It was a lot. They threatened my daughter. They were putting her face on a lot of things and stuff like that in this group as well. And so, I just had to get out of this. I had to get out of where I was living, because of the people that were there. I actually moved out of Alabama for a year.

Etan: Even in the midst of all of that, while you were awaiting jury trial, you organized a community giveback drive for book bags, school uniforms, supplies, and voter registration. Helping people with domestic violence in your home town of Prichard. How do you have the strength and the ability to help others in the midst of you being racially tormented and threatened on the daily?

Clemons: I just feel like it's . . . I don't want to say it's an obligation. I see the people in my community, the things that we go through. I live in my community. I'm an actual citizen. So not only are *they* affected by half the things that goes on in the city, *I'm* affected by it as well. So if our city council members not wanting to come together and help us out, we have to come together and help each other out.

The Waffle House situation, it actually put me in a mind state to give back to people, because we're all we've got. We might not relate to each other as kinfolk, we might not be cousins, but we are in some type of way. And so, if I can be the forefront for these people, to be the voice and help them speak up and speak out about things that concern them, then let me do that. Let me be the pillar for them.

I still suffer a lot of things that go on in this community. Not even just me, just in the world. But we have to look toward somebody. People look toward people for inspiration and strength and energy and dedication and motivation. And let me be that person to do that. And I really enjoy doing it. It's not like it's something being forced on me. This is something from my heart. This solely comes from me, based on me and how I feel my people should be supported. So it may not be much to a lot, but to some it's a lot.

Etan: I've done work with family members of the victims of police brutality. All of you have this in common where you now want to help other people and make sure what happened to you or happened to your loved one doesn't keep happening to the next person. I saw that you were running for city council, and you were involved in the political structure, and you were trying to figure out ways to make a change and make a difference. Tell me a little bit about that.

Clemons: I originally ran for a city council position here in my hometown, Prichard, Alabama, the area that I live in. And so, it's like basic human necessities that we are not receiving. On the streets, we have potholes, literally every other street. We can't even ride in the community without hitting a pothole or getting a flat tire. We have a lot of crime here. If someone gets killed in the streets, no one's going to tell on this person, it's a crime that goes unsolved. We have domestic violence situations that happen a lot here. A lot, lot, lot here in Mobile and in Prichard.

Those things all need solving. And so, by me growing up in this community and seeing those things, and then this situation happened to me, I'm only twenty-seven years old. I'm young. So now I'm trying to make a difference. Running for city council was to introduce a new face, a new generation, running for a political seat to put in some new ideas into office to change some things, to actually bring about change.

Etan: I have so much respect for you. And just a clarification. To this day, the police officers, nothing happened to them? They didn't get fired? No charges?

Clemons: Yeah, that's correct.

Etan: Unbelievable.

Interview with Yamiche Alcindor

Yamiche Alcindor is a PBS White House correspondent, NBC and MSNBC contributor, former writer for the *New York Times* and *USA Today*, and was recently named as the next moderator of the PBS current affairs show *Washington Week*. She sets a shining example for many young Black girls. Sharon Percy Rockefeller, president and CEO of WETA (the DC area's leading public broadcasting station), said of Alcindor, "With composure and tenacity, she has covered some of the most momentous political stories of our time, continually demonstrating the highest standards of journalism."

Etan: I've been a big fan of yours for a long time.

Alcindor: Thanks so much. You might not remember, but you came to my school when I was a freshman at Georgetown University, and you had a lasting impression. I was someone who went to Georgetown not knowing it was a basketball school, and you broke down kind of the NBA, and there was a discussion on the book *Forty Million Dollar Slaves* by Bill Rhoden.

Etan: You were in the audience as a student?

Alcindor: Sure was . . . and since then, I always think about athletes in the lens of the challenges that you face, and it really stuck with me.

Etan: I remember Coach John Thompson was there with a lot of his players in the front. It was a really powerful discussion. You are someone who stands as such a powerful figure, especially for young Black girls. I have two daughters, and seeing them watch you do your thing, read your articles, seeing you challenge Trump, talking about police brutality, everything that you do—how important is that, especially for young Black girls, to see that positive, strong image that you present?

Alcindor: Well, it's probably the most unintended but amazing consequence of doing this work. I got into this work because I heard about the story of Emmett Till, this young boy who was murdered in 1955, and I instantly just knew I wanted to be a civil rights journalist. I wanted to be bringing America these hard truths.

And it didn't really dawn on me until afterwards that I was inspired by Black women like Gwen Ifill and Michele Norris who were doing their thing when I was young. And now I turn around, and there's a new generation of young Black women that are looking at me. And it gives me goose bumps talking about it because it is the thing that I cherish the most now about this work. It's the fact that someone out there, some young girl out there, is looking at me saying, "That girl with her hair curly, allowing it to grow out of her head the way it is, I can still be on TV and do that."

I remember being told by people that I was not going to make it on TV because I didn't look right, I wasn't pretty enough, all these different things. And to then be able to have young girls look up and see me and see Abby Phillip and see so many other women of color doing our thing on TV and saying, "I can do that. I can challenge presidents and also not lose myself in the process."

Etan: You challenging Donald Trump, especially for my daughter Imani, she saw you do that, and her eyes lit up. It was so empowering for her and important to see. And in contrast, she's also seeing other situations, such as when she saw me interview Chikesia Clemons, and she was like, "Wait, so the police weren't held accountable for that?"

Alcindor: I was triggered by that as well.

Etan: Right, and she's looking at Breonna Taylor, looking at Sandra Bland, and it reinforces that notion that Black women don't matter, and that's why it's so important for her to see Black women like you doing what you do.

Alcindor: I think the thing that is always in the back of my mind is that I know overall that this has been a country that has never treated Black people, and especially Black women, as equals. They raped Black women. They sold Black women's children. They, of course, tortured Black men along with Black women. And to me, we are the story of America and the story that I try to tell with every single beat that I'm in, whether I'm covering transportation or education or the White House: How are we trying to get better? How are we actually going to live up to the ideals that we wrote down a long, long time ago, but didn't actually mean.

For me, it's about continuing to press forward. So every time when I was in the White House when President Trump was in office, I would, of course, have the news of the day, stories, maybe China or something going on with the coronavirus pandemic. But in the back of my mind, I would also have on my list of questions stories about civil rights, about kind of blaming African Americans for the fact that they were being impacted more by the pandemic.

In my reporting, I try to remind people all the time that as a Black woman, I know what this country is capable of. I know what Sandra Bland and Breonna Taylor, Ahmaud Arbery and George Floyd, I know the realities that they faced in their everyday lives. And it's not lost on me that we have to continuously remind this country that white supremacy and systemic racism is a danger to our democracy.

January 6, to me, was on full display how much racism really was a threat, not just to Black people and Latinos and Asians, and everyone else. I can say it feels like you feel that you're doing Black people a favor by not being racist. You're doing the country a favor because the very democracy will crumble if these people have their way with our democracy. It's constantly on my mind that we need to shine a light on just how unfair and unequal this country is.

Etan: And I think you're doing that. I know Black people are championing and proud of what you're doing. What is the response that you get from the other side?

Alcindor: Of course there's the really, really critical side of, especially Trump supporters, who have threatened me, who go after me online, who also have been going after Nikole Hannah-Jones, the creator of the 1619 Project, a really dear friend of mine. If you decide to do this work of showing America exactly who we really are, then you know that you're going to deal with an avalanche of critics. Some of them who are heinous, some of them who wear nice suits and say things like, "We are trying to change the history of America," and it's like, "No, we're not. We're just pointing out the obvious."

Etan: Yeah, I saw that criticism of the 1619 Project.

Alcindor: Yes, so there's that, but I'll also tell you, in my newsrooms I've been lucky that I've worked for organizations that have really said, "Okay, let's just let Yamiche go do her thing," because I'm an emotional reporter—if I cry about something, I need to go write about it. I think about Philando Castile. I was covering Bernie Sanders at the time. It was in the middle of the 2016 election. And I saw Philando Castile's video, and that little girl in the back of the scene calming her mother down, and I cried the entire train ride to work. And when I got to work, I was like, "I can't write about Bernie Sanders today. I got to write about Black people today. I got to write about kids today." And the *New York Times* said, "Fine," and I ended up writing this story about all the different children of people who we've seen get killed and what the legacy is.

Etan: I read that, that was a powerful piece.

Alcindor: Thank you. And I wrote about Tamir Rice's sister who lost like fifty pounds after she watched her brother get murdered. I wrote about Eric Garner's grandchildren, who are terrified of the police. There's been this entire generation of young people who are traumatized and have to live with the reality that they know exactly in their own personal lives what the dangers can be when the police see your loved one as a threat.

So I've been lucky in that way because I feel like that's the only way I can do this work. I am not someone who's stoic. I cry. I get emotional. I get mad. Because I'm married to a 6'4" Black man, my brother is a Black man that looks very much like Michael Brown. I'm a Black woman who has an attitude at times, right?

Etan: That's what I think with my daughter Imani.

Alcindor: Right, so when I watch Sandra Bland, I'm like, "Oh, I know what that's like. I know what it's like to be like, 'I don't want to put out my cigarette because my right is I can put my cigarette out if I want to.'" But I also realize that we're living in a country where Black women, your attitude can get you killed, and just being yourself can get you killed. Just walking down the street can get you killed, as we saw with Trayvon Martin, who the prosecutor said was armed with a sidewalk, right? These are the things that Black people have to deal with. And I think you have to continuously start shining the light on it, lest we forget what country we're living in.

Etan: My daughter Imani is a regular preteen, she gets an attitude sometimes if something happens that she doesn't like, and she wants to stand up for herself. And we're looking at Sandra Bland, and I'm scared as a father because our children, our women, our men, get brutalized for doing the same thing that white people do all the time. Literally, I'm interviewing Chikesia Clemons, and she's talking about how she wanted to have utensils. It all happened over utensils, and she wanted to speak to the manager. She was like, *Wait a minute, white people do that all the time.* But white people can do that, and not be seen as a threat. That's a tough reality to have to teach your kids.

Alcindor: Yeah, it's a tough message and I'm not a parent. But I have mentees and my young cousins that I talk to, I think especially the next generation, I'm so proud of them because I feel like they're even more aware of their rights, more aware of where things stand than even I am as a thirtysomething-year-old. But I think that Imani's generation, they're going to have to be told what the generations before them were told, which is, "Get home safely. You can have all your rights. Sandra Bland can have all her rights. But at the end of the day, voicing your rights in this country as a Black woman can get you killed, can get you dragged."

Etan: And it's very, very sad, but I also think that in some ways that is the story of this country.

Alcindor: Exactly, it's reality. It's a real balancing act. It's like if you want utensils at a restaurant, you don't think that that's going to end in your arrest. But I also realize that if I see even the feeling of someone wanting to call the cops, I'm out, I have to completely remove myself from the situation even when I'm in the right, and for me, I can't tell you how difficult that is.

My husband is someone that I talk about a lot. He's the most gentle, sweet guy. But I know, and I realized this, I want to say probably around the time that Trayvon Martin was killed, what I see as attractive in Black men, the taller you are, the darker you are, the broader you are, it's like you're getting more and more threatening to America, and that's the scary thing.

And when I think about if I have children, and they look like me or they look like my husband, it terrifies me because I know I have an attitude. I know I get moments where I'm like, "No, I want my rights, I want my utensils," or, "I want my menu," or "This wasn't done right and I need to talk to the manager." And you realize that those are the moments that can escalate so quickly and turn into something that's dangerous.

Etan: I was watching this case that just happened. It was a nine-year-old girl in Rochester, New York. She's in the back of a police car, calling for her father, and they're treating her like she's hostile. My daughter Baby Sierra is this girl's age, and it broke my heart as a father seeing that. That they would victimize a young girl like that. So it's not even just the age of a grown woman or a teenager like Imani, but then you have little kids like Baby

Sierra's age and the girl in Rochester who are victimized the way that they are. And it's just a terrible state that we're in where you have to argue for our humanity, even a child at nine years old.

Alcindor: It's very, very scary. I think a lot about Tamir Rice because the cops, after Tamir Rice was killed, there was this narrative like, "Oh, well, was he really a man?" And everybody that looks at Tamir Rice's pictures are like, "How is that not a kid?"

Etan: Right. At what point do Black kids stop being cute little kids?

Alcindor: It seems like our cuteness factor ends like around three or four. Where you can see in other races, you'll have a twenty-seven-year-old man who does something that's not right, and it's like, "Oh, well, he's still kind of a kid. He's still growing up." But somehow, a nine-year-old girl needs to be handcuffed. Those are, I think, the things that you have to continuously talk about because it's hard to put into words what that means. It's also hard to explain to people that's the bias, that's the systemic racism in America that continues to be dangerous to people who look like me and you.

You just have to continuously teach people and educate people, "This is what we're up against. We're up against the fact that a nine-year-old girl could be handcuffed and seen as dangerous, even though she was really just being a little kid."

And to go back to Philando Castile and the little girl who was consoling her mother. Imagine how mature you have to be to be able to witness somebody be shot and killed, and then take on the duty of trying to calm your mother down, when that girl was like six, seven, eight years old, an elementary school student who now is in this position where she's trying to calm her mother down. It sticks with me because I just think that that's where we are. We have to teach our kids so early what the stakes are.

Etan: They don't get the chance to just be kids.

Alcindor: Luckily for me, my mom is a proud Haitian woman who taught me very early on about racism, about the history of Haiti being the first Black nation in the Western Hemisphere to be free. In 1804, how we rocked the world. But what we had to endure as a result of that, that to me is the thing that you have to in some ways continuously teach your kids and teach them early. Because it's going to be there confronting them even when you don't think that it should be.

Etan: I want to thank you for what you stand for and the role model and the inspiration that you give to girls all over the country. Who are some of the people who inspired *you*, past and present?

Alcindor: I was really lucky that my mom taught me, and I had this kind of really big encyclopedia of all of these amazing people in history that I could go to and read about. So there were a lot of people like Harriet Tubman, Ida B. Wells, Martin Luther King, Malcolm X, Fred Hampton, Medgar Evers, Fannie Lou Hamer. Those were the people that I grew up with. Toussaint Louverture, I should say, Jean-Jacques Dessalines, the heroes of the Haitian Revolution. These are the people that were the first names that I knew that were Black people who stood for something, and who said, "I am worth something. I should be treated like a human being, and I'm going to demand it." So that's, I think, my early people who inspired me.

As I got more interested in journalism, I started looking at people like Oprah and Gwen Ifill. And now I think, as my contemporaries, there's Abby Phillip and Nikole Hannah-Jones and Trymaine Lee at MSNBC. Those are the people that, as contemporaries, as my friends, I look to them and say, "You're really killing it. And by the way, I had a bad day, can we talk?"

I am mentoring people, and I realize now how much mentoring someone can also be about learning and thinking. Because I feel like the next generation coming behind me, they're even more outspoken about what they know they deserve and their rights. For me, sometimes that can be scary, but for them, they realize that they can use the Internet and they have all these different ways to really call for justice and to really demand what they're worth. This generation, when they're in negotiations, it's like I'm learning from them, like, "Oh, okay, *that's* what we do?" So I think that even younger journalists that are coming behind me really inspire me because I just look at them, and I'm excited about what's next.

Etan: Well, you make sure you take care of yourself. We need you out here to keep fighting for us and keep covering things the way that you have. So much respect to you, and again, thanks again for being a part of all of this.

Alcindor: Thanks so much for doing all that you do and writing and being also a role model. Like I said, as a college student, looking up to you, and realizing that you can have so many multiple careers. You don't only have to be one thing. So that was something that stuck with me when I first met you, so I appreciate that.

Interview with Captain Sonia Pruitt

Captain Sonia Pruitt began her law enforcement career as an officer with the Montgomery County Police Department in Maryland. She served as the deputy director of the Internal Affairs division and was later promoted to administrative lieutenant for the office of the chief of police, where she helped to oversee the department's budget and staff. She has worked as a call taker for the police 911 dispatch center, an investigative sergeant, and a supervisor of the school resource officer program. In 2019, Pruitt was promoted to captain and concurrently served as a duty commander supervising calls for service countywide.

Pruitt retired from policing in 2020. She is the past president of the Coalition of Black Police Officers in Montgomery County, and served as the chairperson of the National Black Police Association.

Etan: Can you explain what you did with the National Black Police Association?

Pruitt: The NBPA is almost fifty years old. It was established in 1972, thirteen smaller Black police organizations from around the country came together in St. Louis and started the charter for the NBPA. And then they went on what I call a tour. They were filing lawsuits, making sure that Black officers had positions in police departments as detectives and specialized units, promotions, etc., all of which were up until that point denied to people who look like us, and they were very successful in that. So fast-forward, we are still in the NBPA fighting that same fight. When I became chair in 2018, I decided that we needed to be more visible. So I started to address issues publicly. Which is what we should do. Now, of course we are not a monolith, but most of us having grown up in the Black community can understand the ills and the trials of the Black community when it comes specifically to policing.

Etan: You all were vocal in supporting Kaepernick from the beginning.

Pruitt: Yes we were. Trump made a lot of disparaging remarks publicly about him and people were attacking him and we collectively agreed that we need to come out in support of him, and we did. So from that point on, we continued to take public stances so that people didn't lump us in with what they think all police feel.

Etan: It's great that you all have the courage to take those unpopular positions despite the backlash that I'm sure you receive from your fellow white officers.

Pruitt: You have no idea. Let me explain this way: In July of this past year, I decided to retire. I didn't want to continue to fight this fight from where I was fighting it from. I was the first Black female police captain in my department. The department has been around for ninety-nine years and I was the first *ever?* That's still crazy to me. So it was a fight from the time I made the decision, and all Black police officers have to make this decision: am I going to be Black or am I going to be blue. Since I can't peel my Blackness off, I decided to go with Black, and blue was just what I did for a living. And it became extremely difficult for me from that point on. It was always a struggle. Always a fight. And I will tell you this, I would do it all again because it was worth it for not only me personally, but those people who were coming behind me and for standing for the public. So I had to make a decision of how I can continue to fight this fight effectively. And since I had amassed enough information in how police departments work, and understanding what much of the public doesn't understand in terms of their rights, I decided, *Let me take this show on the road,* which is why I created the Black Police Experience.

Etan: Tell me a little more about the Black Police Experience.

Pruitt: We're still in our founding stage. This is going to be where people can have a clearing house, if you will, of information. This is where you come if you need to have a workshop on the Fourth Amendment, or the Sixth Amendment—people don't even know what those are or how they apply to their lives. How about the Fifteenth, Thirteenth, and Fourteenth amendments? Anything related to police work or law enforcement, we want to teach the public so that they will feel empowered when they go to the voting booth, when they are pulled over on a traffic stop—we need people to understand what policing really is. It is a science. And yes, it was created to oppress Black people, and yes, it is still working on the same model.

Etan: You mentioned that you have to make a choice of whether you want to be Black or you want to be blue. Can you go into a little more detail with that?

Pruitt: When you become a police officer, there are some things that you will see and hear. They may not mesh with how you were raised as a Black person. You may hear the N-word. I remember a situation I had where I was promoted to a corporal. That's the first real position of rank. And I was off duty and I heard an officer at a 7-Eleven, and there was a group of young Black teens in a car with this white girl, and you could tell that the young lady was intoxicated. It was early in the morning, they probably came from a party or club or something. The young men looked like they were trying to take care of her. They weren't taking advantage of her, they were getting her water. "Are you okay?" They were obviously all friends or whatever. So, the police officers, who were white, decided to insert themselves into the situation. And I said, "Hmmmm, they look like they're doing okay, she's not driving, doesn't appear to be any issue or any reason to interfere." But they did, and there was an exchange of words back and forth between the police and these young Black teenagers, and he called one of the young men a monkey and a MF. So I had to step in, because I outranked him and we had a private conversation and I said, "Don't you ever," and I checked him. But when you do that, he gets to go back to all his little friends and say, "Guess what Officer Pruitt did to me. She's a troublemaker, race baiter, doesn't understand what side she is on."

Etan: Oh wow.

Pruitt: So those are the moments where as a Black police officer you have to make a decision. Do you go along with it, or do you step up and say what's wrong? Now this is a situation where I had rank. But if you're a rank-and-file officer on the street, and you confront one of your fellow officers that you don't outrank, that will be even more difficult. However, like the saying *There's strength in numbers,* that goes with Black officers: you have to have people who will support you if you check someone, and too often, many are afraid to because of the repercussions that will surely happen from other officers.

Etan: I just watched this movie called *Black and Blue* with Tyrese, it's pretty good, but in the movie the Black female police officer witnessed the police kill this guy, and went for comfort with her fellow Black police officer who outranked her, but then she found out that he was one of them. I remember seeing this when I was younger, watching *Boyz n the Hood*, and the Black police officer had Cuba Gooding Jr. slammed on the car, gun pointed to him, was like, "You think you tough? I'll blow your brains out right now, etc., etc.," and that was a Black police officer. Like you said, you have to choose Black or blue, and you have those who choose blue. How do you form alliances when there are so many people who look like us who have chosen to side with them?

Pruitt: Whew, that is a very nuanced situation. It's just like the Black community at large. There are people who we are going to have to throw to the trash. Harriet Tubman would not have been successful, or even wasted her time, trying to save. Same thing with the police department. People have to understand: not all police get into policing for the right reasons. Some are insecure in themselves. Some were bullied and now have power. Some want to enforce white supremacy, and that goes for people who look like us and people who don't. When you are a police officer, you have the power to take someone's freedom, their lives, give them a criminal record so they will have a difficult time navigating through life—that's a lot of power. If you are not well-seated as a person, that power can go to your head. And the blue culture is so strong, when you come in, it's like, "We're all family," it's like a gang or the mob. And to be honest, some Black officers buy into that. Also, some say, "Well, I'm making a good living and I don't want to lose this, so I will do what I have to do." That's the honest truth.

Etan: How is it for Black women in law enforcement? I don't think that's ever really discussed.

Pruitt: Black women, we have our own category in policing. They try to lump us in with white women conveniently, or they want to lump us with Black men, and we have our own separate challenges. If you are a strong and outspoken Black woman on the police force, you are really gonna get it, because they are going to do everything in their power to tear you down. I had some amazing mentors that I definitely needed. As they began to matriculate out of the police department, I had to seek other mentors outside of the department, especially once I reached lieutenant. Why? Because there was nobody like me above me. When I reached out to Black men, my experience only, they did as good of a job as any white person in keeping me down. That was extremely difficult. There were days I would cry in my car. I would never cry in my office or let anyone see. I would cry because I was hurt and sad. Then I would get myself together, go back inside to fight some more.

Etan: While you were the head of the NBPA, there was a series of police killings that you spoke publicly on when there was silence from most police departments.

Pruitt: For me, it was important for us to be vocal about what does represent us and what doesn't represent us. Honestly, the powers that be got us out here feeling like we can't talk about anything, and I just didn't prescribe to that indoctrination, I rejected it. Now, I will say I was a little more comfortable speaking out than what many of the board members were used to, but that's okay, it was important to me and that's why I was the chair.

Etan: You immediately spoke out about the murder of George Floyd.

Pruitt: Yes, that was the one that really made people take notice of us and ask the question, "Where have you all been?" And there were plenty of other cases we had spoken out publicly on, but that one really took the entire country by storm. But I felt that we were at a time where, if you don't say something, that means you're complicit.

Etan: What was your reaction to the US Capitol invasion by the Trump supporters?

Pruitt: I have a friend who calls it "naked racial hypocrisy." Because it's a violation of public decency. And still there were people who tried to justify it on the right and downplay it, but we know what we saw. We saw nooses, Confederate flags, Auschwitz shirts, those are not symbols of democracy. They are symbols of racial hatred. But the bigger picture is, how did the police drop the ball?

Etan: That's really my question.

Pruitt: They didn't just drop the ball, they dropped it and kicked it over the Potomac. We are in the DMV and there are dozens of federal law enforcement agencies as well as local jurisdictions in this area. We are very good at responding to crucial events. This is the nation's capital. This was a riot on January 6. There is overlapping training between organizations in what's called a memorandum of understanding between agencies. So help can come across jurisdictions. Those things exist, even for the smallest event. You do surveillance, you do intel—these folks have been publicly talking about what they were going to be doing for months. It was not a secret.

Etan: Almost like the ball wasn't dropped, but it was—

Pruitt: Purposely thrown. We saw officers taking selfies and opening barriers. But they're not in charge of anything. I'm concerned about the people in charge—why did it take so long to get help? Why was there a denial of help when it was offered? Those questions are going to be very important to get answers for moving forward—not just finding the rioters/insurrectionists, but how did this happen? Why did you not see these people as a threat? They've been threatening people all summer, they were going to kidnap the governor of Michigan.

Etan: Yeah, they announced it.

Pruitt: Exactly. So what did you think they were going to come here and do? That brings us to the whole white supremacy issue where officers are in fact members of these groups. The NBPA did a full press release on this when officers were found to be in white supremacist social media groups and some did get in trouble. What makes us think they weren't in that crowd on January 6? There's a picture circulating of the national guard standing on the steps before this happened, and it looked like an army. That's how it should've looked on January 6. Period. And officers lost their lives during this.

Etan: And how would the whole situation have played out if it was Black people storming the Capitol?

Pruitt: We as Black people would've never even gotten up the steps to get to the Capitol.

Let's just be real about it. I am proud of the Black community right now for what they did in Georgia during the 2020 presidential election. We need to keep that same energy when we push back at what happened at the Capitol.

Etan: I want to do a quick correlation to after Freddie Gray was killed in Baltimore. My cousin William "Tipper" Thomas is a youth advocate in Baltimore, and the situation he described was: High school kids were let out of school, they closed the buses so they had to walk, and the police were ready in full riot gear. One person threw a water bottle and that was justification for their violent response. Compare that to how they responded to the Trump supporters at the Capitol. So you have these two cases, but you're telling people to trust the police, have faith in the police, and look at the police as your friend.

Pruitt: I can't dispute anything you just said. There is absolutely a disparity and a collective trauma to see that clear difference in treatment and double standard and overall disdain for Black people. Even when we are peaceful. Now, imagine being on the *inside* and seeing that? I see the same things you see and everyone else sees. And while I am fighting to change from within, I am simultaneously dealing with being treated differently as a Black woman in the police department. And that contributed to me retiring and trying to fight a different way. Sometimes you have to change strategies. I fought from the inside for a long time. Even us speaking up for Kaepernick was a big thing, and I honestly didn't feel like it should've been.

Etan: I remember when you all spoke out in support of Kaepernick, as Trump was really casting him as being antipolice, but you all explained, "Kaepernick is not saying that, he's saying he has an issue with the police getting away with killing innocent people and not being held accountable." You didn't just say, "We support Colin Kaepernick," you broke it all down. I am definitely looking forward to seeing all that you do moving forward, and you know you have my support.

White Supremacy and the US Capitol

Seems to me that the institutions that function in this country are clearly racist, and that they're built upon racism.
—Stokely Carmichael, aka Kwame Ture

It was a Wednesday afternoon right after lunch; we turned on the TV, and what we witnessed blew our collective minds. My wife Nichole kept repeating, "This can't be happening." I was in shock and couldn't say anything. We watched live as white-supremacist, Make America Great Again Trump supporters progressed with a full assault on democracy and stormed the US Capitol.

We watched them scale the walls of the US Capitol, burst through the barrier, casually stroll past policemen, and literally take over the building. We saw Confederate flags, red MAGA hats, and angry white faces. There was even one guy in a Viking costume including horns (still not sure the relevance of that). They vandalized offices, and were taking selfies behind the desks of congressmen and senators. It was complete and total mayhem.

Baby Sierra asked, "Why are they so mad? Did a white person get killed by the police?"

I replied, "No, they're upset that Trump lost the election."

Malcolm said, "Stop playing, Daddy, that cannot be the reason for all of this."

Nichole chimed in, "They have been saying since the election that this was coming. Trump has been leading the charge. He even pinpointed the date January 6. I saw the tweet with my own eyes. They should've known this was coming. Why weren't they prepared for this? All summer with every Black Lives Matter protest, they had tanks and military gear and tear gas and everything within minutes. Where is all of that now?"

Nichole's questions were valid: Donald Trump indeed led the charge in what happened that day, and there's proof.

On April 17, 2020, Trump tweeted his support of armed protests against COVID-19 measures in three states with Democratic governors. The first, *LIBERATE MINNESOTA*, followed by, *LIBERATE MICHIGAN*, then finally, *LIBERATE VIRGINIA, and save your great 2nd Amendment. It is under siege!*

It appeared to be somewhat of a dress rehearsal, the occupation of state capitols and a foiled plot to kidnap the Michigan governor, as well as activities of Proud Boys and other far-right extremists.

Former acting US assistant attorney general for national security Mary McCord wrote that Trump had "incited insurrection" in his own country.

"The time line [of the Capitol attack] tracks 365 days that built up to that moment," said Professor Ryan Goodman, Just Security's co–editor in chief. "It shows how the president often glorified violence as a tool to confront perceived political enemies. It is no wonder the mob followed through." Just Security highlighted Trump's backing of his supporters in Texas who just days before November's presidential election surrounded a Joe Biden campaign bus and nearly forced it off the road.

I LOVE TEXAS! Trump tweeted at the time, alongside a video of the incident. *These patriots did nothing wrong,* he added when the FBI started an investigation. Just Security also highlighted a string of *Stop the Steal* tweets made by Trump ahead of the US Capitol invasion, in reference to baseless rumors that the election was somehow fixed in Biden's favor.

Following months of rousing speeches by Donald Trump, tweets, statements, and messages, an estimated eight hundred people stormed the building in a melee shocking in its intensity and sustained violence. This resulted in over 140 injured police officers and five dead (including Officer Brian Sicknick, forty-two) either shortly before, during, or right after the attempted coup. This total does not include two officers who helped fight the mob and later committed suicide. Officer Jeffery Smith (thirty-five) was still fighting to defend the building when a metal pole thrown by rioters struck his helmet and face shield. A few days later he took his own life.

Noticeably absent from all of this was the Blue Lives Matter crowd. But what was on full display was white supremacy, and Donald Trump gave the orders.

So who were the rioters? And what motivated them to attack the seat of their own government?

Shortly after the insurrection, the FBI arrested key members of the pro-Trump Proud Boys and two militia groups, training the spotlight on far-right organizations. Yet researchers, including a team from the University of Chicago, have concluded the majority of rioters were not members of far-right groups and just part of Trump's political base.

"What we are dealing with here is not merely a mix of right-wing organizations, but a broader mass movement with violence at its core," Robert Pape and Keven Ruby of the Chicago Project on Security and Threats (CPOST) wrote in a report. "All of them had been egged on by Trump to march on the Capitol and 'fight like hell' to prevent Congress from certifying Biden's electoral college victory, which Trump for weeks had falsely called a fraud."

To gain insight into the backgrounds and ideologies of the rioters, the University of Chicago researchers examined more than 1,500 court documents and media stories about more than 220 people who had been arrested at that point.

The majority were white and male. Sixty-six percent were thirty-four years or older; 85 percent had jobs; 13 percent were business owners, while 27 percent held white-collar jobs. In other words, they were regular people who we see and interact with every day of our lives.

Interview with Jemele Hill

Jemele Hill is a journalist who writes for the *Atlantic* and cohosts Vice's *Cari & Jemele (Won't) Stick to Sports*. She worked for nearly twelve years for sports conglomerate ESPN. In February 2017, Hill and Michael Smith became co-hosts of SC6, the six p.m. (ET) edition of ESPN's flagship *SportsCenter*. Hill remained in that role until February 2018, when ESPN moved her to their website, The Undefeated. She joined the *Atlantic* in October 2018.

Etan: Those who now agree that Donald Trump has proven to be the white supremacist you called him back in 2017 say that ESPN owes Jemele Hill an apology. Do you agree with that?

Hill: That's a tough question to answer, because corporations don't do that.

Etan: True, but shouldn't they? Corporations can be wrong, can't they?

Hill: Yeah, sure. They can certainly be on the wrong side of history. This is a complicated answer. Do I believe ESPN, in many ways, was on the wrong side of history? Of course. They were, but I guess the idea of them owing me an apology is, in many ways, a little hard to grasp because I don't regret what happened. I've got to be honest. I don't think they do either, and so we're both in the places that we need to be. They're a network that is focused on sports content and providing live games to people. That's what they want it to be about, and while I very much understood their business initiative and business objectives, which is to get as many people as possible to watch, I had a different objective.

That objective was telling the truth and making people understand the imminent danger that was in the White House and how this wasn't just about what we were experiencing in the moment with Donald Trump. This was about the culmination of one hundred years of history, leading us to the moment. In fact, it had led us to *many* of these moments. This was just the latest one . . . This speaks to something when my memoir's finally released, that I'll talk about a little bit more in detail. Put it like this: a lot of the people who were in charge, or at least enough of them, the one thing that they never said was, "I disagree." I'll just leave it at that.

Etan: Oh, I see, they didn't disagree, they just didn't want you to say it. Gotcha.

Hill: That doesn't give ESPN a pass or anything, but it is to say that I think very much any decisions they made related to me were business decisions, and I don't think they regret them. I certainly don't regret the decisions they made, only because it led me to this moment in this time and talking to you and being able to be in a media space where I can say what I want, and I really wouldn't give that up. A lot of people are like, "They should have you back." I don't want to go back.

Etan: I didn't think you did.

Hill: My time was my time there, and it was great. I got out of it what I needed. It was the platform I needed it to be to jump me to something else. I was like, "I don't really miss it, and I don't want to go back." I guess an apology would feel a little empty because I can't really see ESPN making a different decision, even knowing what they know right now.

Etan: Even after the attack on the US Capitol?

Hill: The reason I wasn't suspended right away after the Trump thing was because I think that they saw that, while there were certainly a lot of people who objected to what I said, there were a lot of people who agreed with it. A lot of those people were athletes they do business with. It became one of those things where they wanted it to go away and they were under the assumption that this was not going to be something that I would be speaking on, and that wasn't the assumption I was under. It is what it is. So to answer your question, I'm not necessarily sure if there's a different outcome, even if it happens in 2020 or 2021.

Etan: I want to discuss the Trump phenomenon. He built his entire platform on racism. He had no other qualifications. He hadn't held an office. It was just racism, and what does that say about where we are in society today, that somebody can actually get to the White House when that's the only thing they have?

Hill: We've seen versions of Donald Trump before. They were just more polite, and they actually believed in the function of government. There's really not that much difference between some of the things that he says and some of the things Richard Nixon said, definitely very little difference between Donald Trump and Ronald Reagan. The more traditional Republicans in the Republican Party consider the party to be the party of Lincoln, for example, and the party of Ronald Reagan, because they looked at them as people who were patriots, who believed in the function of government, but they still said a lot of the same racist things that Donald Trump did. They just said them nicer.

Etan: That's a good point.

Hill: Again, the key element here is that Nixon may have been a crook and he may have stepped outside the laws that were established, but Nixon believed government worked, and there was a certain decorum he believed needed to take place in office. Donald Trump did not believe in norms and decorum, and that's really the only difference, but when you start looking at the War on Drugs and some of the other policies, Nixon very much, especially a lot of the things that he said about civil rights, there's really no difference. Donald Trump was just the unapologetic, politically incorrect version of what previously we had seen from this party before.

Abraham Lincoln plays a very important role in our history, but Abraham Lincoln did not believe Black people were equal. He had some very ingrained white supremacist views, where he didn't think Black people needed to be political equals. He didn't think that we deserved the right to vote. He did not think we were as smart as white people. This is all laid out. He said these things publicly. He just thought slavery sucked, but in terms of considering us full human beings, no, Abraham Lincoln did not believe that. I think that, really, Donald Trump, in many ways, it was the chickens coming home to roost.

Etan: And it's crazy for him to come right after President Obama. I think that illustrated the two Americas we live in.

Hill: Look, what it took for Barack Obama to get to the White House, and when you think about all the things he had to accomplish, even when you want to look at his personal life, to have a wife like Michelle Obama, to have children like Sasha and Malia, he had to check every single box. For Black people overall in whatever profession, but particularly those in prominent roles, we have to be perfect. Not only perfect, we have to be exceptional. We have to be stars. Then for them right after that to have somebody who, frankly, wasn't as educated . . . We all know the story about Trump's educational history and what that was really about, to never have held a government office, to have come from reality TV, to have been married multiple times. Literally, this is America showing the hypocrisy, the double standards, the privilege.

There was only the racism. That's why I was very frustrated with the American media for trying to come up with all these things that it wasn't, when a lot of Black journalists and journalists of color saw exactly what it was. Birtherism showed you what it was. To give that kind of racism, to mainstream it and give it a platform, was just really a disgusting legacy that the media left.

All of these things that he said were normalized, and they were never seen within the context of, "This is what a racist would say." Because of that, it became about "economic anxiety," which it was never about. It was about one simple thing: backlash to a Black president. This world, this country, is getting a little too progressive. You're going to follow a Black man with a woman? Oh no. This was the last chance for a lot of white people who know this demographic change is coming and there's nothing they can do about it.

What has always been at the root, I think, of a lot of the racial problems we have in this country, and the reason why a lot of white people act so afraid of us and so afraid of this changing world, is an expectation that we'll do to them what they did to us. But we never have. We've never done that. We've never, ever established any platform that has been about retaliation or revenge. Unfortunately, we're having to deal with white supremacy working through its issues, and we have to bear the brunt of dealing with this all the time. Trumpism is not going away.

Etan: That fear came after we were freed, and they feared retaliation, which they feel is what they actually deserve.

Hill: At the end of the day, deep down, in a place that they don't talk about, that's what it is. It's like they know they deserve that retaliation and revenge. We know that will never get us anywhere.

Etan: Right, and that's how the KKK formed, from that fear. Then the fear of Black men around white women results in lynchings. Trump invoked that time period as his calling card, and it worked. I'm looking at some of your old tweets, and your old tweets have aged very well.

You said, *Donald Trump is a white supremacist who has largely surrounded himself with other white supremacists.* You're going down the list. When you're talking in terms of white supremacy, where are we in society now that it could work to have somebody be the president of the United States when that's their only platform?

Hill: I don't like to give Donald Trump credit for much, but I'll say either he or the people that made him, maybe like Steve Bannon or Stephen Miller, it was very clear they used a blueprint, like a playbook. They went back and looked at the playbook of Republican presidents and what worked and what didn't. Let's say post–Lyndon B. Johnson, because that's really the era of Republicanism that we're dealing with right now. Ronald Reagan used the slogan Make America Great Again. That was his, so he taps into this idea of patriotism, and Richard Nixon did the same, of patriotism being something completely co-opted by white people. It's just that in today's world with technology, especially Donald Trump and people who think like him, are able to be unchecked on these platforms. It made the messaging much more dangerous, and we saw the combination of that danger with the riots at the Capitol.

It says a lot. I tweeted this the day we were observing Dr. Martin Luther King Jr.'s birthday, because it just struck me, and it was actually kind of depressing. *Martin Luther King Jr. was less popular when he was murdered than Donald Trump is today.*

Etan: That's absolutely insane.

Hill: That pretty much shows you, based off polling, how few people approved of Dr. King, and to know that there was more hatred for him at that time than there is for Donald Trump right now says everything about where white supremacy has taken this country.

It feels like this country was built on a pretty brochure, and nobody looked inside to see what they were basing the brochure on. We've got the greatest brochure in the world, democracy, equality, all the things. We've got a Statue of Liberty that says, *Give me your tired, your poor,* and all these other things. Then you do a little digging, and you realize that it's not exactly the country we are. It's the country we *want* to be, but it's not the country that we are. Mostly, a lot of the things we tell ourselves, like "greatest on earth," these are all affirmations. They're not actually true.

Etan: Right.

Hill: The only way they can be true is if we confront and defeat white supremacy, and I don't know if this is something that will happen in our lifetime. I do know I was very hopeful that Joe Biden literally, his first day as president, he called out white supremacy. See, Donald Trump? It's not that hard, right?

Etan: Right.

Hill: First day in office, he was like, "White supremacy's got to go." It's like, "All right. At least we're all on the same page with that one." That's a good starting place. I don't know if it'll be accomplished, but that's a good starting place. I hope that 2020, with all we've been through as a nation, was a real wake-up call, because now we're at the fork in the road where we've got to decide what kind of country we're trying to be right now. There's some of us that want to be the kind of country that does live up to the brochure, and there's other people in this country, millions unfortunately, in fact, that don't want us to become that country. They want us to be something that is, frankly, regressive and not indicative of the type of people who actually live here.

I'd be very curious as to see the long-term damage that comes out of what Donald Trump became, because I know people think that just because he left office that that's going to be the end of Trumpism. It's like, no, because it's only stronger. They realize that there are seventy-plus million people who actually want that kind of leadership, and that is tantalizing bait for the Republican Party, for conservatives right now, so they're still placating the seventy-plus million that voted for, who thought that after all they'd seen for four years, thought, *You know what? We need another four of this.*

Etan: I heard a lot of people say, "Maybe this is a wake-up call." I'm like, "Did y'all forget what happened in Charlottesville? *That* wasn't a wake-up call?"

Hill: Right.

Etan: This is along the same lines. It only happened a few years ago. They didn't even have their hoods on. Those are regular white people that went from Charlottesville back to their jobs as policemen, as firemen, as teachers, as everything. That should have been wake-up call enough.

Hill: It should have been all the evidence we needed about the type of danger that was festering out here. I guess it's never too late, but for all these social media platforms to suddenly suspend Donald Trump after the fact, it's kind of like, "But you've allowed him to go unchecked for this long. People are already radicalized. His message is already out there." Yeah, but unfortunately, you can look at our history and know one thing for sure: we don't actually learn from it.

We continue to repeat the same mistakes over and over again, and I hope people understood that about both Charlottesville and the Capitol. You mentioned something really important. Nobody was wearing a hood. Nobody was in secret. Nobody felt ashamed of what they were doing, and you have to dig and ask the bigger question of why. Why would a bunch of white people think it's completely okay to go into a Capitol, storm it, with the intention of trying to kidnap and/or assassinate our political leaders? Why would they think that was okay, and then have the gall to do it openly? The reason why they think that it's okay, which led, unfortunately, to the police officer that lost his life and some of the other lives that were lost, the reason why it's been okay is because any function of law and order has never been meant for them.

It's only been meant for us, and we saw that play out right there on that Capitol. There is a very different fear when it comes to the police. They don't have the fear, because in their mind, the police work for *them*, to check us, to keep us in check. I hope it doesn't take something even worse happening, because I don't know what it's going to take. Where is the line going to be? It feels like we don't have one. That's scary, that there is no bottom for what we saw there.

Etan: They don't feel they did anything wrong. The amount of white privilege is amazing. You talk about white privilege and people will say things like, "I didn't grow up with a lot of money." It has nothing to do with money. Your white skin allows you to be treated differently in a situation where I would have been killed, and that's the part that they don't connect.

Hill: Let's be honest. Black people couldn't even have the thought bubble of trying to storm the Capitol. We would have gotten taken out right there. As soon as we whispered it out loud, we're all arrested. They'd be running us all up.

I keep waiting on this moment for a certain portion of this constituency, of our American constituents, to wake up. I don't know that it's just a question of them waking up or it's just that they find it that acceptable. As a citizen of this country, you need to be outraged, because we can't be a functioning government to have people who try to delegitimize and then, upon thinking they're grieved in some way, think a perfectly natural and normal response is to use violence to intimidate, threaten, harass our elected officials.

That can't work, which is why all those lawmakers who helped to incite what happened need to be expelled. You can't work with people like that, that don't think it's legitimate. Anybody who is a conservative or, really, anybody, even though we know this is coming from one side. If you're an elected official and you're still saying this election was rigged, you need to go. You need to go, because you are undermining and you are a threat to our democracy.

Etan: Republicans don't ever want you to put them in the same box. Don't say, "All Republicans are racist." My response to that was, "All racists and white supremacists certainly seem to support Trump."

Hill: Clearly.

Etan: Trump didn't invent racism, but he gave them a spokesperson, somebody to fight for, and they turned toward him. That's really undeniable. Either you're on this side, or you're on that side. There has to be a line in the sand, and they're still, even right now, as we're doing this interview, they're still reluctant to jump on one side or the other, and that just amazes me.

Hill: Yeah. It's amazing. It's appalling. It's a lot of things, and especially the thing that upsets me about, really, any politician, is that—and you can tell the ones that do this—this is a game to them. That's what's so offending to me. They're not looking at the damage they're doing every time they say this election is rigged. What they're looking at is the seventy-plus million people who voted for Donald Trump, and they're trying to tap into that so they can stay in power. It's all just a role play for them. It's like they're cosplaying right now and inciting something that you can't control.

Frankenstein's monster was Donald Trump, and he got out of hand. You're only doing it to preserve your own power and importance. I'm just really disappointed in a lot of these officials that allow themselves to be morally contaminated for basically power. At the end of the day, this was about individual gain. This was not about serving the American people, because I think we sometimes forget that being an elected official is a position of service.

That's why there was no indication that Donald Trump would ever be a good president in addition to the racism and the white supremacy and all that. He's never been a servant. That's not what he is. Barack Obama was a grassroots organizer. To do that, you have to have a level of service that's in you to other people. If you don't have that, you can't really be or make a great elected official, and Trump does not have that. He's selfish, and he's entitled, and he lacks empathy, which are three of the worst characteristics to have when you're supposed to be elected and in charge of governing everybody.

Interview with Jake Tapper

Jake Tapper is the lead Washington anchor for CNN, and hosts the weekday television news show *The Lead with Jake Tapper,* and cohosts the Sunday-morning public affairs program *State of the Union.*

Etan: I appreciate your journalistic integrity. Not only the past few weeks since the US Capitol invasion and at the inauguration, but for many years now. You called the coup attempt on the US Capitol one of the darkest days in our nation's history. Can you explain why you described it in those terms?

Tapper: Well, I think first of all, any act of violence is a moment for reflection and it should be taken seriously. But what distinguished this from say other riots or acts of violence, including those where people have been killed, is that this was not just political violence, which is to say terrorism—that's the definition of terrorism—but terrorism that was incited very directly by powerful people. That's not to excuse riots from unpowerful people, but I think Martin Luther King said something one time about riots as a voice of the oppressed; he was arguing about when people get desperate. This was not that, this was desperation but an all different kind, this was the most powerful person in the world, who had been rejected by voters in a democratic election, telling a very big lie, and this lie was supported by not just the president but his supporters in Congress and in the media.

And it infected people like a virus. And ultimately they were convinced, whether normal, average, everyday Americans or far-right groups like the Proud Boys, to commit an act of political terror, which was not just to protest an act with which they disagreed but to try to reverse it. So I don't think we've ever seen anything like it, really, because it was a powerful man trying to hold on to power. And even if the most charitable interpretation you could have is that the president wanted his supporters to go to Capitol Hill to intimidate members of Congress to not certify the election. That's the most charitable interpretation.

Etan: Yeah, that's pretty charitable.

Tapper: Don't get me wrong, that's definitely not the argument I'm making. But that, too, is a) based on a lie that the election could have been overturned, and b) that's still physical violence, whether you throw a punch or not. If you're getting in somebody's face, it's violence or the threat of violence. I know a little bit about history, and I've never seen anything like it in the United States since the early days of the American Revolution.

Etan: Can you talk a little bit about how some of the rhetoric that was coming from the right and from Trump also contributed to what we saw at the Capitol as well?

Tapper: Well, he had been setting the stage for the general strategy, not necessarily the insurrection, but the general strategy, since before the election. Obviously because of the pandemic, there were a lot of states, Democratic states and Republican states, in terms of who the governors were that were trying to make it easier for voters to vote. Because as a general principle—although I know even saying something like this is controversial—the more legal votes that are cast, the better; it's democracy of the representative, we want to make sure we have as many people as possible raise their hand as to who they want representing them. And so there was all these different vote-by-mail maneuvers in different states. I think before the pandemic, it was going to be about ten states that changed their vote by mail, and then it became even more.

So there were people objecting to that, and that happens every time there's any change people object to, and there's legal avenues and all that. But what President Trump started to do was say that this would constitute cheating, and it wasn't. And so he was setting the stage for months before the election that he was going to challenge this. Because we knew that Democrats were overwhelmingly voting by mail, and Trump was telling his people not to do so, to vote on Election Day. A lot of people were saying, "This is what he's going to do, he's going to come out on election night and say because the votes that had already been cast, because a lot of them were cast that day, Election Day, he's going to declare victory ahead of time."

Etan: So basically Trump was lying to everyone.

Tapper: Yes, that was his plan. To lie and say that all the votes that are counted after that are fraudulent, which is not true. So this just became his strategy. I don't know if he believes it or not. I've said one of the challenges of the Trump era is figuring out who's cynically lying, who isn't smart enough to explain, understand what's going on, and who has a psychological issue, and I can't diagnose that. But the lie was out there and it took hold of people. And then the president pursued every legal path to challenge the results in court, lost dozens of court cases. I think he won one which had to do with ballots that came into Pennsylvania polling places after Election Day. And so Pennsylvania put those ballots aside for any later-date challenge, so those weren't counted.

But other than that, he lost everything else. And then he tried everything else: intimidating state legislatures, intimidating election boards, calling county canvassers. Again, we've never seen anything like it. And then finally, he had exhausted everything and somebody had told him that Mike Pence could challenge the results and House Republicans and Senate Republicans could reverse the election, and they couldn't, but there were enough House and Senate Republicans willing to engage in this kind of like Kabuki theater about what they could do, and then the mob ran to the Capitol.

Looking back on it, you can see how it was a straight line to that day. And obviously all of us who were covering it were worried. You can find things that I said on air a month before the attack, saying, "When you put out all these lies, you can't control it." This is when Georgia Republican election officials were getting death threats. So regrettably, it ended up the way it is, and in a way, in a sad, sick way, we're lucky that it wasn't more violent than it was.

Etan: The images from that day of Confederate flags, Nazi flags, is it deeper than just telling lies? Trump struck a chord, he had a specific strategy with a specific targeted audience. And a lot of people in the media were very reluctant to call that specific target audience. Why were you not as reluctant to call it like it was?

Tapper: There are gradations of this stuff. There is like the run-of-the-mill, vaguely racist voter, and then there's just a line from that person to neo-Nazis and Klan. Then there are also in this same group people that might not have any racial or racist animus, but find themselves voting for that same person that they all support. So I find it important to distinguish. I personally do not think that seventy-four million Americans who voted for Donald Trump are racist. I just don't think that. Hillary Clinton said half of his voters are deplorable—I have no idea what the number is, but certainly there are a number of them that are deplorable.

Etan: But you call those racists out—however many of them there are.

Tapper: When racism rears its head, it needs to be called out. There's a long history in this country—and it's not just Republican politicians, it's Democrats too—of racist dog whistles. Democratic politicians have done it too, not just in the South but in the North as well. This is not just Republicans in the South, this is a complicated, ugly history in the United States and around the world. But then, at a certain point, it goes from racial tinge or racist dog whistles to *racist*. And Donald Trump very clearly early on in 2016 was making a play for racists. He wanted racists to vote for him and I saw it firsthand.

Etan: That was quite clear from the beginning.

Tapper: Yes, I knew he was a bigot from the very moment he came down the stairs, the escalator, and started talking about Latinos. And then from December 2015 when he talked about banning all Muslims, that's bigotry. And then when he came on my show in February 2016 and he refused to condemn David Duke, and I did not see that coming. That's the easiest layup in politics. A Klan leader? "Yes, of course I condemn him" should've been his answer.

Etan: You would think any nonracist would have no issues condemning an actual KKK leader.

Tapper: You would think, right? So from then on I was just very keenly aware of what was going on. And I would get attacked a lot by bots and trolls for being Jewish. And there's a very conservative Republican named David French, who I think of as a guy with a lot of integrity. And he had adopted a daughter, I think from Ethiopia, and he started getting attacked a lot for having a Black daughter. And it just became very obvious what was going on. And so I think Donald Trump played footsie with these far-right groups throughout his presidency. He would say what he had to say when Jared Kushner gave him a piece of paper, but then ultimately when left to his own devices, he wouldn't. So he said to the Proud Boys, "Stand back and stand by." And they did. And then they attacked the Capitol.

Etan: I was watching this movie a few days ago, *BlacKkKlansman.* There was a part where they were talking about David Duke. You never saw him in a KKK hood or anything like that, but he was in a suit and his sights were set on politics. And he probably wanted to make a run for the White House or something like that. And John David Washington's character laughed. He was like, "America would never vote for somebody who is an outright bigot."

Tapper: Pretty ironic, huh?

Etan: Yeah, and the guy looking at him was like, "Are you serious?" And I thought that was such an interesting parallel about how David Duke sold hate. And now going back to Trump, you have to see the correlation. As far as selling hate and going to that specific base. It worked then and it almost worked again. To the tune of seventy-four million people who voted for him again. So what does that say about where we are as a society?

Tapper: Well, it's a great question. I have to believe, just because of who I am and how I try to look at the world, I have to believe that most people were not voting for the uglier sides of Trumpism. That might be naive, I don't know, but I will say this: there is clearly still a lot of ugly racist politics sometimes beneath the surface and sometimes way out there above the surface. Whether it's seeing the Confederate flag, the guy marching through the Capitol—he's not there because he cares about states' rights, that's not what that flag symbolizes. And in fact, I think in Germany, because the Nazi flag has been banned in Germany, I think they use the Confederate battle flag of the United States in Germany to symbolize what they want it to symbolize.

Where are we? We're in a world where twenty years ago, George W. Bush won the Republican nomination saying that he had no problem with the Confederate battle flag flying in South Carolina. And John McCain did the same thing. And then, after the election, he went back and apologized and said, "That's not what I think and I shouldn't have done that." And so I think we are in a continuum where these things are changing and evolving. And you know what Dr. King said about bending toward justice. Progress is never a straight line, things go up and they go down. You see Mitt Romney marching for Black Lives Matter. I think it was Will Smith who said, "Racism . . ."

Etan: Something to the effect that "it isn't new, it's just that everybody has cameras now."

Tapper: Yes, it was something like that. And so I think people are seeing that. And look, there's a lot of people who make a lot of money or accrue power by telling citizens, "The problem isn't you, the problem is these other people." You see it every night on Fox. And that is a message that people are susceptible to. Anytime in my life where I've had a setback, it's much easier to feel like, *Well, I'm not the problem. The problem is this system works against people like me who are so beautiful and deserving and righteous.* It's an easy trap to fall into, but I do think that we are generally bending toward justice and generally making progress.

And I don't think that somebody should look at the election results of 2016 or 2020 and say, "This means I live in a horrible country full of racists." But I do think it means that we have a long way to go still. And a lot of the progress that needs to happen now is not in our laws necessarily as much as it is in our hearts. And education does a lot, but obviously there's a lot more to do, but look, I'm a privileged white guy saying that. What do you think?

Etan: I agree. But another question: maybe every one of the seventy-four million people who voted for Trump, I'm not saying that they're all racist, but is it safe to say that racism wasn't a deal breaker for them?

Tapper: I think that's fair, but also you have to look at the fact that it's not like he only had white people voting for him.

Etan: And that's fair too.

Tapper: African Americans and Latinos and Asians, Jews, people who are Muslim, women, people who are parts of groups that you could argue that he has expressed animus toward—they supported him. And I don't think that comes down to, "These people hate themselves and therefore they voted that way." I think that maybe they thought that there was reason to think the media is not always fair to Donald Trump. I hear that all the time, and whenever anybody says that, I think, *Okay, well tell me . . . Give me an example of what you're talking about.*

Etan: When people say the media isn't fair to Donald Trump, I always say holding someone accountable doesn't mean that you're not being fair to them, it means you're holding them accountable. I watched a program where you talked about where the media enabled some of his rhetoric to continue by bringing people onto the platform and allowing them to spread untruths that go challenged.

Tapper: Yeah. And I don't hold myself up as some sort of exemplar that bears no responsibility for that. People have certainly said things on my show that

I wish I had called them out about. I try to do my best, but I don't always succeed.

Etan: Of course there are going to be some that you missed, I'm not talking about that, you're not perfect, you're not going to always catch everything, but in general . . . the media did buy into a narrative from Trump and the right, even though they knew that narrative was not factual. But they allowed it to permeate without challenging it. And so in some cases, does the media bear some of the responsibility for allowing or sharing untruths that led to what we saw at the Capitol?

Tapper: I do think so, because reporters don't like to be players, reporters like to be observers. I think that's failing viewers, that's failing the public.

I look back on the Trump era and I think in 2015 . . . the very moment he started attacking Latinos as, "They're sending rapists, they're sending drug dealers and some I assume are fine people." Like, that's racist. That's not an accurate description of who's coming into this country. Of course, there are some criminals coming into this country, but most of the people who come into this country illegally are trying to escape countries that are racked with poverty or civil strife and/or make better lives for themselves, and to cast them as criminals is racist. And then in December, when he proposed a ban on Muslims, I look back on it and I expressed outrage at the time and I covered it at the time.

But for both, I moved on. And to me, I think, well, what if that had been about . . . What if he had been saying . . . just to pick random groups. This sounds stupid, but Canadians. He's casting Canadians as a certain way. Maybe, say, a little bit more personal, what if he says something . . .

Etan: Say, Jewish people?

Tapper: Right, any sophisticated conversation that has to do with extremism, it's bigoted and insane to say that we need to ban Muslims from entering the country. And I look back and I think, *God, if he'd said that about any other religion that white people are predominantly, would I have covered it differently?* And I probably would've. I probably would not have let go of it because that's just bigoted. And it offended me and I made it clear on air, but then I moved on. And so I beat myself up a lot more for how I covered the Trump era. It's easy to say, yes, I was going further than most other anchors were.

Etan: Which is what I was just going to say. So you took the words out of my mouth.

Tapper: I will admit that part of what I felt at the time was, *God, I'm already so far out there and nobody else is saying anything.* With the ban that critics described as *prejudiced.* No. It's bigoted. So I hold myself responsible for not going far enough.

Interview with Mahmoud Abdul-Rauf

Mahmoud Abdul-Rauf was Kaepernick before Kaepernick, protesting during the national anthem in 1996. His career wasn't cut short because his skills were diminishing or because of injuries—it was the result of the controversy he sparked for calling the flag of the United States a symbol of oppression and racism and explaining that standing for the anthem would conflict with his Muslim faith.

Etan: I've been reading about you since high school. I appreciate everything that you've always stood for and the sacrifices that you've made so athletes like myself had the ability, while I was playing, to speak freely.

Abdul-Rauf: Thank you, man. I appreciate it. It means a lot to me.

Etan: A lot of people don't know what happened to you as a result of you taking a stand against white supremacy. This notion of what the flag means to different people, and what the symbolism means. So I want to read this third verse of the national anthem that was taken out, because that'll open everyone's eyes to the original intent of the "Star-Spangled Banner."

Abdul-Rauf: I know that verse very well.

Etan: I'm sure you do. It says: *"No refuge could save the hireling and slave,* *from the terror of flight, or the gloom of the grave. And the star-spangled banner in triumph doth wave, o'er the land of the free and the home of the brave. O thus be it ever, when freemen shall stand, between their lov'd home and the war's desolation. Blest with vict'ry and peace, may the Heav'n rescued land, praise the power that hath made and preserved us a nation. Then conquer we must, when our cause it is just, and this be our motto, in God is our trust. And the star-spangled banner in triumph shall wave, o'er the land of the free and the home of the brave."*

I remember reading that in high school and I was like, *What the devil is that? Why are we still singing this? Why am I supposed to honor this?* Right around that time I started learning about John Carlos and Tommie Smith, so I started doing the Black Power salute, and everybody that remembers me playing at Booker T. Washington High School, that's what I did during the national anthem.

And then I read about you and the reaction when you said the words, "You can't be for God and for oppression." And that really stuck with me. No matter what religion you are, you can't be for both. I think there's only one way to interpret what I just read from the third verse. Talk to me about what the flag represents.

Abdul-Rauf: Well, first, man, I'm glad you read that, because the thought that came to my mind was it doesn't matter if they deleted the third stanza or not. They never deleted the way they treated us and the policies that affected us. So, not having it in there never really changed the way we were perceived and the way we were treated historically. So, words or newly crafted words would be nice, but when it's all said and done, there's a saying, *What you do speaks so loudly in my ears that I can't hear a word you're saying.* I think Emerson said that. And so, really, actions speak louder than words.

But to answer your question, Etan, yes, it means so many different things to a lot of people. I think as it relates to whether you're talking about African Americans, whether you're talking about just people of color, when you're talking about the Native Americans, our perception of it is quite different than if you're talking about a European American, who reaps many of the benefits that this country offers not to everyone. They have a leg up from the beginning.

So for a lot of us, when we think of the flag—and yes, we know that there's always a mixture of good and bad in society—it can never just be totally bad, because it wouldn't last. But I would just say that for many of us, when we think of the flag, or if you're talking to a Native American, we think of phrases like sexism. We think of terrorism. We think of racism, right? These are the things that come to our mind. We think of militarism. We think of imperialism. There's so many words that come to mind when you think of it.

Etan: Not so much freedom, justice, and equality for all.

Abdul-Rauf: I wish that was our reality, but it wasn't and isn't. When I was in the league, I began to read more. I began to be introduced to a lot of material, and those things, learning about what's happening globally and domestically, really opened my eyes. But the more you're reading these books, whether it's by Noam Chomsky, whether it's by Randall Robinson . . .

Randall Robinson said something that still resonates with me. He said, "Never before in history have millions of people been deprived of everything except respiratory function." Language, religion, culture, mothers, fathers— we've been deprived of those things. And he said, "Even genitalia." And he said, "Still considered menaces to society." And so, this is something that has been with us from time immemorial. And until things change, I think many of us will continue to see it that way. And no amount of woo-hoo-rah speeches, soft words . . . will change that, because it's about what's happening on the ground, and how we're being affected.

Etan: For a white person to look at a Black person and say, "I don't understand why you don't look at this 'Star-Spangled Banner' and this national anthem the same way that I do," I think it's absolutely ridiculous. For them to look at a Native American person and say the same thing, and say that you should be required to stand at attention and put your hand on your heart and all of that, knowing the history . . . It'd be different if you didn't know the history, but you know the history.

Abdul-Rauf: Some people know only *their* version of history. And that's all they were ever fed. And even if you're being fed that, you have to engage, and ask these questions, dig a little deeper. But not everybody's willing to do that, so there are some people that don't necessarily know, but I think the majority of them do know.

Etan: I don't see how they couldn't know at this point, or maybe they just accept what they know not to be factual because it benefits them.

Abdul-Rauf: That could be true too. People are constantly being fed this sense of America as an exceptional nation. There's a great book called *American Exceptionalism and American Innocence*. That notion of being so great and wonderful and exceptional and superior is constantly being pushed. It's unique, nothing like it. And at the same time, everything by and large that America does is from a position of innocence, like we made a mistake. It wasn't intentional. We didn't mean slavery. We didn't mean to come and bomb your country into the next galaxy. We wanted to bring democracy and freedom to you. We wanted to do this.

And so, this is constantly what you're being fed. And if you're constantly reaping the benefit, and I'm specifically talking about by and large European culture, you're going to perceive America as this great, exceptional, wonderful nation, until you come on our side of the track and go through *Black Like Me*.

And you live that experience. And then even, even if you had to paint yourself Black and live that experience, you always can escape it and go back. We can't. And it's amazing that people have the audacity to utter these things, but it comes from a condition. It comes from an education. They're confident in saying it, because this is their experience. This is their knowledge base. And some of them, like you said, know it, and it's just an arrogance: "How dare you not appreciate what we've given you."

Etan: In the education system, from the time they're in kindergarten, they're taught white supremacy. They're taught things that they know are not true. Like say for instance, Christopher Columbus discovered America, even though people were already here, but they said that they discovered it, and they refer to the natives as savages—that's teaching white supremacy from a young age. And then it just builds on from there. So you're told, "You're better. You're superior." From a young age. And you hear people now say, "We don't know how we can uproot this racism, and where did it come from?" And I'm like, "You all been taught it since kindergarten."

Abdul-Rauf: Yeah. There's a book called the *The White Architects of Black Education,* by William Watkins. And he made a statement that was so profound. He said that in justifying colonialism, we can add in justifying white supremacy and justifying all of these things. They use the textbook as often as the bullet. We're all being duped. There's a saying that what you concentrate on grows. So what you allow continues.

And so, of course, engaging the issues is so critical. But unfortunately, not a lot of people do that. And not a lot of people feel they have the time with the society that we live in—the work schedule and all the stresses upon us. But this stuff has been happening from the beginning. Even a lot of the things that existed then, we have these conversations a lot, even about slavery. And there's a thing called "slavery by another name," and the book that the sister Michelle Alexander wrote, *The New Jim Crow.*

We can deal with and talk about that. It's like, "Are you serious? You talk to me about *my* position on a flag?" And then, even that, you're trying to switch the debate and make it about the flag. Now let's talk about policies. Let's talk about condition. That's just what I'm using to get your attention to deal with these things. Let's not make it about the flag. That's minor compared to all the other stuff.

Etan: I remember being in high school and asking, "Why would America even use that same song?" Why wouldn't they create a new song? Maybe recognizing the sins of the past? Not just skip over them like they never happened, but recognize and have a complete atonement for the sins of the past, in the song, and talk about moving forward collectively, or something like that? Why would you use the same song that has the lyrics specifically about slavery? That was just mind-boggling to me.

Abdul-Rauf: Right, right, I agree with you. I mean, even after this became public—because a lot of people didn't know—there should have been major talk about how we need to come up with something else. But even then, the argument with us would be, when it's all said and done, man, we don't want your songs. We want change. As Dr. Harry Edwards would say, not all change leads to progress. So, change that leads to progress. You've said things to us since we've been here on the shores, and a lot of what you say to us is just double-talk. You contradict yourself. You give us tokenism. You give us bits and pieces to where we think that we're moving ahead. But in all actuality, we're not really moving ahead. And so, we don't want the songs. Yeah, change, it sounds good, but we want *policies*. We want progress.

Etan: A few years ago, my daughter Imani asked me, after seeing Trump's Make America Great Again slogan, "What specific time are they talking about when it was great? And are *we* included in that time period when it was great, because it wasn't never great for us." She said, "It couldn't have been slavery. It couldn't have been lynchings and the KKK era after slavery. It couldn't have been Jim Crow and segregation. What time are they referring to?" This is a thirteen-year-old girl asking this.

Abdul-Rauf: I know you're being humble, and you said she's reading history, but also, she's growing up in your household, so she's learning a lot more than normal thirteen-year-olds.

Etan: Okay, that's fair. So when this happened, going back to 1996, which wasn't that long ago—it's not like we're talking about going back to the sixties, when it's black-and-white TV and we're fighting Jim Crow—I was in high school. You came up with a compromise and said that you were going to stand and pray a silent prayer during the national anthem. And people still had an issue with that.

Abdul-Rauf: Still weren't happy. And that's saying it nicely. They just find reasons to argue and to not be happy and to be disgusted. But yeah, it's ridiculous.

Etan: Could you describe the level of hatred that you were bombarded with at that time, because people kind of gloss over it. But you basically said, "Well, this is a symbol of white supremacy," which it is. That wasn't an opinion. Those are facts.

Abdul-Rauf: Oh, man. I mean, you saw it represented in the media. You saw it represented in the newspapers. I received a lot of death threats as a result of it, a lot of hate mail. And as you said, which is very important and should be brought to people's attention, which Dr. Harry Edwards brought to mine in a way that I didn't even think about, which is why he's considered who he is and the scholar that he is. But he said, "Mahmoud . . ." He wasn't trying to knock anybody at all, but he was just making the point that, because we didn't have social media, it changed things, the dynamic of how things turned out. He said, "When you did what you did, and Craig Hodges did what he did, it was different than when Kaepernick and Muhammad Ali did what they did."

I said, "What do you mean?" He said, "Because during those times they had a movement to attach it to, the Black Power movement. Kaepernick, the Black Lives Matter movement." He said, "When you did what you did, and Craig, there was no movement to attach it to. So you guys were like on an ocean without a paddle, all by yourself." And the media and people could frame the issue the way they wanted to. And so you're right, no social media during my time, they didn't have it, as you said. And so, the media could control the narrative.

Here's a fact that many people don't know: yes, I received tons of hate mail, but I also received a lot of support mail as well

Etan: I didn't know that.

Abdul-Rauf: Yeah, from Jews, Christians, Muslims, atheists, agnostics—agreeing with the position. They can say, "We're going to focus on this. We're not going to show all the people, all different religious persuasions, ethnicities, and cultures, that think the same thing." This is not what they want the world to see . . . But because there was no social media, the media can just focus on more so the hate, right? Tyranny? Oppression? "Who does this guy think he is? Making millions of dollars? How can he talk about oppression?"

Etan: So it became: "Ungrateful, anti-American athlete, Black radical Muslim. Let's vilify the messenger." What toll did that take on you?

Abdul-Rauf: I ended up having to go to the hospital twice, because I'm trying to process it. I'm angry. I'm listening to all of these diatribes and epithets being used. And I'm saying to myself, *I just wanted to go out, man, swinging.* I'm listening to people that I trust about our value, their opinion, and I'm processing it all. And in the process of doing that, I went to the hospital twice, because I had ulcers.

Etan: Oh, wow.

Abdul-Rauf: Yeah. And I had to have IVs in me and everything. But yeah, it was serious anger and hate, man, coming from everywhere. And it did take its toll on me. And even at the games, people coming to the games and then talking about their love for the anthem and why the anthem is this and that, but they're too busy booing me and disrespecting the anthem while the actual anthem is playing. [*Laughing*] I can laugh about it now, but yeah, there was a whole bunch of contradictions going on.

Etan: So [*laughing*] they were booing you while you were praying, but they were booing during the anthem?

Abdul-Rauf: Exactly. And I'm sitting there, man. I'm like, *You all are just* . . . [*laughing*].

Etan: Good lord [*laughs*].

White Privilege

We don't hate nobody because of their color. We hate oppression.
—Bobby Seale

My son Malcolm often traveled with me during my college book tour for *We Matter: Athletes and Activism*. Sometimes he opened with a poem, or he would just sit and listen to the discussion or presentation. One time at Penn State, before an audience of mostly white males, a student told me he hated the phrase "white privilege" because it was, in his opinion, overused in society, similar to the word "racism." He said sometimes he thinks people "play the race card" far too often to get out of taking responsibility for their actions.

I asked him if he had ever been pulled over by the police, and he said yes. I asked him his first thought when he was pulled over. He said that he hoped he wouldn't get a ticket—and the few Black people in the audience laughed. The white people were not sure what the joke was. I explained that they were laughing because the furthest thing from our mind when we get stopped by the police is if we will get a ticket. But he still didn't understand.

I asked them to look at Malcolm. I told them he would be of driving age in a few years and I would be scared for his life to the point that I wasn't sure if I even wanted him to drive. I told them I had been teaching him what to do when he gets stopped by the police, even though he was still several years away from driving. Lessons like, "Don't make any sudden movements, keep your hands visible at all times, don't ever put your hands in your pockets." I then told the student, "You all can cuss out the police, be drunk, spit in their face, tell them you'll have their badge, but me and Malcolm, and all of the other Black people in this room, have to follow a different set of rules. We have to do everything right in order to de-escalate a situation that is only es- calated because of the color of our skin. And you, and all of the white people in this room, do not have to worry about that." I told him there are two separate worlds in this country, and that is white privilege. The crowd fell silent.

I asked him if he had ever been told by any teacher that he was slow and would never be able to write complete paragraphs. He said no. I told him that happened to me in fifth grade, with Ms. Scalet. I asked if he had ever been accused of cheating because the teacher didn't think he could get as high a grade as he did on a math test. He said no. I told him that happened to me in sixth grade, with Ms. Stewart. I asked him if he had ever been told that he needed to sit down when he spoke to teachers because his stature was too intimidating, even though there were other kids the same height and even bigger in the class. He said no. I told him that happened to me in seventh grade, with Mr. Shoemaker. I explained that I had stories all the way through calculus at Syracuse, when the professor, on the first day of class, asked what I was doing there, and announced I was in the wrong classroom.

Afterward, the student, with friends, approached and told me that nobody had ever broken it down for him like that before. We took a group picture and they hung around after the book signing and had a great and lengthy conversation.

That experience showed me that a lot of white people really don't see the privilege they live in. It's all they know. One of the young men said he grew up around all white people, and only saw the world through the lens of his own experiences and reality. Another said he felt bad that the only reason this even got on his radar was by hearing athletes, specifically LeBron James, discuss it. I told him that was one goal of my book: utilizing athletes to bring attention to issues that affect a lot of people.

There are also white people who are actually very aware of their privilege, but don't want to admit it.

A few years ago, I came across a series of videos by Jane Elliott. Ms. Elliott, a white woman, is a race educator, international lecturer, and diversity trainer who gained notoriety when her "Blue Eyes/Brown Eyes" experiment went viral. Utilizing an all-white third grade class, she illustrated how easy it was to indoctrinate feelings of supremacy in children. She wanted them to experience what discrimination felt like. In an interview about the experiment, she stated, "An educator is one who is engaged in the act of leading students out of ignorance, and you can't do that in a system in which you teach that all of the wonderful things that have been done on the earth were done by white males."

In another video, Ms. Elliott said to an auditorium full of white people, "I want every white person in this room who would be happy to be treated as this society, in general, treats our Black citizens, if you as a white person would be happy to receive the same treatment that our Black citizens do in this society, please stand." Unsurprisingly, no one stood. She then said, "You didn't understand the directions. If you white folks want to be treated the way Blacks are, in this society, stand." Again, nobody stood. Then she said, "Nobody's standing here. That says very plainly that you know what's happening. You know you don't want it for you. I want to know why you're willing to accept it or to allow it to happen for others."

With this chapter I interviewed white people who speak about white privilege. We need allies—they can influence white people who will hear it differently from other white people. There's some white people for whom it doesn't matter if LeBron says it or Steph Curry says it. They're only going to hear it if Gregg Popovich or Mark Cuban says it. That's just the way it is. So for any white person to have the moral courage to be able to take a stand on things, that might not necessarily directly impact you, but it might help you to develop the empathy to be able to say, "Well, it's still wrong that this impacts *anybody*." And that's what creating empathy is all about.

Interview with Sue Bird

Sue Bird was first pick in the 2002 WNBA draft, and is a three-time WNBA champion, the all-time WNBA assist leader, an eleven-time WNBA All-Star, and a five-time Olympic gold medalist.

Etan: After the video of Jacob Blake's shooting went viral, both the NBA and WNBA went on strike, and we were guests together on *Meet the Press*. You mentioned the impact that listening to the pain of your Black teammates had on you, as a white person. Could you expound a little bit more on that point.

Bird: I've been really lucky to be exposed to a lot of different cultures. Just from being a basketball player, growing up in New York. I was from Long Island, which was predominantly white, but growing up in Queens and going to high school there, a lot of my teammates were obviously Black. So I've experienced a different world. Playing in Russia, I've been exposed to tons of different cultures. I bring that up because I feel like I have a fairly well-rounded outlook.

Simultaneously, when I talk to my Black teammates, especially during this last year or so, what I've realized is, I can watch the footage and be appalled and disgusted and sad and hurt. And yet, listening to my teammates, how it makes them feel, and seeing that it's bringing up old trauma for them and they all have a story. Whether directly with them, or a family member or a friend. Whether it's police brutality or racism. And the truth is, I'm not going to be able to experience or really relate to that, in that way. So that's when I know, that's when I have to listen, and that's when my learning curve kicks in.

I realized two things. One, there's times to shut up and listen, to be honest, and take a step back. As a white person, a white player in this moment, there's times where I can help amplify from using my platform, using my voice. But that was really the learning process, understanding in that moment that this was retraumatization happening. Seeing it firsthand helped me learn. Which is a huge thing—you got to be educated. But it also helped me see where I can help.

Etan: When we were on *Meet the Press*, Chuck Todd asked if we could do more. And I was like, "Of course," and I talked about my family, my daughter, and what I think about with my son. And it kind of threw him a little bit and he paused. When we talk about white privilege, it's a bit of a hot-button topic, and sometimes people don't quite understand what it means. But it's a privilege to not have to think about your children and your family every time something like this happens, right?

Bird: Oh, absolutely. And I feel like part of my privilege is now what I need to use. Right? Like I need to use that privilege, if you will, in ways to make a positive impact. But the other side of it . . . When you tell somebody they've had privilege, they internalize that as if they didn't work hard.

Etan: Right, and they take offense.

Bird: Exactly, and not that they didn't work hard for the things they got, or got it the wrong way, or they were given. And I'm like, "That's not what I'm saying. But you still had privilege. And those two things can exist at the same time." I think some people view them as, it's either one or the other. And it's not.

Etan: Oftentimes you'll hear people say, "Well, I didn't come from money." But this doesn't have anything to do with money. I played over a decade in the NBA, I have money. But when my son is stopped by the police, my money doesn't save him. And that's the connection that is missed sometimes.

Bird: It's interesting you say that because . . . this is something that in the back of my head, I knew. But when the WNBA executive committee was in negotiations about wanting Breonna Taylor on our jersey, *Say Her Name* on our shooting shirts, and *Black Lives Matte*r on the court, Layshia Clarendon said, and a lot of athletes have said it, but it really hit home, having this one-on-one conversation with her, she told me, "When I take my uniform off, I *am* Breonna Taylor." That's when it really clicked for me. So to your point, does it matter? Money? Fame, no fame? Status, no status? This is the reality for Black people in our country.

Etan: Talk to me about the conversations that you have with other white people, beyond your teammates.

Bird: I've definitely had some interesting, tough conversations. There were just certain things that I thought everybody knew. Whether it's about Black culture or the walk of a Black person in our country, just because I've been able to listen to stories. I've heard firsthand, different experiences. It really opened my eyes to how little it's talked about in our mainstream media or just in society. So a lot of the conversations are just me sharing a story that a teammate told me and a friend or a family member being completely shocked at what I've shared with them. A lot of times it comes from a place of ignorance. They just don't know, but I'm like, "That's the thing: you have the privilege to not have to know."

Etan: Exactly. In sports you might be introduced to people who maybe you wouldn't have crossed otherwise. People outside of athletics, they're not interacting with people from different cultures in the same way. That plays a big difference. Do you agree?

Bird: I'm like, "We have it figured out in sports, you guys," like politicians, all kinds of people. "You should come see how sports teams interact, how we operate." I'm sure you could speak to this. We've been on teams where people didn't like each other.

Etan: Of course.

Bird: That's just how it is. But the culture of team sports is, regardless of, you like them, you don't like them. You believe what they say, you don't. You agree, you don't agree, whatever it is. You're like, "Okay, but no. We're all equal on this team. We're all here, trying to win. So we have to push these things to the side and do what's best for the team." Actually, thematically, it's how the whole world should operate.

Etan: That's a great analogy.

Bird: Tell me to shut up and dribble? I'm like, "Oh, I've lived in this eco-system where I see that you're Black, I know that I'm white." It's not that we don't see it. We do see it. But we respect it, and we're here for the better of the team, no matter what.

Etan: And it's crazy that in 2021 there are people who only interact with Black people in movies, TV, and music. I can understand maybe back in the sixties. But *now*? People who have no interaction with Black people at all? That's amazing to me.

Bird: I know. And as terrible as the insurrection was, it pulled back the veil, and now we're forced to deal with it. So my hope is that, because we're forced to deal with it now, it can start real change. Not just this Band-Aid change. Like, "Oh yeah, we'll just fix this with a Band-Aid." No. We need real surgery.

Interview with Kyle Korver

Kyle Korver played seventeen seasons in the NBA and ranks among the most prolific three-point shooters in league history, ranking fourth all-time in three-point field goals made and third all-time in three-point field goal percentage. In 2019 he wrote an article for the *Players' Tribune* called "Privileged" where he discusses white privilege, what it takes to be an ally, the role white people can play in pushing the movement forward. His article opened up the eyes of a lot of white America to white privilege because he used himself as an example, which alone is a truly selfless act. Nobody likes to publicly criticize themselves, but when it's done to make an overall point, that message can definitely resonate with the masses.

Etan: Let's start off with Thabo Sefolosha. He was your teammate, and he was my teammate in Oklahoma City for a year. Talk about the incident with the NYPD, and how that affected you.

Korver: I would say initially it didn't, and that's the problem. We played in Atlanta the night before, then we flew to New York for a back-to-back against Brooklyn. We finally got to New York. Guys want to go to dinner, go out a little bit, see the city. But we had a big game the next day and then a lot of us were focused in.

When we woke the next morning, I hear Thabo got into an altercation with the police. We didn't know his leg was broken at the time, only that he got hurt and spent the night in prison. I love Thabo. He's one of my favorite teammates, one of the most interesting teammates I've ever had. Conversation is very rarely about basketball. We talk basketball when we need to, but we're talking life, we're talking culture, we're talking much bigger things. I played with him twice, once in Atlanta, once in Salt Lake. My first thought, even though I know who Thabo is, my first reaction was like, *What was Thabo doing out on the night of a back-to-back, and what did he do to get his leg broken?* My first reaction was to side with the police, because if I was in that situation, as a white man . . . and I didn't put this together in that moment, but I would've had to have done something significant for the police to do that to me.

And so it wasn't until sometime later, looking back on this story, and was like, *Wow, look at my privilege. Look at the way that I experienced this country in this world. What a messed-up moment.* I claimed to be Thabo's friend. He's one of my favorites. But in that moment, somehow I trusted the police more than Thabo? It's a hard story to pass along because I don't really want to admit it. But it's, I think, a story that a lot of white people can relate to.

When I was trying to put together this article, I thought about it for a good long time. How do you talk to them? You probably wrestled with this much more than me, but this is a real thing. How do we bridge this gap? How do we get people to see the story differently? And ultimately, what I've landed on is to share my stories. And they're not fun to share. They're mostly embarrassing. They feel like confessions. But when I do that, it seems like there's not this attack or this defense that gets put up right away. Like, "Oh, you're willing to admit where you've been complicit and where you've been part of the problem, maybe I'll consider it a little bit differently."

And so that's what that piece kind of felt like. There's more stories around it, I do want to be a bridge because I care deeply. I have many Black friends who I love and who I don't just see as equal, but I see as better than me. They're better people, better dads, better athletes, more creative, stronger, braver, more courageous than I am. And I'm also connected to a whole lot of white people who I know to be generous and who I know to be kind and who I know to be loving and they do love their country and their families, but there's this huge gap between us and how do we step into the middle and really bridge this?

And you can't just point fingers at each other. I can't just shoot missiles at my white friends. It doesn't work. And so how do I lead with my own stories to show where I've had blind spots and how I'm doing work to try to be better in this space? And so, anyway, that was the heart of that piece, and you have to come strong with these things, right? You're not trying to water the message down. That's important not to do, but ultimately this is a space that we need more white men to step into, I believe.

Etan: There is a segment of mainstream America who are only going to be able to hear it if it comes from another white face. Do you think that's an accurate assessment?

Korver: I think it's sad, but true. I could have you or another Black man who can speak twice as intelligently, twice as articulately, twice as well as I ever could, but for some reason white people will listen to me a little bit more and open that first conversation. For me, it's like, "Okay, but there's people who can do this way better than me." And so it makes me not want to step out all the time, because I know that I don't know.

But I think it's important, especially for white men, that we try to humbly walk this journey and align ourselves where we are listening to Black voices who are educating us and giving us the right messages to say. Oftentimes, where white men get into trouble is with our privilege, we just want to fix problems. Like, "This law doesn't work. Change the law." Or, "This person's not seeing things the right way, let me just explain this to him better." So for us to *not* try to do that, because we get ourselves in a whole lot of trouble trying to take our own understandings, which we don't have, and fix these huge horrible problems in our country. So how are we aligning ourselves so that we're listening to Black voices, but then taking that message to our white networks? This is the work for us right now.

Etan: One of the things you also talked about in the article was an incident that happened with Russell Westbrook, with a fan in Utah. Can you talk about how that affected you as well?

Korver: We were playing Oklahoma City a couple of years ago, right before the article came out. This was kind of the last thing that happened in my life before I felt the need to put that out there. There's been stories like this, unfortunately, playing there where you have a lot of white fans, and this is not the first time this has happened.

Etan: I know what you're saying, and no, this definitely isn't the first time this has ever happened.

Korver: Right, so someone said something very ugly to Russ, and Russ responded, defending himself as he should. I didn't hear the comment that was said, I didn't know what happened. And still, because I didn't hear that, I was just like, "Russ gets into it with the fans. This is what happens." He's a fighting guy. He's going to respond. So I just automatically took that side of the story. And it wasn't until a few hours after the game that I learned about what had actually happened. And I was just like, *Man, how did I not side with Russ? I know Russ's heart. I know who Russ is.* We're not super close, but I know enough of him to know who his character is and what he's all about. And so that was another moment where, as a white man, I just assumed that . . . I put Russ at fault.

And from then, we had lots of discussions as a team, and it was super emotional. Ironically, Thabo was on my team having these conversations again. And I'm sitting there and I'm like, *Okay, I've thought a lot about this since that happened, but have I done anything or have I just been complicit this whole time? Even though I've had all these thoughts and I've read these books, I'm still a part of the problem. How do I be a part of solution?* And so that was ultimately a powerful moment for me to be like, *Okay, if I want to be a team-mate, a good teammate, a good friend, I've got to start stepping into this more.* And then that's ultimately where that article came from.

Etan: One of the things that struck me about the piece was that I made a direct correlation to what happens in mainstream America every time a Black man is killed by the police. That a lot of times white America immediately sides with the police before even knowing any of the facts. And that's when you hear, "Well, before we jump to conclusions, let's just wait until the facts come out." And that's usually code for, "Let's wait for the police explanation of what really happened, not what the family says happened." But that's also what is so profound about you admitting that, even though it was in a basketball sense—there was a direct correlation to the bigger picture of what happens in real life.

Korver: I totally agree. In my conversations with white folk, unfortunately, a lot of white people don't have any Black friends, but they know some cops. And they know the cops to be mostly good people who protect them. And if they call 911, they're going to be there for them. And if they get pulled over, there's a chance that if they weren't doing anything really wrong, they could be let off. They might just get a warning. And so that's their experience with police.

And we're not great, as a society, at trying to seek another perspective. We just kind of hold on to what we understand and what we think is right and what we think is fair. And I think that's a big part of this, why diversity is so important, because you can't get other perspectives unless you're seeking them out, if you're living next to people who can give you another side of the story. All that to be said, you can live in diversity and still not see the other side of the story. And I think that's where my story . . . I was born in Paramount, California. It's a bit of a long story here, but I think it's important.

Etan: Take your time.

Korver: I was born in Paramount, California, where me and some of my family, we were the minorities in the city. And we went up through the Rodney King riots. We went through a whole bunch of things and we saw all that. Moved to a small town called Pella, Iowa, which has ten thousand white people in it when I was twelve. So I lived for twelve years in LA, when I was in the minority, then I was in a complete majority in Iowa. Then I was at Clayton, some diversity. My rookie year in Philly, I was the only white guy on the team. I played there for two years, then I go to the Jazz in the NBA, Chicago, Atlanta, Cleveland. That's when a lot of the stuff, the anthem was first coming up, I'm starting to see things differently for the first time, just because of the conversations I'm having. But I still don't fully understand. Go back to Utah and Milwaukee, which some say is the most segregated city in America.

So I've been in diversity. I've been in the minority and then I've been in the majority, and I've literally gone back and forth every single time that I moved. And so because of that, I always assumed that while I surely wasn't an expert, I probably knew quite a bit. And I certainly wasn't part of the problem. But it really wasn't until those years in Atlanta, and then through the anthem stories with my teammates in Cleveland, that I was just like, *Wow.* It just blew me away that I've been in diversity, I have lots of Black friends. Not just friends, but people I really care about and who I've gone through the limits with physically and emotionally in these basketball seasons and playoff rounds, I'm emotionally invested in, and I still don't get it.

And that blew my mind. It blew my mind. And that's why I'm so passionate. And I'm trying right now in this space because I can't sit here and be like . . . as far as my posture of just admitting my blind spots, because if anyone should get it, it should be Kyle.

Etan: And you felt guilty about having those blind spots.

Korver: Definitely, I still had all these blind spots. And you learn it's because white supremacy is just so intricately laced into all of the systems, all of our culture. White people, we don't understand we have a culture and that we've set what we think is normal based on our culture. We don't understand it's important to have eyes for these things.

So, to come full circle, just because you're in diversity doesn't mean that you're seeing things properly. And so I can't just be mad at my white friends or networks that don't see it, because you don't know what you don't know. But that's why it's important for us to be messengers and try to be bridges in this, because there's a whole different America that these white networks will never see, will never experience, if we're not trying to bring this message. Just because you're in diversity doesn't mean you can see, doesn't mean you know. There's a lot of work that has to happen in your heart.

Etan: I think one important thing is creating empathy. And this is a tough thing to do. In my previous book, *We Matter: Athletes and Activism*, I interviewed a lot of different athletes to discuss how these situations of police brutality or killings affect us personally.

Before COVID, I did an event with Emerald Garner, Eric Garner's daughter, at Columbia University. Afterwards, one of the students said, "Listen, we hear these stories and we've read your book—it was required for us to read it. And we're reading your interviews with Dwyane Wade, Russell Westbrook, Eric Reid, and Anquan Boldin, and that's just not our reality. We don't know that." And he said, "It's terrible what happened to Eric Garner, I can say that it's wrong for that to be anybody's reality, but if I don't necessarily experience that, how can it be on my radar?"

Korver: So it's not even on his radar, and that's the problem, and it wasn't on my radar either, but I feel that it should've been.

Etan: And that's the interesting part, because there are two worlds. For instance, you have children, I have children. My son Malcolm is fifteen. So we're thinking about him driving and it terrifies us. That's a real concern of ours, but it's not a concern for white America.

Korver: That's so terrible that that's the reality for you and for Black people all over the country.

Etan: Right, but what your article did was open the eyes of many white people, because they have to learn in order for things to change.

Korver: I could not agree more. And I think that in trying to be helpful as a white man, it's kind of like Racism 101. We can't really get to the deeper levels because we don't know. And if we try to wade too deep in those waters, we just get ourselves in trouble and probably make the problem worse. But there is a lot of talk about privilege, talk about white supremacy, share our stories, make it personal. Black Lives Matter, what's wrong with the response of, "All lives matter." All these things that we can handle, these questions. And honestly, you guys don't need to talk about this anymore. Like I'm sure that you guys are exhausted trying to explain to white people. I can't imagine. But *I* can do that.

Like you said, empathy. How do we do that? I think you have to humanize people's stories. And so I think for me, being able to share some of my stories as a white man, I think maybe that's a way to help them, but this is big work. And the more you step into this, the more you realize how deep and how painful and how hard this is. But we all have a role to play.

Etan: In the article you stress how important it is to listen. Craig Hodges told me, "Oh man, I just had this great conversation with Kyle Korver." And that's how we even connected. Talk to me about trying to learn more and listening to people like Craig Hodges.

Korver: How do we know that there's anything changing in the world right now? I think the only thing you can do is look at yourself and say, *How am I growing? How am I getting better? What am I doing differently that I wasn't doing before?* One of the things that I've tried to really sit in is, *Who are the voices that have authority in my life? Who are the voices that I'm seeking out?*

Because I'm a white man, it's been very easy for me to only listen to white men. I think you have to be intentional about, *Who am I seeking wisdom from?* It's one thing that I ask about basketball, it's another thing to really seek in life and faith and the fear questions. Have I given Black men and women permission to be that voice in my life? And that's a huge . . . What comes in is what's going to come out. And so if we're not putting in different voices and voices who really know, who have lived experiences, how are we ultimately going to be helpful?

I've found that there's just incredible deep wells of wisdom and life in the Black community that, not purposefully, but just naturally, I wasn't seeking before. Listening and learning has been a huge part of the journey and it's an important part of the journey. I think a lot of us want to be about the action right away and we want to fix the problems, but I can't teach things that I don't know. I have to listen before I can know anything. And so that's a big part of this story.

Interview with Rick Strom

Rick Strom serves as executive producer, lead host, and content coordinator of *The Young Turks Sports (TYT Sports)*. Rick originally joined TYT Network in 2011 and grew the subscriber base from 4,000 to 120,000-plus, and 511,000 video views to 100,000,000-plus video views. He has interviewed countless athletes and celebrities, and consistently uses his platform to point out white privilege. What he is doing with *TYT Sports* is really needed, not just for entertainment purposes but for educating and properly informing an entire population of people who might have just skipped over these stories and never observed the differences in treatment that happens in America when it comes to police, the justice system, who gets to live and who dies, and just overall white privilege.

Etan: I've been following you for a long time. I'm a big fan of your work.

Strom: There is no way that I could possibly show enough gratitude for the words that you just said, because I feel like I'm just doing a very small part in this world. To hear it from you as an author, a leader, and a community activist, it truly means a lot. Thank you very much.

Etan: You're showing and exposing white privilege in a way that most white people are not reporting on and talking about. In the Black community, we're having those conversations, but then to turn on the Young Turks and you're reporting the same conversation that we're having, talking about white privilege in particular, that's not normally done. And that's why it's really important that you do that and show that level of differences in justice, treatment, police brutality, white privilege, all of it.

Strom: Because I think if more people understood, especially people who look like me and sound like me and don't have to worry about how loud they played their music or not using a turn signal or driving when it's dark out

. . . Just to make a quick segue, Richard Pryor gave this interview in 1977 that I did a story on recently, that was like, "If we started talking about these things, then people would start talking to one another and there wouldn't be all these differences in the world. And racism, not that it would come to an end, but it would be marginalized and minimized." I think it's important for someone who looks like me to do this because, for the racists in the world, if they keep hearing the same story, which is an absolute injustice, over and over and over again, from someone who doesn't look like me, then the racial undertones will continue to exist in their minds and thinking, *Well, he's just complaining about it. Blah, blah, blah.*

Etan: Right. But it's different coming from you.

Strom: Right. If it's me, I do think that there is potential, at least, to reach someone who does look like me, say, "Well, wait a minute. Why is he saying this?" I think if more people who are Caucasian talked about these issues, understood them and just gave their own minds the chance to process all of it, then we wouldn't be seeing what we're seeing. And as we have seen with Dr. King, as we've seen with Muhammad Ali and many others, this is a life-long fight, but I'm committed to it.

Etan: At Liberty High School in Florida, one of the resource officers slammed a girl to the ground, she's knocked unconscious. I'm thinking, *Yeah, they wouldn't have done a little white girl like that.* But you do segments on it. Talk about some of the segments that you've done.

Strom: Sure. I'll go from the most notable to the local. If Colin Kaeper-nick takes a knee, he is canceled, and Republicans love to rail against cancel culture and how bad it is. And Kelly Loeffler literally using her team, the Atlanta Dream, said, "We must stand up against this cancel culture." They canceled the guy who didn't do anything violent, but took a knee. Mean-while, you have someone like UFC president Dana White, who wants to be like Trump, if you saw in his media compilation bit that he did. And they will, along with ESPN, promote somebody, have them on their shows, and continue to push Colby Covington, who is a bigot, whether he thinks he is or not, or whether he's playing the character or not. You are a David at this point. Look at what happened with him and Tyron Woodley. Look at what he said about Black Lives Matter.

Now, you go back to someone like Kaepernick, who's saying, "That racism thing is kind of bad," and they let him go. And they whiteball him and they don't let him back in the league.

Then you go to the local levels. I don't remember the man's name. It's probably best I don't. But there was a video that I literally thought was from *America's Funniest Home Videos*, where a guy, white guy, is naked, running around a neighborhood. The first time I saw this, I'm thinking like, *Where is "Yakety Sax"? Why aren't we hearing this crazy music playing over it?* And then you learn the story. This is a guy who killed a Minor League Baseball player's family, ran around his town naked, charged at a police officer who's also white, and . . . no bullets. No fear for your life. Nothing. There was another one where a white guy, clearly, clearly crazy, going after an officer with a knife—the officer didn't fire a shot, didn't do anything.

Etan: Happens all the time, unfortunately.

Strom: Meanwhile, someone like Philando Castile will get shot to death. Because he's Black? He told an officer that he was a registered gun owner. There's countless examples. We're just trying to expose the injustices one at a time and hopefully the cases come to a close.

Etan: My son, he's fifteen. And he was reading about Kalief Browder and what happened with him. He was held at Rikers Island for three years, serving two in solitary confinement, because he allegedly stole a backpack. And then, tragically, he committed suicide. Malcolm's looking at this and at the different crimes that white people commit. And he's asking me about two separate worlds and what can be done about that. And it's tough because I don't have the answer for him. How can we change that? How can we expose it? You are consistently exposing on the large platform of the Young Turks. And it's so important that you continue doing it.

Strom: I will. There's going to be no shortage of it. There was another case that I recently discovered and there are tons of them, unfortunately. Marquis Dixon, who they alleged that he stole Nikes. He's a teenager and also allegedly flashed a gun. When cops searched his home, they did not find a gun. The eyewitness did not come forward after initially seeing this. Meanwhile, he is in an adult penitentiary with rapists and murderers and true criminals. And he's underage. Now the greatest, most glaring example is the interaction that took place on January 6. We want to talk about two Americas.

Etan: I live in DC, and people here remember Miriam Carey back in like maybe 2013. She did a U-turn there and broke the barricade around the Capitol and they immediately shot her down. No questions, no hesitation, shot her dead through her car. And without a care in the world on January 6, those people went into the Capitol. They didn't go in there with a fear that something could possibly happen to them.

Eventually they said, "Domestic terrorist." But at first, the media was trying to not really say those words. They were saying, "Well, you know, they just want to be heard. They're upset with the election and are protesting," almost sympathizing with them. So, talk about that level of double standard in the media.

Strom: Well, you could point to the example recently of Chad Wheeler from the Seattle Seahawks, where we're not hearing domestic violence. We're not hearing this guy almost killed his wife. It is, well, mental illness. And here's the thing: mental illness is really important. My issue is, that can't be the first line of defense for someone who's white and they don't use it for someone who is not.

Etan: Isn't it interesting that when you have the mass shooters, the first thing they talk about is mental illness or "lone shooter" and they start talking about their past? And as soon as they start doing that, I automatically say, "Oh, the person's white." Before they give a name, before they show a picture, I know immediately this was a white person, just by their description.

Strom: Oh, no question. You automatically know. You could close your eyes, listen to the news report, and know automatically what race they are. But even when there is a picture, notice the depiction in which media paints someone who is white and who is not white. If it's a white person who committed a crime, you'll see something like family photos, showing they're a family man or woman. You'll see pictures of them at graduation where they look great. And then if it's a person of color, you will see the literal complete opposite.

Etan: That's definitely true. How do you speak to other white people about white privilege? White people who don't get it.

Strom: If someone says something wrong in the context of a conversation, I'll quickly correct them, but I'm not going to tear them down because I think that's part of getting someone onto your side. When I hear something, I go and talk. Now, if it's someone that I don't know and we just met a day, a week, a month ago, go in even softer. But if it's someone that I do know and they understand the issue, but don't really go deep enough, that's when I'll explain it to them. It's frustrating.

To know that we could achieve so much more if we're in it together. And then to hear things that are baseless, that just don't exist. To hear how they don't understand their privilege, incredibly frustrating. And there's billions of stories, even in the conversation that we've had, or as it happens in present day, for that to just fly over someone's head, incredibly frustrating. I would just say if I come across it, and this goes for a lot of people who may be reading this, maybe this is their family member or their friend or whatever, go and talk, because they literally don't know. That's about all I could say.

Etan: When you say go at them "soft," give me an example. I want this to be a tutorial for white people about how to talk to other white people who don't understand white privilege.

Strom: Sure. I think it was just not being aggressive in the way that I phrased something. So when I'm trying to explain something to someone, I'm going to talk with my voice low. I'm not going to be super aggressive. When they say something that is totally blasphemous and wrong, I don't fight fire with fire. I just don't think that's the way to accomplish our end goal. I think it's more like, "Well, actually, there's this case about Sandra Bland, on how she got pulled over for nothing. And she died, did you know that? She died in police custody." "Oh my God. I didn't know." You know, instead of being like, "No! Actually, you're wrong and here's why!" I just don't think that's the best way to try to get somebody on your side, especially if it's someone that you view as fighting for the cause but maybe they just don't know it yet.

Whitewashed Education and Media

Do you see law and order? There is nothing but disorder, and instead of law there is the illusion of security. It is an illusion because it is built on a long history of injustices: racism, criminality, and the genocide of millions. Many people say it is insane to resist the system, but actually, it is insane not to.

—Mumia Abu-Jamal

When I was growing up in Tulsa, my middle school, Carver, was seven minutes away from what had once been Black Wall Street. But I didn't learn about that in school. I learned about this tragedy at home, from people in my community and my church. I was then surprised to discover how many people were unaware of what happened. It wasn't taught around the country. Only recently, because of the depiction in the HBO shows *Watchmen* and *Lovecraft Country*, are people becoming aware of its existence.

In 1921, Tulsa's Greenwood District, also known as Black Wall Street, was one of the most prosperous Black communities in the United States. The community was self-sustaining, with hotels, doctors, theaters, grocery stores, and schools. Greenwood wasn't just surviving, it was prospering, without the participation of white people. Then, on May 31, 1921, the *Tulsa Tribune* reported that a Black man, Dick Rowland, had attempted to rape a white woman, Sarah Page.

Hannibal B. Johnson, author of *Black Wall Street: From Riot to Renaissance in Tulsa's Historic Greenwood District*, was quoted as saying, "The *Tulsa Tribune* published a story titled 'Nab Negro for Attacking Girl in an Elevator.' It was a false narrative to keep Black people in their place and to reinforce white supremacy." It must be understood that whites were long jealous of how the exuberant community was thriving. Refusing to wait for the investigative process, whites sparked two days of unprecedented racial violence. Vicious mobs of whites, many of them deputized and provided guns and ammo by city officials, attacked Black residents and businesses in Greenwood. Thirty-five city blocks went up in flames, three hundred people died, and eight hundred were injured. Defense of white female virtue was the expressed motivation for the collective racial violence. It has been called "the single worst incident of racial violence in American history."

Delegate Marlon Amprey from Baltimore, Maryland, summed it up with this tweet:

> *Stop saying that Black Wall Street was destroyed by nebulous "white mobs." Black Wall Street was destroyed by white supremacy as judges, state attorneys, a city council, a mayor, a governor, white media, policemen, fire fighters, the national guard, pilots, and insurance companies.*

I remember once, during an economics class at Syracuse University, the professor referenced Black Wall Street, and aside from some people from Oklahoma and Texas, hardly anyone else in the big lecture hall was aware of what had happened. After the professor briefly explained some history, a student from New Jersey expressed confusion because she had never heard of masses of white people being involved in anything this violent and vicious. In fact, most of the lecture hall shared her surprise and disbelief. They actually thought the professor didn't have his facts right, or that it was a mistake.

They were never taught this in school. I remember sharing that Tulsa was not in fact an anomaly, but one of many cities all across the country that were intentionally destroyed by white supremacy. Men, women, and children lynched, businesses burned to the ground, in conjunction with the police and fire departments. I pointed out that this missing information from their education had warped their perception of history. They only saw history through white eyes. This was one thing I definitely learned in college: the danger of not teaching white people true history.

In 2019, for the four hundredth anniversary of the arrival of the first enslaved Africans in Virginia, the *New York Times* published the 1619 Project. It is a long-form journalism project developed by Nikole Hannah-Jones and writers from the *New York Times* and the *New York Times Magazine*, which "aims to reframe the country's history by placing the consequences of slavery and the contributions of Black Americans at the very center of the United

States' national narrative." The project time line begins with the year enslaved Africans were brought to Jamestown, revealing how slavery and racial injustice have been an integral part of American history.

Many historians attempted to discredit the project and dedicated themselves to challenging the accuracy of certain aspects. In an essay for the *New York Review of Books*, historian Sean Wilentz accused the 1619 Project of cynicism for its portrayal of the American Revolution, the Civil War, and Abraham Lincoln. Lincoln, commonly taught as someone who loved and freed enslaved Black people, according to Wilentz, is "rendered as a white supremacist."

I recall challenging my history teacher for saying that Lincoln thought slavery was morally wrong and that many white people—abolitionists, Quakers, and "good Christians"—agreed with him, and that's why they ended slavery. But in a letter to Horace Greeley, Lincoln wrote:

If I could save the Union without freeing any slave I would do it, and if I could save it by freeing all the slaves I would do it; and if I could save it by freeing some and leaving others alone I would also do that. What I do about slavery, and the colored race, I do because I believe it helps to save the Union.

Based on my research, I believe that emancipation was driven by the goal of crushing the main economic source of the Confederacy, and it just so happened that source was slavery.

The clash regarding the 1619 Project and historian critics represents a fundamental disagreement over the trajectory of American society. Was America founded as a slavocracy based on white supremacy, and are current racial inequities the natural outgrowth? Or was America conceived on principles of liberty, freedom, justice for all, and the principle that all men are created equal, which schools have been teaching students for decades?

Former president Donald Trump's response was the creation of the 1776 Commission "to promote patriotic education." Trump vowed to "encourage our educators to teach our children about the miracle of American history," and promised, "Our heroes will never be forgotten. Our youth will be taught to love America with all of their heart and all of their soul."

To further support history being taught the way it has always been—

through a white revisionist lens—Republican-controlled legislatures are working hard to prevent alternate teachings in schools. HB 1775, which prevents the teaching of the academic theory that holds racism is ingrained in the history of the United States and still impacts current laws, is being discussed in half a dozen states. Oklahoma governor Kevin Stitt (R) has already signed a bill into law that bans the teaching of critical race theory in schools.

Stitt explained in a video statement on Twitter, "Now more than ever we need policies that bring us together, not rip us apart. I firmly believe that not one cent of taxpayer money should be used to define and divide young Oklahomans about their race or sex . . . We can and should teach this history without labeling a young child as an oppressor, or requiring he or she feel guilt or shame based on their race or sex."

Why are they so outraged and afraid of an accurate portrayal of American history? Do they want to teach that slavery wasn't horrific, using language similar to the Texas Board of Education, which printed history books such as the one that says the Atlantic slave trade brought "millions of workers from Africa to the southern United States to work on agricultural plantations"? (After national outrage erupted, they claimed this statement was simply an error.)

Amna Akbar, an assistant professor of law at the Moritz College of Law at Ohio State University, slammed all of the efforts by the right as catchall attempts to suppress conversations around racism. "The term critical race theory is being used by Republicans in a loose way to capture all sorts of critical thought about the histories and legacies of racism in this country," Akbar explained. "It's a bogeyman that they're constructing around critical attention to the history of the country."

MSNBC national correspondent Joy Reid brilliantly summed it up with a tweet that read:

A-They enslave you
B-They reluctantly free you & say "pull yourself up by your bootstraps because we owe you nothing"
C-Somehow you build a community
D-They get mad and burn it down
E-They mock your neighborhood's poverty & blame YOUR character
F-They erase A from history books

If Black children are old enough to experience racism, white children are old enough to learn the truth about it. Sugarcoating history isn't going to bring anyone together, it will only continue the very long pattern of whitewashing education in this country.

Interview with Cenk Uygur

I discussed the danger of misinformation with Cenk Uygur, the founder and CEO of TYT Networks, which is one of the largest online news platforms in the world.

Etan: What made you want to start the Young Turks?

Uygur: That's a great question. I don't get asked that that often. Back in 1998, I wrote an email to my friends saying, *I think that online video is going to beat television.* They wrote back, *You're nuts.* To be fair to them, they said it would take at least twenty years. On that they were right, but here we are.

The reason: you need billions of dollars to start a TV station. You need almost nothing to start online video. The TV guys think, *Oh, we're professionals and so we're going to be better at this.* I always thought, *That's not remotely true. You guys generally suck at this.* When it comes to TV news, by definition, it has to be brought to you by multibillion-dollar corporations.

As a result, the news will be brought to you by a multinational corporate lens. There's no way of avoiding that in television, it's inescapable. I thought all the way back then, if you start doing news online, it will be more honest, more successful. It will resonate with people more. As it turned out, we were right about that.

We went from zero, with no resources, no money. We started in my one-bedroom apartment without a nickel to our name. Now we get five hundred million views a month. The Young Turks's audience overall is larger per month than Tucker Carlson, Rachel Maddow, or any show on cable news. We were right. Online video won, and we're just getting started.

Etan: Malcolm X once said, "The media is the most powerful entity on earth. They have the power to make the innocent guilty and to make the guilty innocent, and that's power. Because they control the minds of the masses.

Uygur: I agree 1,000 percent.

Etan: Specifically, Fox News and the way that they have mind control over their supporters. They'll say something that you know is not factually correct, but they'll repeat it over and over. Then other people start repeating it as if it is factually correct. I have to give them credit, because they do that brilliantly. But it's important to have truth tellers.

Uygur: We're not trying to out-left people. What we're trying to do is out-correct people. Present news and positions that are based on real facts. We're not doing the news that we are because we're progressive, we're progressive because of where the news led us.

Malcolm X, as usual, is 100 percent right. "Number one Fox News" and all those guys, they created Frankenstein. They constantly misled their own audience and fed them misinformation. They did that for a couple of decades. Frankenstein always rises up and always attacks its creators. Now it is attacking the Republican Party and Fox News itself.

Now Newsmax and OAN are saying, "Well, we're even more nuts than Fox News, we'll like you more thoroughly, and we'll give you whatever pretty little dreams that you want. Black people are inferior, of course, we'll tell you that, no problem. Immigrants that cross the border without a dollar in their pocket are the most powerful people on earth, of course, we'll tell you that. What other lie do you need? Muslims are about to take over Tulsa, Oklahoma, so you need to pass a law against Sharia law in Oklahoma. You need that lie, we'll tell you that lie because we're just trying to get an audience."

The right-wing mind is deeply conspiratorial, filled with fear and usually loathing and hatred. If you're going to do a right-wing network, you must appeal to fear and hatred.

Now, Fox News is getting beat at their own game. But by definition, that wing of media must tell you lies, because if they told you that Muslims are not taking over Oklahoma, but the biggest problem in the country is corporate donors to politicians, instead of Brown people and Black people, well, then you might get angry at corporations like News Corp that owns and runs Fox News. Then, you might get angry at all the tax cuts that they're getting, the deregulation that they have, and the fact that they can keep your wages low. The very last thing they want you to do is to focus on those real problems. Hence, they must distract you with fear and hatred, and for the right-wing mind, that's perfect.

Etan: We experience a lot of police terrorism, and with almost every case you'll see the *victim* being put on trial. Malcolm X talked about this as well. When he talked about police brutality, he said they will criminalize the victim, so white America feels that the police are justified in whatever they have to do to maintain law and order. It's a media trick that has been happening for decades.

Uygur: You're exactly onto the right issue here. Let's think about it logically. When Malcolm X, Martin Luther King, and Shirley Chisholm were around, let alone Frederick Douglass, they all said the same thing. There was no Fox News, but they all had a problem with mainstream media.

American media pushes stereotypes in ways *they* don't even understand. For example, the local news. Folks have traced this, and when local news did stories about white-on-white crime, it didn't scare people or grab their attention enough. It didn't drive ratings. White-on-Black crime—they didn't like that at all because the audience is majority white. They just viscerally react and say, "I don't like that. That looks like that's an attack on me. I'm going to turn it off. I'm going to the other news station."

Black men committing crime on white people got them great ratings. So they repeated that over and over, until it drilled into all of our heads, the mythology that unfortunately has been present in America for so long. That was the reason why it was successful in the ratings in the first place, because it's a vicious cycle. The mythology was already in their heads. Then it is reinforced and made deeper. That mythology dates back to slavery, reconstruction, etc.

Jim Crow, *The Birth of a Nation*. That was the original first feature-length film. It told America, "Black people are violent and they will come for you and your women." A lot of white folks don't know this and I feel like it's okay to educate them. I know some folks say, "No, it's not my job to educate them." Well, I'm a talk show host and I do news, so it's literally my job to educate people.

Etan: I hear you.

Uygur: The education in this process is the reason why blackface is so offensive, because among other things, the white actor in *The Birth of a Nation*—a deeply racist movie, that literally, very literally, celebrated the Ku Klux Klan—was in blackface, and he did all of these terrible things that put these thoughts into people's heads that Black people are violent.

This is going to deeply bother white right-wingers. When I say this stuff, they get triggered because the truth bothers them so much. If there was one race in the history of America, in particular, that is more violent, is there any question which race it is? Of course not. The white race was far more violent, by an order of magnitude. A hundred million times more violent than the Black race.

Not even close—white people were *vicious* to Black people. Tore the skin off their back. If you ever read the description of a lynching, how much fun they had at the "picnic," how they took home charred body parts as mementos to show their kids, kids who were at that barbecue, where they lynched an actual human being.

Etan: It's like something out of a horror movie, only it's based on real events.

Uygur: Right, so to turn around and say Black people are the ones who are violent toward white people in this country? It is the height of absurdity. Absolutely insane.

Interview with Tim Wise

Author and antiracism educator Tim Wise breaks down the dangers in education. Miseducation happens in many forms in this country, and the ramifications have proven to be catastrophic. Since 1995, he has given speeches at over six hundred college campuses across the US. He trains teachers, corporate employees, nonprofit workers, and law enforcement officers in methods of addressing and dismantling racism in their institutions.

Etan: The first description on your Twitter handle is "antiracism educator." Talk to me about what that means.

Wise: Well, the thing about Twitter bios is they're very limited in terms of characters, so you can't say a lot. So you try to say as much as you can in as few characters as possible. And that's more or less how I describe myself. I'm trying to distinguish what I do from what I think is really some of the more important work, frankly, that activists and organizers do. I've been an activist and an organizer also throughout the course of my life, but that's really special work. I don't want to claim that kind of grassroots organizing that I have historically done but I'm not doing now.

I want to stay in my lane and give homage to those who were in the other lane. I call myself an educator because principally the way I view my work is as a writer, a speaker, and someone who educates without a fixed classroom. I'm not, obviously, a professor or a teacher in that sense. I'm an educator without a formal classroom who speaks to hundreds of thousands of people a year, maybe millions, by way of writing and other things that people see. Just trying to raise awareness around the issues that activists and organizers are then organizing around so that we can all sort of work in tandem and contribute to the larger antiracist project of dismantling systemic racism in America.

Etan: And it sounds like you're very careful about not wanting to step on anyone's toes.

Wise: Yeah, trying not to. I mean, there are times that I'll get introduced and somebody will say "antiracism activist." And it's like, okay. I mean, in a way, sure. But I really think activists and organizers are so special, and especially the folks of color who do the vast majority of that work, Black and Brown folks, I don't want to over-claim what it is I do. I do my piece, other people do their piece. I think part of being an ally or a cocollaborator, coconspirator, whatever term people prefer—I know there's debate and dissension about that—part of that is having enough humility to know what your role is, right? To know sort of what your lane is.

As a white man doing this work, I narrowly define that. For me, my lane is mostly speaking to other white folks, challenging them around our racialization. A lot of times white folks think racism isn't an issue, or it's an issue for folks of color more broadly. And it obviously *is* an issue, because we created this thing as a system and as a category of thoughts. So it's only an issue for Black and Brown folk because we made it one. Therefore, we have an obligation to explore how and why we did that, and the consequences of it.

I think white folks in this work should stay in that space where we are not trying to speak to Black truth. I can't talk about Black truth because whatever I might say, Black folks can say better. I can just point you to them. But I can certainly speak about what it means to be white in a society created for people like me, because I have fifty-two years of experience knowing how whiteness operates. And that's where I think I can be of some assistance.

Etan: Let's talk about how you try to create white empathy.

Wise: Well, how do we move beyond empathy? There's no question that white supremacy historically has necessitated that white people essentially crushed our own empathy. You have to, because if you're a human being, the natural impulse is to reflect on other people's pain and sort of flinch when you see other people in pain. We have these things called "mirror neurons." So if you see somebody trip, your natural instinct is to go, "Oh!" because you know that could be you and you've probably done that yourself, right?

That's a natural human impulse. Well, magnify that. If white people are being told for hundreds of years, "These folks are not human and you need not treat them as human," over time your ability to empathize has to be crushed because there's that part of your humanity that is saying, *Wait a minute, that's not right.* But yet your family, your society, your government, your culture, the economy, everything around you is telling you, "No, no, it is okay." So you have to split yourself off, right? In order to do that, you have to have some type of empathic collapse, which is actually very dangerous. Once I make myself immune to feeling the pain of other people, I eventually numb myself to my *own* mind. And it makes me not as loving a person in my own family, or even with other white people.

So it's actually really dangerous, but it absolutely happens. Part of this project is reattaching those people to their natural humanity, adding in the empathy piece. However, it's also about going beyond the limits of empathy. Why should I be able to put myself in the place of a Black person in order to understand that what's happening to Black people is wrong? Because empathy basically says, *Imagine that you were George Floyd.* Well, I shouldn't have to imagine that. I should be able to *see* what happened to George Floyd or *hear* what happened to Breonna Taylor, and, based on the fact that George Floyd and Breonna Taylor are human beings with a right to life, liberty, and the pursuit of happiness, say that is wrong and unacceptable. I shouldn't have to say, "Oh my God, what if it were me?" Or, "What if it were *my* kid?"

So we have to also ask for more than empathy. And I think in this case, the one beneficial thing that's going to come out of COVID because of the relative sort of isolation that we're experiencing, we're much more cloistered in a way and sequestered from one another. What that has done is given us just enough quiet to see, hear, and feel what I think many white folks weren't seeing, hearing, and feeling before.

That has opened a window white folks now need to go through to really connect in solidarity with Black and Brown folks who are leading this struggle. The question is, when we get to the other side of COVID, will that window close or will we keep it open? And that's the challenge, because everything in this culture tells white folks to look the other way and collaborate with this system, just like men are told every day to look the other way and collaborate with misogyny and sexism. Resisting that is not easy in a culture that rewards you for doing what it told you to do. So it's a long struggle, but I do think that there's an opening right now for us to potentially take advantage of.

Etan: You said something really important: it shouldn't take imagining yourself as George Floyd for you to say that it's wrong.

Wise: Yeah, there's two things. Number one, any white person in the United States today is however many generations of so-called white people. Only "so-called" because we weren't called that in Europe, that was something we created in the colonies. However many generations of people who have been told, at least since the mid-1600s, that they were better than Black people.

In fact, that was the one thing they could always count on, even if they were poor, right? Even if they had nothing. This was an identity that gave you a badge of superiority—no matter how bad things were, you'd always be better than somebody. Meaning Black folks, indigenous folks, anyone who was not white. And if you were told that for hundreds of years and it keeps getting handed down the way that the armoire that your great-grandmother left your grandmother who left it to her mother who left it to you gets handed down, at some point you are going to internalize that.

Etan: That's a great analogy.

Wise: The second thing, in addition to that sort of direct line of inheriting that mentality: We live in a society where we are told, every one of us, white, Black, and otherwise, that wherever you end up in America is all about your own effort, right? Anybody can make it if they just work hard, which means if you didn't make it, it must be something wrong with you. If you did, you must be superior. So in other words, if we don't learn to question the basic ideology of America, which is rugged individualism and anybody can make it if they try, if you don't learn to challenge that by understanding systemic racism, the class system, discrimination, all of these things that get in the way of that being true, then you will naturally conclude that white people are better. Whoever's on top must be superior and whoever's disproportionately on the bottom must be inferior. That becomes the default position in a country that teaches us that.

So the work that we have to do isn't even just about challenging the direct teaching of racism, which is hard enough, it's the *indirect* teaching, right? If a kid is told wherever they end up is all about him or her, then that child grows up to say, well, I guess if I'm doing better, it must be because I made better choices, I have better values, maybe I'm genetically superior and those people are damaged. And once you accept that, you'll never try to fix it because you think inequality is natural. So that's the real challenge.

Etan: So if somebody has programmed that from the time that they're young and it's passed down from generation to generation, how do you reprogram that?

Wise: We have to give our young people a sociological imagination, which is really just fancy language for a critical eye, right? An ability to understand why things are the way they are. Kids are interesting, they always ask questions about why things are, right? Where does that come from? Why is that like that? Because kids are always trying to figure things out. But when it comes to things like inequality or de facto racial segregation—the Black and Brown folks on that side of town disproportionately, white folks on this side of town, or Black and Brown folks mostly in that school over there, and white folks mostly in this school—we don't equip our kids to understand why that is. We just sort of assume, well, we're not supposed to talk about that, right?

And so we have to, as parents, those of us who are, we have to really talk to our children about this. And I learned this talking to my own kids. I mean, driving my kids one day from the school they attended to the dance studio where they were in the dance company, and it's an eight-minute drive and right in between just a few minutes down from their school's a public housing community, and we're stopped at the red light and we're waiting for it to turn. And we've made this trip every day for a year, but on that day the ten-year-old in the backseat looks around and she realizes the demographic of the neighborhood. And she said, "Daddy, why is everybody in this neighborhood Black?" That's a great question. And it's a question that most white parents either wouldn't know the answer to, or just don't want to talk about, right?

Daddy, in this case, has the answer, because that's like the one thing I know, right? So she asked me that I'm like, "Good, we got four minutes before we get to the studio, let me break down the last hundred years of inequality." And I did it in a way that my ten- and my twelve-year-old, I hope, could understand—they seem to. But the problem is, if I don't know the answer to that question, if I don't know the history of redlining and housing discrimination, if I don't know how the government created public housing for white people initially, and then after a couple years subsidized those same white people with FHA loans, VA loans, the G.I. Bill, to move out to the suburbs—and if I don't know that, I can't tell my kid that, and then my kid just concludes, "Well, I guess those white people moved away from the city into 'nicer areas' because they were harder working. And these people are left behind because they're less hardworking."

I teach my kids differently because of my background and my training and what I know, but how many parents don't know the answer to the question? I would say the majority, and even the ones that do know don't know how to talk to a ten-year-old and they're like, "Oh, look, there's a bird over there." They'll just change the subject.

Etan: I remember talking with a white student in my class about the segregation of schools. She believed Black people wanted to be next to white people because they were superior. I argued it was because white schools were getting more funding than the Black schools. So they thought, *If we go to the white school, we'll be able to enjoy some of that funding as well.*

Wise: You were in Tulsa—the Black community in Tulsa was doing just fine when they had Black Wall Street.

Etan: More than just fine. We didn't need white people for anything, and they knew that.

Wise: Right, so white folks decided to burn it to the ground in 1921, which as you know, growing up in Tulsa, is something that the city fathers in that town wanted to cover up so badly that they literally cut the stories out of the Tulsa paper. They just excised that from the local papers, so you couldn't find anything.

Now, of course, there are people in Tulsa trying to really face and confront that history finally, after about one hundred years, right? But yeah, Black folks weren't trying to get next to white folks so that some white superiority would rub off, it was white folks making it real clear, "If y'all are over there, you're going to get nothing but fire and bombs and violence and inferior schools, because you're inferior."

Etan: Exactly, and that's the difference. It's really about education and educating. In your latest book, *Dispatches from the Race War*, you talk about the consequences of white supremacy in all its forms. It's a great book, you have essays on what you call racial class points, white denial and violence, and the manipulation of fear in America today. Can you talk about the manipulation of white fear and how that plays into white supremacy as a whole?

Wise: The fear issue is side by side with the issue of contempt. So I have a piece in the book where I'm talking about the incident in Central Park with Amy Cooper, the white woman who called the cops on Christian Cooper, no relation to her, an obviously Black man who was birdwatching in Central Park. And she called the cops because he told her to leash her dog, which she was supposed to do in that particular part of the park. And a lot of people responded to that by saying that she'd been socialized and conditioned to be afraid of Black men. Now, I don't have any doubt that that's true because that's a longstanding thing in this country—trying to cast Black men as hyperviolent, hypersexual, dangerous, aggressive—but I also insist that that wasn't all that that was. That might've been a *part* of what that was, but more than fear, it was *contempt* for Black bodies, and his Black body in particular.

Because if you're really afraid of something or someone, do you mess with it? If I'm in the woods and a grizzly bear came up, I wouldn't get in its face, wag my finger at it, and yell . . . I would freeze, I would hide behind a tree, I would run, I would hide under some leaves. I wouldn't yell at it. So it seems to me that a lot of times white folks say we've been conditioned to be afraid of Black people, yeah, that's true, and more than that, we've been conditioned to actually detest and to look down upon and to inferiorize Black people and to believe that we have the right to control them. So take that, and then you think about a society like ours, where the demographic of the country is changing, so we know within twenty, thirty years, white folks will no longer be a statistical majority, and that scares them.

So combine an economic insecurity that we're not used to, cultural shift that we're not ready for, demographic shift. Oh, and we had a Black president, which also shook up the idea of who the leader ought to be. You have all that happening at once. And if you've been taught to not only fear Black and Brown folks, but to have contempt for them and to think of them as inferior, when you look out at the country that's changing in a way that is now becoming Browner and Blacker, it makes sense that you would think to yourself, *Oh my God, the wheels are coming off this thing.* Or, *How are we going to maintain a wonderful country if these people are running it?* That's what happens when you teach not only fear and then manipulate that, but what you're really being taught to fear is the notion of their inferiority and what it'll mean for you if they get control, and if you're not the dominant hegemonic control of the society.

So that's why we're seeing this existential crisis right now. I wrote about that in my book *Dear White America*, back in 2012. But now with Trumpism, it's been ramped up to the nth degree to where we have people who, when they say, "Make America great again," what they are manifesting is this fear of progress.

We have white folks who were being led to believe that if their dominance and control slips, that everything's coming to an end, because if you have experienced and enjoyed this white privilege, anything else feels like oppression to you, right? Having to share the toys when I had all the toys. If I've been sharing the toys from the beginning, I could share my toys with some more people, it wouldn't be a big deal. But if I've had *all* the toys to myself, right, and now I got to share them with you, it's like, *Wait, no, that doesn't work for me*, right? We've been set up for this moment. That's why Trumpism is the logical result of a society that has trained white people in the entitlement mentality, entitlement to control one's power. And that's where it leads.

Etan: That translates to the violence and anger we see in so many Trump supporters. There was a rally in DC and the Proud Boys were vandalizing Black historic churches. You watch the videos, and you're like, *Wow, they look angry.* Talk about how and why that has translated into the violence and anger that we've seen from Trump supporters.

Wise: Again, the great irony is these are people who for four years have been in power. I mean, they won in 2016. They've been in power, they've been packing the courts. But what they are realizing is that they don't really control the culture, right? The culture continues to shift toward more pluralism, more multicultural acceptance, greater sort of equity in the cultural sphere, and they can't control it. And what they realize, I think, is that they can't be happy until they control *all* of it. It's not enough for them to have the presidency and the courts. They want to make sure that their way of thinking is *the* way of thinking. And if anyone challenges that, if anyone challenges their assumptions about the way society ought to be, they view that as oppressive, which is why these are people who think that if you talk about white privilege and systemic racism, that's racist against white people, because they're not used to having whiteness challenged.

They're more than happy to challenge Black folks and Brown folks, right? But when you start challenging whiteness, it drives them batty. Why? Well, because if you're used to having 100 percent, you get angry at the thought that somebody might share that. And so part of that rage is about realizing they can win the politics, but they're losing the culture, and politics is downstream from culture. Culture actually determines the direction of the country, make no mistake about it. And these folks know that, because once young people are acculturated, particularly in a more pluralistic and multicultural society, that affects their politics going forward.

That doesn't mean that all the young folks are progressive and antiracist and all that, because they're not. But it does mean that ten, fifteen, twenty years from now, when these young people's political beliefs are being set in place, in part because of their cultural connections, they are going to be probably more progressive than these folks on the right want them to be. And they know that, they can see it coming. They can see that their America is dying. And rather than say, "Survival of the fittest," which is what they always said to other folks, right? They always said that. "Well, y'all will be the ones that will die out, because we're the strongest in the bunch." Well, apparently not, because the hegemony that you thought would always last isn't going to last. Folks are moving forward and I think they realize this is their last gasp to hold on to that cultural power.

Interview with Chuck D

Chuck D is the leader of the rap group Public Enemy, which he cofounded in 1985 with Flavor Flav. Chuck D helped create the original politically and socially conscious hip-hop music of the mid-1980s. Public Enemy, Ice Cube (after he left NWA), and X Clan were my regular rotation of music in middle school. They were my teachers outside of my classroom and my home. I wanted to ask Chuck D about particular tracks that really spoke to me the most.

Etan: *Fear of a Black Planet* is an album that really captured the fear of mainstream America and still holds so true today, especially after the rise of Trump and Trumpism.

Chuck D: What *Fear* did was create a movement that showed the world rap and hip-hop could produce as significant an album genre as rock, forcing respect. It was a musical and political statement that, like you said, resonates to this day, as we are currently seeing. All of the issues and topics we covered are still relevant. Rap and hip-hop altered the musical soundscape audibly and visually with shrapnel impact from many different directions. That impact was felt way beyond the music. The music ignited it, then it spread. The music informed and educated, then you saw the impact afterwards. When the world heard "911 Is a Joke," led by Flavor Flav, it made them think, examine what he was saying and why he was saying it, all while making you bop your head and dance at the same time.

Etan: I remember how Public Enemy was the first group to walk away from a $1 million contract when y'all left Def Jam. I remember reading you did that so you could have creative freedom. I really respected that.

Chuck D: Our thinking was this: What the hell is a $1 million contract when you don't have control of your stuff? That $1 million is never going to be spent by you. It's going to be spent on your behalf by someone who's just pressing buttons and pushing numbers. And at the end of the day, you've got what? Because they've spent your money trying to make their profit while you're working on a percentage. That's one of the biggest reasons why I jumped into the Internet in 1996.

Etan: Let me ask you about "Burn Hollywoood Burn." I loved that track too.

Chuck D: Well, first, it was groundbreaking for a lot of different reasons. It was the first time you had artists from different labels collaborating. Cube was Priority. Big Daddy Kane was cold chillin' with Warner Bros. And we was Def Jam at that time, Sony. So every record label was against it because they wanted it to be on their label. People didn't do that back then at all. Now, like when we did the "Fight the Power" remake, Questlove brought us all together—Nas, Rapsody, YG, Black Thought, and Jahi—like it was nothing, but back then it wasn't done. But we wanted to put Hollywood on blast for the images they were showing of us and historically showed of us. Currently and historically. We knew they weren't gonna like it talking about Hollywood, but putting them on blast and exposing their dedication to showing negative images of us was more important.

Etan: What do you remember about creating "By the Time I Get to Arizona"?

Chuck D: I remember being angry. And my anger was focused on Arizona and New Hampshire because they both were refusing to honor Martin Luther King Jr. as a holiday. I took it as a smack in the face that needed to be addressed. I looked around and didn't see anyone else addressing it, so I did.

Etan: Any particular reason you went with that title?

Chuck D: I'm a big Isaac Hayes fan, and his version of "By the Time I Get to Phoenix," the Jim Webb, Glen Campbell song, it was a creative play off of that.

Etan: What did you expect the reaction to be from the song?

Chuck D: Well, we weren't making songs to be popular, we didn't care if the mainstream approved of what we were doing. We were taking a stand. Social, political, or for our people. That's what it was all about. Not a popularity contest. We didn't expect to climb anyone's charts or anything, we wanted to send a message.

Etan: So you wanted to educate the masses. I remember in middle school having an argument with a white student who didn't know what the big fuss was about a holiday. I played him this song. He listened to it three straight times and then went home and watched the video, and all he said when he came back was, "Okay, I get it." Didn't say anything else. Just, "I get it."

Chuck D: [*Laughing*] Well, I guess he got it. But that's what we wanted to do. On one hand, speak for the powerless. And on the other hand, we try to give some logic, balance, and understanding to the privileged. Enlighten the masses of minds. Open their perspectives. Bring something to them that they never considered, through the art of music. People like your classmate. People are equipped to not act immediately. We've got to be able to give them energy to think outside of their surroundings, themselves, and their community.

Etan: Yes sir, y'all definitely did that.

Chuck D: People can't be sheep. Let me bring it to the present with Black Lives Matter. A lot of white people in the United States of America think that it's a violent movement. Why? Because that's what they're shown when they turn on the news. They see the eruptions from a failure to get justice after a police killing, and they label an entire movement.

When I look at Black Lives Matter as a movement, it's a push for peace that involves everybody. A push for humanity that everyone should be able to get behind. Black and white and everyone else. How can you be *for* the police killing Black people with no chance of jail time? But the way it is presented affects how someone formulated their opinion about it—that's with everything in life. So when someone says they don't know what the big deal is, we have to show them what the big deal is, then they will get it. Well, *some* of them will get it.

Hip-hop culture brings human beings together on the same accord. That's the beauty of rap music and hip-hop at its beginning. [Hip-hop] came out of a cultural olive branch. Collectives and revues is how hip-hop was meant to be. It doesn't always manifest itself in that form, but that's how Public Enemy has always operated. That was our focus.

Etan: Talk to me about the track "Fight the Power" and how all of the elements you were capturing are still relevant now. The song can be utilized as the same teaching tool it was back then, and you mentioned the remix bringing it to the present.

Chuck D: Okay, let's start with the original, if that's okay.

Etan: Ummm, you can start wherever you want, you're Chuck D [*laughing*].

Chuck D: Oh stop that [*laughing*]. Okay, so back when "Fight the Power" was first released, it was the summer of 1989. Public Enemy was able to give the generation at that time something that the prior generations had, which is something that captured the entire pulse and feeling of the community. Sam Cooke, Curtis Mayfield, Miriam Makeba in South Africa—they shouted against the oppression of our people. When James Brown did *Say It Loud—I'm Black and I'm Proud*, they all captured an entire feeling of rebellion against the atmosphere that was working against Black people for hundreds of years. But we wanted to make it palatable to the current generation. We weren't reinventing the wheel, we were following the traditions that were laid before us. Freedom songs and protest songs came out of the Black community when the talking voices weren't loud enough.

Etan: Y'all were teaching too.

Chuck D: I see the theme you're going with about the teaching, and I hear you on one hand, but then on the other hand, if you couldn't tell that racism existed and was running rampant throughout the country, you had Howard Beach in New York, Rodney King in LA, and every place in between. So if you couldn't see that was happening, you had to be deaf, dumb, and blind. Same thing today—if you don't see what Trump is doing, and what's happening with the police, you gotta be deaf, dumb, and blind.

Etan: Yeah, but a lot of people didn't see it then and still don't see it today. Or they pretend not to understand.

Chuck D: That's true. They know, they just don't like when someone who has influence says it. Look at the [Dixie] Chicks. You had three white girls talking against the establishment and George Bush and Iraq; around the same time you came out talking about Iraq when you was with the Wizards.

Etan: Wait, you remember that?

Chuck D: Of course, but my point is, they caught a lot of heat just like *you* caught a lot of heat, just like Public Enemy caught a lot of heat, but it all needed to be said. And bringing light to a situation and utilizing your platform and your craft is important. Speaking for the people. So "Fight the Power" became the CNN for Black America because *World News Tonight* wasn't covering what was happing with us. They weren't covering *our* voice. And we had the opportunity to be that megaphone for the world. We saw a need, we saw an opening, and we stepped in.

Etan: Talk about the remix with Nas, Black Thought, and Rapsody you did last year. That was powerful.

Chuck D: Don't forget Jahi and YG, but this was a teachable moment and a reachable moment, and I had a lot of help from my friends. I put my differences with Def Jam aside and said, "This is the time to do this, not the time for petty differences or real understandable differences." Now, Flav helped me get there, but this isn't the time for differences. That's what Chuck D learned. I ain't perfect. I'm not gonna sit here and say I always look at things in the bigger picture—no, I was in my feelings, like the young people say. But Flav helped me see it's bigger than that. So we created something very crucial to our society right now. Even with debuting it in the BET Awards, I could've . . . Listen, I have had my issues with BET, and still have my issues with them, but all that's put aside for the bigger picture, and I gotta thank my friends, especially Questlove, for being able to see that.

So the real question now is, what you gonna do when the grid goes down? You gotta recognize hate when you see it and gotta call it out and make sure everyone else sees it. You gotta have people who roll up their sleeves and get in the trenches with you, so that's what happened with this track.

Etan: I'm glad the wisdom of Flav rained down on you so we could get this done, because it was special and very timely.

Chuck D: Flav ain't always right, but he was right on this one. Let me say it like this: I was just watching 45's speech last night, did you watch it?

Etan: Unfortunately, yes, I suffered through it.

Chuck D: Okay, so this is what it boils down to. If you are Black, it's simple: there's the side you're on, and the side that hates you. Simple as that. When they say you don't matter or your lives don't matter, that's hate. They can cloak it in whatever package they want, that's what it is. So right now, it's a reachable moment . . . the same way it was back in 1989 with Reagan and Bush. So bringing "Fight the Power" back, this is the continuation of the same hatred now that was going on back then. It's just in a different form. That's why Prince said, "This is a time to manage your gadget or it will master you." Our gadget is music, rap, hip-hop. So bringing "Fight the Power" only seemed right in this day and age, because we are still fighting the same enemy in a different form.

Whitewashed Christianity

You don't have to teach people how to be human. You have to teach them how to stop being inhuman.

—Eldridge Cleaver

Frederick K.C. Price of the Crenshaw Christian Center in Los Angeles examines the history of racism and white supremacy in the white evangelical church in the series *Race, Religion & Racism*. He was my wife Nichole's childhood pastor, so we watched it as a family.

In one episode, Pastor Price plays excerpts from a taped sermon in which another pastor says that young white Christians should not date people of other races. He states, "We can be friends with everybody. We are not prejudiced. But we are not going to date this group of people. It's not in our culture to do it." He goes on to discuss how he started ingraining this into his children during kindergarten, because you can't wait until they are older.

He even misquotes Proverbs 22:6, saying, "The Bible says if you train a child up in the way you want it to go, when it gets older it will not depart."

This is a distortion of the actual Scripture.

The speaker was not identified, but as soon as I heard it, I recognized the voice. It was from Pastor Kenneth Hagin Jr. of Rhema Bible Church, a megachurch in Tulsa.

Hagin's father, the Reverend Kenneth Hagin Sr., was known for pioneering the Word of Faith Movement and Rhema Bible Training College, and was a mentor to Pastor Fred Price, who was now telling his 16,000-member church and his television audience that he was forced to break his fellowship with the minister because in his words, "Principle means more to me than friendship."

Tulsa is in the heart of the Bible Belt. I remember watching right-wing evangelicals growing up and telling my mother, "These folks don't like us, I can feel it."

For a while we were members of Higher Dimensions Family Church under Carlton Pearson. He prided himself on bringing white people and Black people together in a way that had never been seen, at least not in Tulsa. Sunday morning, even in the nineties, existed as the most segregated hours of the week.

At that time, there was a nationwide conference for evangelicals called Azusa, held at the Oral Roberts University Mabee Center in Tulsa. It attracted about forty thousand people from all around the world. Carlton Pearson was the founder of this conference, so we went every year. Even though I was young, I could feel the subtle tone of racism that would slip out of the pastors from time to time. After having interactions with some of the white people in the church, I remember saying, "I don't know if these Christians like Black people too much."

I remember seeing Kenneth Hagin onstage with Carlton Pearson, and I also remember reading what he said in the sermon that Pastor Price was referencing. I wanted nothing to do with Christianity at that point in my life if these people represented the faith.

So, I wasn't surprised in early 2021 to hear that a former white evangelical youth pastor, Matt Rowan, had gone viral when his hot mic caught him directing a hateful slur toward the Norman High School girls' basketball team as they knelt during the national anthem. "They're kneeling? F**k them," Rowan said. "I hope Norman gets their ass kicked . . . I hope they lose. C'mon, Midwest City. They're gonna kneel like that? Hell no." He then called players the N-word. Scott Sapulpa, his broadcast partner and head football coach at Hulbert High School in northeast Oklahoma, didn't object.

I was shocked to hear Rowan blame his comments on his type 1 diabetes. His official statement says, "While not excusing my remarks, it is not unusual when my sugar spikes that I become disoriented and often say things that are not appropriate as well as hurtful." He had consulted with his legal team, friends, and family, and came up with the excuse that racism was a side effect of diabetes.

In 1996, my high school team beat Norman 70–55 to win back-to-back Oklahoma state championships. I was leaving the arena at Oral Roberts University, and encountered some Norman parents who were mad that I had done the Black Power salute during the national anthem. I will never forget the anger, hatred, and evil in their faces as they shouted, "Who the hell do you think you are to disrespect our country?"

I responded, "*Our* country? Do you not know I was born here too?"

Mabee Center security guards approached me and treated me as if I was the one causing the disturbance. They asked for my ID, even though I was carrying my Booker T. Washington High School bag. They asked the parents if I was threatening them. They called for backup, said that someone was being belligerent. Six more security guards came running from both directions, all of their eyes focused on me.

These security guards had big crosses on their uniforms and I remembered them from Azusa. These Christian security guards sang, clapped, and praised Jesus at different stations throughout the building. They also stood together praying in a circle before the tournament started. Now, after winning the state championship, I knew I had to play it cool with these guards or it would end badly for me.

After that incident, it made me sick to my stomach every time I would pass by ORU, or see the ORU Christians at the mall asking if I knew Jesus or if I wanted them to pray with me. I didn't want anything to do with them or what they believed.

I interview Christians in this chapter in order to have a real discussion on the history of racism in Christianity. Many young people have had negative interactions with white evangelicals, or watched Trump supporting white evangelicals. Others have read the history of racism in Christianity as a whole, and have the same feelings I had about white evangelicals in my childhood. It's sad that not much has changed, but it's good to hear Christians stand up and say that those people don't represent Christianity.

Interview with Bishop Talbert Swan

Bishop Talbert Swan is the pastor of the Spring of Hope Church of God in Christ, assistant general secretary for the National Church of God in Christ, national chaplain of Iota Phi Theta Fraternity, Inc., executive director of COGIC Family Services, president of the Springfield, Massachusetts, branch of the NAACP, an author, radio talk show host, and longtime community activist. In addition to being a gifted preacher, administrator, and organizer,

Pastor Swan has been at the forefront of civil rights issues throughout the region and nationally for over two decades.

Etan: I have been following you on social media, and I watched your speech at the March on Washington. What gave you the courage to speak in a way that most men of the cloth are not speaking right now, in terms of racism, the Trump administration, and white evangelicals?

Swan: The way that I interpret Scripture leads me to the point of believing that speaking against injustice, condemning wickedness, standing up for the vulnerable is just an extension of ministry, it's a part of what we ought to be doing. My signature Scripture is in Luke, the fourth chapter, when Jesus starts his public ministry. After he's baptized in the Jordan and he's tempted in the wilderness, he goes into the temple. His first public message, he says, "The spirit of the Lord is upon me, for he has anointed me to preach good tidings to the poor."

Then he deals with several demographics of people. He talks about the poor, the sick, the imprisoned, and the oppressed. He spends the next three and a half years of his ministry really empowering, inspiring, advocating on behalf of those demographic groups. So I don't believe you can be authentic in your Christianity if you do not stand for those that Jesus stood for. If you don't stand for the principles that he stood for. The late James Cone put it best. He said, "Any authentic theology must affirm that God is on the side of the oppressed." That's how I live out my ministry and my life. That's what compels me to do the things that I do.

Etan: I imagine you get quite a bit of backlash, but what type of reactions do you get as a whole from other fellow members of the clergy?

Swan: Yeah, there's quite a bit of backlash. There are many who are stuck in a paradigm in which they believe that preachers shouldn't be political. That the job of the church and of the faithful is simply to pray. Although the Bible clearly says, "Faith without works is dead." They believe we ought to have a hands-off approach to being directly involved in the political sphere or in any civic engagement. So there are those who say, "Swan is too political." Or, "Are you a politician or a preacher?" And, "You ought to stop spending so much time talking about social issues and just preach the Gospel." What I try to explain is I *am* preaching the Gospel and this is part of ministry.

The unfortunate reality is we have gotten far away from where the church has been. When you think about the Civil Rights Movement in this nation, the human rights movement, it was a church movement. The leaders came out of the churches, had their meetings in the churches, and got the bodies to sit at the lunch counters out of the churches. Then as we progressed, had legislation passed, and it seemed like we were making some inroads toward justice, the church shifted, started talking about health, wealth, prosperity, and a number of other things. Now here we are being reminded in a great way over the last four years with this covert in-your-face racism, and with the rise of Black Lives Matter and a generation of activists that are not connected to the church. People are saying, "Well, now, where is the church?" Because historically, the church has been the voice for the Black community.

Etan: Definitely. I grew up in Tulsa, in the middle of the Bible Belt. Talk about the racism in the white evangelical church in particular, because it's so strong and it's so evil. Their racism is really turning a lot of young people away from Christianity, because they think those people represent all Christians.

Swan: Yeah. You talk about Tulsa, I mean, you're right there where, of the history of the destruction, of what we call Black Wall Street, of the murder of Black people, simply because they found themselves being able to create community, and do for themselves. White evangelicalism is nothing but white supremacy in drag. The reality is they still hold on to a slave-holder religion that sees no contradiction between blatant racism and their claim to be Christians and people of God. It's just like the slave holder could lynch a Black man on a Saturday night and roast marshmallows as his body burned from a tree, and then praise their Jesus on Sunday morning.

White evangelicals today have no problem with watching a George Floyd being lynched in the street, or a Trayvon Martin being murdered, or Tamir Rice being killed. Defending their murder, and then worshipping their Jesus on Sunday morning. They still are of the opinion that somehow God has cursed Black people, some biblical curse or mandate for us to be subservient, be less than they are. That it is God's will for there to be a manifest destiny. So they justify all of the atrocities that were done in the name of

God, because when you think about it, slavery was justified using the Bible, as was the slaughter of Native Americans. Even now, on the heels of this election, we have white evangelicals who are adamant that their God is calling for Trump to be president, and he's going to flip this election upside down.

If that means we need to negate the votes of Black people in Philadelphia, Atlanta, Milwaukee, and Detroit, in order to keep this white supremacist in office, then so be it. Their religion is white supremacy. The perpetuation of it, sustaining it, keeping it in the forefront. The one good thing about the Trump presidency is it really exposed the depths of their hypocrisy. Because for so many years, they talked about family values and the family unit. Marriage, between one man and one woman, and the importance of fidelity, character, and integrity. When a Black man who had one wife of twenty-nine years and two children by the same wife; a man who was active and raised his family in church; he did everything by the book according to white right-wing evangelicals; Black people ought to work hard, pull themselves up by their bootstraps—he did all of that. He became president of the United States, and they turned around and called him the antichrist.

Along comes this guy, three wives, countless mistresses, whose abortions he paid for, who had casinos and gambling joints, who slept with porn stars and *Playboy* bunnies, who cheated on all of his wives, who was a pathological liar, who didn't pay his employees, who had all kinds of failed ventures because of his crookedness, stole from his own charity. They turned around the party of family values. 81 percent of evangelicals said, "This is God's anointed. God would have us elect, and this is who is going to uphold Christian values for us." You know their religion cannot be Christianity, it has to be white supremacy.

My friend Dr. Freddy Haynes says, when he talks about white [evangelicals], "They've been too busy being white. They haven't got around to being Christian yet."

Etan: [*Laughing*] That's a good one. I'm going to have to use that one.

Swan: Feel free, because that's the reality of it. They have been caught up in their whiteness, protecting their whiteness, protecting the privilege that comes with their whiteness. They have not been concerned about being Christian. To the younger audience, they have to understand that you don't throw away the value of the lessons that you learned in Christianity simply because some people have bastardized and perverted Scripture, and have not been a good representation of what a Christian should be. That's exactly what is happening with white evangelicals, they are a horrible representation of what a Christian should be. So I completely get why people are turned off by it. If that is their example, if that is their focus, they will be turned off all of the time. I've said it myself, been taking a lot of heat. I tweeted one time, I said, *If heaven is going to be full of white evangelicals, I'll take my chances on hell.*

Etan: What is your reaction to younger people nowadays who say this is the white man's religion?

Swan: I wrote a book some years ago called *No More Cursing: Destroying the Roots of Religious Racism.* It dealt with the myth of Black people being cursed. It also dealt with the perversion of Christianity by white Christians. I get why people say that, but when you really look at the history of Christianity, first of all, the oldest Christian church in the world is the Ethiopian Coptic Church, okay. Christianity spread in Africa long before European whites got Christianity. Long before Constantine adopted Christianity and it became the official religion of Rome. Before the rise of the Roman Catholic Church and Catholicism and all of that, it was already in Africa. That's what people have to understand. Simply because our foreparents who were enslaved in America were introduced to what I call a whitenized version of Christianity does not mean we give Christianity to white folks and let them claim it as their religion.

Now, we believe full-heartedly that Jesus was a Black man, right? He was born in the cradle of Africa. I know folks resist that because, "No, Bishop, he was born in the Middle East." There was no such thing as the Middle East. The term "Middle East" didn't even come into existence until the 1850s, after they built the Suez Canal, a man-made waterway that separates northeast Africa from what we now call the Middle East. Matter of fact, it was all northeast Africa. So Jesus was born in Africa during the time where there were Black Africans living there. So how can the religion inspired by a Black man who lived in Africa, who was followed by Black people, because remember now, if you read the Bible, the only white folks in the Bible are the oppressors. When the Romans show up in the New Testament and colonize Israel, that's when you have white folks in the Bible. Otherwise it's a story about God's relationship with Black people.

How can you have a religion that is inspired by a Black man, that is about life in the cradle of Africa, that first ran throughout Africa, and call it a white man's religion? Simply because white folk perverted it does not mean it is their religion. Our ancestors, thank God, reclaimed Christianity, because when they were being taught on the plantation, "Slaves, be obedient to your master," when they learned how to read, they flipped over to the Old Testament. We read about Shadrach, Meshach, and what I call a bad Negro in the fiery furnace. They read about Daniel in the lion's den. They read about Moses and the children of Israel being freed from bondage. They understood that the God that they serve wanted them to be free. So they developed a completely different hermeneutic from what they were being taught on the plantation.

They began to sing songs, *"Go down Moses, way down in Egypt land, tell old Pharaoh to let my people go."* They were singing in code language, they weren't talking about Egypt land. They were talking about Alabama, Mississippi, Georgia, North Carolina, South Carolina. They weren't talking about Pharaoh when they said, *"Tell old Pharaoh, let my people go."* They were talking about Master Swan, Smith, and Thomas. All of them. So they followed the completely different hermeneutics. Like Maxine Waters says, "Reclaiming my time." They reclaimed Christianity for us. So no, I reject the notion that the Christianity that I was taught by my ancestors was a white man's religion. It wasn't stained with the perversion that the white man put on.

Etan: Talk about the very strategic and intentional reason the white man changed the image of Jesus to look like him.

Swan: Absolutely. So if you are going to push the myth that people without melanin are superior, or darker-hued people are inferior, by the edicts of deity; if you are going to push the myth that the subjugation of Black people, and Brown people, and nonwhite people, is ordained and sanctioned by God, to get them to buy into signing off on their own oppression—then you cannot depict deity as Black folk or Brown folk. In order to be consistent, if you're going to push white supremacy, then deity, Jesus, God, and angels all have to look like they look, because you cannot show the true art.

You can't show true Egyptian art. You can't even show art from Europe. The oldest picture of a Madonna and Child in Poland is of a Black Madonna and a Black baby Jesus. But you can't show that and push white supremacy. They were very strategic in terms of depicting Christ, angels, and everybody in the Bible as white. So when a pope sanctioned the painting at the Sistine Chapel, and all types of other painting and artwork, of course they sanctioned them painting Christ looking like a white European. Because if I'm going to be the spokesperson for Christ, he's got to look like me. He can't look like you. Of course, America and other parts of the world adopted that false notion that Christ was some blond-haired, blue-eyed surfer guy.

For years, even Black people had pictures of white Jesus hanging up in their churches, and hanging up in their homes. But we debunked that whole myth that we know that Christ could not look like them. Moses could not look like them. Even Paula White, when she was praying that Trump would win the election, she was calling on the angels to come from where? From Africa.

She admits it, she knows the real deal. So yes, of course they've got to depict deity like that. If you ever noticed, when you talk about Christ, and if you ever say, "Well, Jesus was Black," white folks will readily admit, "Yeah, we know he wasn't white." And they'll push back and they'll say, "Well, no, he wasn't Black. He was a Jew, and the religion has something to do with the color of his skin. No, no, no, he was olive-skinned. He was brown. I always tell them, I say, "Well, I'm brown. You call me a Black man, right?" They will call him anything but Black, because they cannot allow Jesus to be Black.

Etan: That's absolutely right. I appreciate the way that you use your voice. We need more people using their voice, more clergy, more pastors, more preachers using their voice in the way that you do. So please continue to do that. I can't say enough how important it is, because right now we have a whole younger generation being bamboozled away from Jesus.

Swan: Further, not only the representation of white evangelicals, but also the silence of Black Christians. That's also turning them away as well. So we definitely need more people like you to speak up. So please you keep doing what you're doing as well.

Interview with Chris Broussard

Chris Broussard is known to many as a basketball analyst. But what some people don't know is that he started a group called the K.I.N.G. Movement, with a mission statement that reads, "To empower men to reach our God-given potential in every realm of life through the power and grace of The Lord Jesus Christ / To help us become the husbands, fathers, leaders, citizens and role models God created us to be / To present to our families, communities, nation, and world an image of men as God-fearing, family-oriented, moral, loving, intelligent, responsible and productive / To glorify The Most High God by walking in true biblical manhood." He is also unafraid to call out the history and current white supremacy within the white evangelical church.

Etan: We're both strong Christians. Strong in our beliefs, and vocal about our Lord and Savior Jesus Christ. We have the evangelicals who have fully embraced Trump, someone who doesn't have the desire to be on the path of anything that resembles Christ. And they act as if they represent Christianity. So some young people are like, "Well, if this is what Christianity represents, I don't want no part of it."

Broussard: I totally agree with you. They have done harm to the Gospel for embracing Trump. When Bill Clinton had his issue with Monica Lewinsky, it was all about character, right? Character of the president, and he represents the highest office in the land. Yet when Donald Trump is on record as talking about grabbing women in their private parts, and all his divorces, and the issue with the porn star, all that stuff, then now all of a sudden character doesn't matter. It is hypocrisy at the highest order. President Obama, nice family, no scandals, and yet they don't embrace him. They have done a harm to the cause of Christ. They look like a bunch of hypocrites and it's shameful. I know white and Black Christians who voted for Trump.

Etan: Sadly, so do I.

Broussard: There are books and studies that have been written to show they're less understanding of racial issues for Blacks than whites on the left who aren't Christians. Their problem is, one, they're very miseducated. And I mean historically. We notice, Etan, one of the ways that white so-called Christians . . . and I don't even call them Christian, but so-called Christians, the reason they justified slavery was to create this myth that it was necessary to enslave the Africans to bring them to Christ. That's part of their ideology. And then after Reconstruction, you can study it with the Daughters of the Confederacy, they changed all the books, the textbooks in the South, to talk about slavery as almost a benevolent institution.

"It wasn't really that bad. The Blacks were happy." White evangelicals have been raised in that line of thought. "America was this great Christian nation, and the city on the hill, and manifest destiny," and all of that erroneous stuff, to say it nicely. And that's where the whole "Make America Great Again" comes from, because as African Americans, we're saying, "Was it great during slavery?" Actually, for all these issues, this is the best time in America for Black people. This general last fifty years or so. As bad as it is, it's still much better than this period of time they are pointing to. So that is a problem with white evangelicals. They really think America used to be such a great Christian nation. I never say America was a Christian nation, because how could you be a Christian nation and your government policy is enslaving and dehumanizing people who are created in God's image?

In a book called *Divided by Faith,* which talks about white and Black Christians and racism, they quote studies that found that white Christians viewed racism, for the most part, as an individual thing. If a white evangelical knows you, Etan, they're cool with you and your family, they got no problems individually with you, they think, *I'm not racist. What are you talking about?* It also found Blacks view racism correctly as systemic.

I've had arguments with white evangelicals and pastors about this, and they want to say it's just individual. "We just need to go to church together and worship together." I'm like, "No, because that policeman in your congregation might end up shooting the cousin of a Black person in your congregation who was unarmed." How is that going to help them in the same church? It is a big problem with the white evangelicals. They don't understand that racism is systemic.

And that's why I said they've been miseducated on American history. They only see it from a white perspective. They don't look at it from the perspective of all people that have been in America: Blacks, Native Americans, Hispanics, Asians, etc. I do feel we need to unite from a Christian perspective, on a Kingdom agenda. Embrace the biblical values of justice, equality, all of that. And also I think values that strengthen the family.

Etan: You talk about justice and the way justice is described in the Bible. We've had atrocities where Black men or Black women have been killed and brutalized by the police, and it makes the news for a little while, then it goes away. George Floyd was literally everywhere. I don't know if it was the pandemic, but I saw more white people protesting in the streets over a Black man being killed by the police than I've ever seen in my lifetime. Yet there was this silence from the white evangelical church. How do you unite on a Kingdom level when there's silence from that side?

Broussard: White evangelicals that I knew and talked to about the George Floyd murder, they were appalled. They were upset. But again, they looked at it as just an individual thing. Like, "Oh, that was unfortunate." They didn't see that it was systemic. And I think part of the answer, Etan, is that African Americans who fellowship with white evangelicals have got to stand up and speak on these issues.

Too often Black Christian brothers who fellowship with white evangelicals, they don't really go there. And one of the benefits of my platform is I do have a wide range of fellowship within the Body of Christ. So I've spoken at white evangelical churches, traditional Black churches, multiracial churches, Hispanic, Asian, charismatic, Baptist, whatever.

Also, it's important to note that Dr. King, he said essentially the same thing you and I are talking about in his letter from Birmingham: the white Christians are not supporting us in what we're trying to do, and they don't understand biblical justice. And they were either against Dr. King or indifferent to what he was doing. Most of them—I'm generalizing—did not get on his side and fight against it. They often say, "Well, those are social issues. We just preach the Gospel and stuff." But here's the hypocrisy—when it comes to social issues that impact them, they have no problem speaking out, fighting. Whether it's abortion, same-sex marriage, now religious liberty. All of these social issues that impact them, they fight for all that. But when it's talking about fighting for racial justice, which is a social issue, then they say, "Oh, just preach the Gospel." And that's the hypocrisy. And like I said, African Americans that are in those spaces need to speak up about it. And if not, to your point, the Gospel, it is a deterrent to people coming to Christ.

Etan: How couldn't it be?

Broussard: And so as far as uniting with them, I think it's just a matter of we have to show them this. This is what's going on, this is our agenda, this is what we see as the Kingdom agenda. And if they don't want to get down with it, then to your point, unfortunately, we probably can't unite. And that is stopping the Body of Christ from flourishing or being what God wants it to be in this country.

Etan: I saw a really interesting panel discussion this past summer with Lecrae. It was the CEO of Chick-fil-A, and it was Pastor Louie Giglio. Did you see it?

Broussard: I didn't see the whole panel, but I saw the clip where he was saying he views it as a white blessing . . .

Etan: So Lecrae is trying to break down why we have to unite from a Kingdom standpoint and how you have to look at me with empathy as your Christian brother, and if this is happening to me, you feel upset about it. You feel this injustice just as you would if it were happening to you. And the white pastor starts talking about the phrase "white privilege" as being something that's offensive to white people and how white people don't want to think they have privilege. He talks about slavery, and the necessary evil of it, and then he says something like, "We should think of it more of a white blessing." And when he says it, Lecrae looks shocked. Like he doesn't even know how to react to it.

Broussard: Oh yeah. And Lecrae caught a lot of flak about that too.

Etan: A lot of flak. Lecrae addressed it later and basically said, "Listen, I was kind of caught off guard. I didn't expect him to say that." My point isn't so much about Lecrae's reaction, it is the fact that this was the actual ideology of the pastor. And he's just not some local storefront-church pastor, he's Pastor Louie Giglio the Visionary Architect and director of the Passion Movement.

Broussard: Decades ago, a white Christian said to me, "Well, slavery was like just a little blind spot," and I'm like, "Blind spot? That's what the whole country was based on." For Americans across the board, Christian or otherwise, Black or white, whatever, I think it should be mandatory that every school in America visit the National Museum of African American History and Culture in Washington, DC.

Etan: Especially that bottom floor. You have to start at the bottom floor and then work your way up, but spend a lot of time on that bottom floor.

Broussard: It makes it clear, Etan, this country was built on slavery. The cotton, rice, tobacco, and sugar industries are what made America the wealthiest nation in the world. Took me three days to get through it. I spent a whole day on the bottom level. And a whole day on the second level.

Pastor Giglio refers to it as "white blessing." This is the same thing with the racial wealth gap, right? Whites having eight times more wealth than African Americans. That wealth gap and these white blessings were not created from just working harder than everybody else. Like everything was equal, and whites just worked harder—that's not what happened. And they have to be honest about what really happened.

So this white blessing, as you want to call it, this wealth gap that you have over us, these great white suburbs that you have while we're stuck in the inner city—that is all the result of systemic racism, oppression, discrimination, terrorism, all of that. And the wrong has still not been righted.

And that's why his statement was incredibly offensive. And obviously, Louie Giglio came out and apologized for it.

Etan: He apologized, yeah, but did he apologize because of the public backlash or is that what he really felt?

Broussard: But not just him, that's how a lot of those so-called Christians feel. And that's why I said they were miseducated. They're reading the Bible, they're reading history, from a white perspective. You can't just consider American history from a white perspective. You have to consider it from the perspective of Blacks, Native Americans, and everyone else as well. If they did that, they would not come to a lot of the conclusions that they come to. And that's a part, Etan, of what has to change as we try to erase white supremacy from this country and this world, because it is idolatry.

It's an offense to God, because they're lifting up whiteness as God. And you know that historically, because everything is submissive to whiteness. Christianity was submissive to whiteness in this country. So that Christianity changed, well, *Do unto others as you'd have them do unto you.* No, not really, because that doesn't match with white supremacy.

So that shows you that white supremacy is idolatry. But part of getting rid of white supremacy is addressing theology, history. When you go to most American seminaries and you study the history of the Christian Church, you're not really studying the history of the Christian Church. You're studying the history of the European Christian Church. In Rome and Europe, and all of that.

But you're not studying about the Ethiopian Orthodox Church, the first or second Christian nation in the world. You're not talking about the Indian Orthodox Church. You're not talking about the Egyptian Coptic Church. You're not talking about the Nubian Church. So consequently, white Christians have been taught—not as much as they used to be, but it's probably still there—that they did us a favor. "Slavery was horrible. Yes, it was brutal. But you know what? You learned about Jesus." But if you knew *real* church history you'd know, "Well, hold on, Christianity was in Africa before Europe."

Etan: Yes, way before Europe.

Broussard: If they understood all of that history, they would not be like, "Oh, we did y'all a favor. It was brutal, but like you said, kind of a necessary evil." "No. You don't understand, y'all were just wrong. Period. Don't try to sugarcoat it, whitewash it, nothing. It was wrong." Even if you don't know the history, Etan, you know this as a Christian: that's wrong. You don't have to know history to know you shouldn't do that to somebody.

Interview with Steph Curry

Steph Curry plays for the Golden State Warriors. Many analysts and players have called him the greatest shooter in NBA history. He is credited with revolutionizing basketball by inspiring teams to regularly utilize the three-point shot. A seven-time NBA All-Star, Curry has been named the NBA Most Valuable Player (MVP) twice and has won three NBA championships with the Warriors. He is also a devout Christian and someone who is unashamed to stand up for what he believes. He has publicly denounced Donald Trump, racism, police brutality, and white supremacy, all while simultaneously speaking about the role faith and his devotion to Jesus Christ play in his life. His courage is unique and important in this day and age.

Etan: You have been very vocal about your spirituality. Have you had any backlash with that, and what has made you feel so comfortable in speaking so freely about your faith?

Curry: A lot of my foundation and the way I see the world is through the gifts that I've been given and trying to find my purpose. And in terms of how I try to represent myself and my family, and understanding that I'm always a work in progress and trying to be as authentic as possible. Sometimes there's an insinuation of Christianity as perfection and being blameless, but a lot of the faults I've had are on full display, and I'm not afraid of those moments. The only backlash I've received is when people don't understand that me being a follower of Christ doesn't mean that I don't make mistakes, it just means that I'm still on the journey to do better.

Etan: Do people expect you to be perfect?

Curry: Some do. I remember one time when I cussed on the court during the playoffs a few years ago, and people came after me. Said I wasn't representing Christ the right way on the court. And I honor the fact that I've been given this gift and this stage to impact the Kingdom, and my faults will be on display for the world to see, but that doesn't change my drive to still represent Christ in everything I do.

Etan: I coach an AAU team for my church, and we have the words *I can do all things through Christ* on our warm-ups. My players have seen you write Scripture on your shoes and stand up for Christ, and they've been inspired by that. Why did you choose that Scripture in particular, and what does it mean to you?

Curry: That goes back to freshman year in college. My mom texted me that Scripture in particular to encourage me on the new challenge and new journey I was embarking on. Her favorite verse was Romans 8:28: *"And we know that all things work together for good to them that love God, to them who are the called according to his purpose."* That was the message she lived by, and she told me to find something for myself that I could find strength from every time I put on my shoes, so I started writing Philippians 4:13: *"I can do all things through Christ who strengthens me,"* and I did it before every practice and game since then. And it reminds me that no matter what I go through in life or on the court, that's where I gain my strength. And I know that I'm not doing any of this without the strength that comes through my faith and what I believe. And it's a great way to share a testimony and have a witness, and I don't even have to say anything, the Scripture speaks for itself. And people like the players on my team have taken notice and that makes me feel good that I can be that positive influence on anyone.

Etan: What do you want people to know about Christ?

Curry: There is definitely a lot of what you are describing in religion and in the traditions of religion—hate, judgment, pretentiousness, hypocrisy, etc.— because that is in every walk of life. That's not what Christianity teaches, and not everyone who claims to represent Christ is really representing him. Being Christlike or striving to be Christlike is none of those things. For me, it's about your walk and your personal relationship with Jesus Christ. Not about a denomination or a custom. I read the Word and try to follow what the Word says, not make it mean what I want it to mean—and that's the difference.

I want to rely on him and his wisdom and strength and direction. That's my focus.

Etan: Do other fellow Christian athletes reach out to you?

Curry: Definitely, I have a great circle of Christian brothas in the league and we all lean on each other. When Mark Jackson was my coach, we went to chapel, and we were really close while he was here. We still are, we talk and encourage each other and it's definitely something that is needed.

Etan: I interviewed Oscar Robertson for my previous book, *We Matter: Athletes and Activism,* and he talked about how much respect he has for you because of how you stood up for yourself with Trump and Under Armour. Explain to me what happened with that.

Curry: It started when we won the championship in 2017. Trump was in office and there was conversation about going to the White House or not. The team was going to make that decision the following training camp and have everyone give their input, to make a unified decision. Before we got to that point, Trump tweeted me specifically and said I was hesitating, so the invitation to come to the White House was withdrawn.

Etan: *Were* you hesitating?

Curry: Well, me personally, I wasn't hesitating at all. I didn't want to go, but I wanted the team to have a united front and I wanted their input. But Trump doesn't have the ideals that I have, that I root my entire belief system on as a Christian, so how could I support him? I can't support hate, racism, and bigotry, and that's just how I felt about the subject. We would be here all day if I listed all of the reasons why, and it's not like I'm judging anyone, but he hasn't shown to even attempt to exhibit anything even close to Christian values, so just from that perspective alone I couldn't support him.

Etan: Understood.

Curry: Now as far as Under Armour, Kevin Plank was invited to this council that Trump had put together with other major business CEOs, and the smoke screen was that they were trying to figure out how to bring jobs back to America. A lot of people saw through it in terms of it being more of a PR stunt, but others didn't. Our CEO made some glowing comments about Trump being an asset to American businesses and as a person. I chimed in because I had a very different opinion and position on Trump. He's shown exactly who he was on multiple occasions and I didn't think it was anything worthy of praise in any way, shape, or form, and I stood up for what I believed in . . . And as a Christian and as a Black man, it really wasn't a hard position for me personally to take.

Etan: And the CEO, Kevin Plank, backtracked on his statement after that? Because that was the part that Oscar Robertson loved the most.

Curry: I called Kevin before I talked to the media, and I had a lot of questions around what his intentions were and where his mind was in regards to promoting and endorsing Trump, and his plans for working with Trump moving forward. I explained how Trump's ideals didn't align with mine. When you're connected to people from a business perspective the way that I am, I'm in a position to hold their feet to the fire, and that's what I did. He respected my position and understood where I was coming from.

We as athletes, with the microphones in front of us and people caring what we have to say, we have an opportunity to be true to who we are and stand up for what is right and against what is wrong.

White Allies/Accomplices

Some people say you fight fire best with fire, but we say you put fire out best with water. We say you don't fight racism with racism. We're gonna fight racism with solidarity.

—Fred Hampton

During Martin Luther King Day weekend, my family watched the movie *Selma*. Baby Sierra was both intrigued and nervous throughout the movie. She was being exposed to a world she had never seen portrayed. She is a talker during movies, and she had questions throughout. "All of this because they wanted to vote?" She couldn't wrap her young mind around it at all.

At one point she paused the movie and asked a question that was visibly bothering her, confusion and disappointment splashed across her face. She said, "Did *all* white people feel this way about us, and if they didn't, why didn't they say anything or support us?" The majority of the white people in the movie up until that point were the police who were beating, arresting, turning water hoses on, and siccing their dogs on protesters, and the angry mobs who were opposed to Black people voting.

I told her to just wait, and through skeptical eyes, she did just that. She watched as the police attacked protesters in a very traumatizing and disturbing scene, then she saw when white pastors and clergy all across the country stood with Dr. King as they were attempting to cross the Edmund Pettus Bridge. She watched the same police now pause and stop attacking. Baby Sierra let out a sigh of relief and said, "Okay, good, so it wasn't *all* white people." Then she said, "So the police only didn't beat them because there were white people standing with them? While it's good that they stood with us and supported us, it's terrible that that's the only reason why they didn't beat us."

What Baby Sierra witnessed, unfortunately, holds very true today. Some white people have acted as allies, while others have remained quiet, complacent, unbothered, or simply in denial.

Judas and the Black Messiah, the movie about the life and death of Chairman Fred Hampton of the Illinois chapter of the Black Panther Party, briefly illustrates how the chairman aligned with what he called the "hillbillies." In one scene, he leads Black Panthers into what looks like a Klan meeting with an oversized Confederate flag on the wall. They can't take their eyes off the flag, and as they whisper about it, someone says, "It's just up there to remind us of our Southern heritage." One of the Panthers responds, "When I look at that, I don't see no flag hanging. I see my uncle hanging from a tree, and a bunch of white devils like y'all smiling around his body." Someone then chimes in, "Who the f**k do you think you're talking to?" The leader then says, "Okay, cool it, we oppressed your people for a long time," but he is interrupted by another white man: "I didn't oppress sh*t. And my folks grew up poor. They were sharecroppers." A Black Panther responds, "Aka the overseer," at which point Fred Hampton says, "What if the overseer had banded with the slaves and cut the master's throat?" And everyone falls quiet.

Hampton breaks down the common enemy of both groups. He discusses the terrible education and how they pay the same taxes and get abused by the same police. He shows the commonality between the two groups and convinces them to stand together. A brilliant concept.

If you were poor in Chicago in the 1960s, it didn't matter what color you were—you were catching hell. Issues of poverty, unemployment, police terrorism, substandard housing, inadequate schools, and a lack of social services were affecting all groups. As a result, ethnic and racial groups created their own activist networks to fight against the various forms of oppression they were facing.

The Young Patriots Organization (YPO) was based in "Hillbilly Harlem," an uptown neighborhood of Chicago populated by displaced white Southerners. Many YPO members were indeed racists and embraced the idea of white supremacy, and flaunted the Confederate flag, even though they weren't directly benefiting from it.

Fred Hampton dedicated himself and the Black Panther Party to putting aside differences and even tolerating the Confederate flags while focusing on the bigger issue: forming a "Rainbow Coalition" of working-class and poor people of all races. He did, however, require the Young Patriots to denounce racism.

Eventually, many Young Patriots rejected their deeply embedded ideas of white supremacy—and even the Confederate flag—as they realized how much they had in common with the Black Panthers and Latino Young Lords. Once sworn enemies, they formed an alliance to stand together in unity. They went on to work with other groups who also faced the same issues. This coalition had Southern white migrants (Young Patriots), Puerto Ricans (Young Lords), poor white ethnic groups (Rising Up Angry, JOIN Community Union, and the Intercommunal Survival Committee), students, and the women's movement all under one umbrella, standing in solidarity, combining resources and strategies, to fight for change. And they were successful. They provided community services and aid for their various constituents that the government and private sector would not provide. Their initiatives included health clinics, feeding homeless and hungry people, and legal advice for those dealing with unethical landlords and police brutality.

Their alliance was eventually duplicated by other Black Panther chapters across the country. Former Black Panther Bobby Lee was quoted as saying, "The Rainbow Coalition was just a code word for class struggle." Bobby Seale said, "We had a grassroots, real people's revolution, complete with the programs, complete with the unity, complete with the working coalitions, where we crossed racial lines."

In contrast, during the 2016 presidential election, Donald Trump embodied Lyndon B. Johnson's approach of, "If you can convince the lowest white man he's better than the best colored man, he won't notice you're picking his pocket. Hell, give him somebody to look down on, and he'll empty his pockets for you." It got Trump into office, and almost worked a second time.

Trump won the white vote across all demographics, doing especially well among working-class white voters: 67 percent of whites without a college degree voted for him. White working-class people voted against their own interests by supporting a billionaire businessman tycoon whose policies hurt them all around. Who provided their kids with the same terrible education, gave tax breaks for people outside their economic bracket, took away social programs, and empowered police to exert more terrorism. None of Trump's positions would benefit them, yet they voted for him in record numbers. He bamboozled them with hatred, racism, and white supremacy, the same way the "hillbillies" were duped by it before they met Chairman Fred Hampton.

For this chapter I talked to four white people who have stood as allies and used their voices and platforms to speak out in support of Black lives. They call out racism, bigotry, and the criticism they receive for doing so. It's important that white people understand they are either part of the solution or part of the problem.

Interview with Rex Chapman

Rex Chapman is an NBA legend, king of Twitter, and host of *The Rex Chapman Show with Josh Hopkins*. Following a McDonald's All-American career in high school and a memorable two seasons with the Kentucky Wildcats in college, Chapman spent twelve seasons in the NBA.

Etan: You got on social media and took off, touching on a lot of hot-button topics: race, Trump, white supremacists, police brutality, Karens—you don't pull any punches. How did that start?

Chapman: About seven years ago I had about fifty thousand Twitter followers from basketball. I came back to Kentucky from LA, and started doing some stuff for Kentucky basketball. Pregame stuff, just enjoying a slower pace than what I've been used to out west. Twitter kind of grew from that—seventy-five thousand, then a hundred thousand followers. Then I started putting up the silly block or charge videos. I posted a video of a guy paddling in the ocean when a dolphin jumped up and hit him square in the chest. I tweeted, *That's a charge.* People thought it was funny, so I started doing that. I kept to that for quite a while.

Etan: Those were funny, and then your tweets changed . . .

Chapman: Yeah, they did, and that's because I was having a really tough time with Donald Trump, Mitch McConnell and Rand Paul, Kentucky representatives and senators. This is a red state and people here hated it at first. People don't want to be told on. What I'm saying is not wrong, but it hurts their feelings. But the worse Trump got, the more overtly racist he became,

I felt like I needed to speak up a little more. Then George Floyd, Breonna Taylor, and Jacob Blake, and on and on and on, I just got fed up.

Etan: I've heard you say you felt guilty that you didn't speak up before.

Chapman: Well, this is stuff I've known for a long time. Since I was a teenager. I did feel like I let a lot of my friends down by not speaking out at a younger age about some of these things. I tried here and there, but there comes a point where you have to. Now, I've been through a lot of stuff, and to be quite honest, I've been very, very fortunate. I'm happy to feel healthy and alive at this point for my kids. But I'm not going down without trying. I've felt very strongly about this racial issue in this country since I was a little kid growing up in Kentucky. I just felt it was time for me to say some things.

Etan: You have a podcast with BasketballNews.com now, and it looks like you are going to cover a little bit of everything.

Chapman: Since so many people are into this little silly Twitter channel of mine now, I am going to use that. There's no shortage of people I can get to from an entertainment background, acting, politics, and I've been able to really connect some dots through this. It will be a pretty liberal safe haven for people, for lack of a better term, to come and talk politics and sports. Hopefully through that we can find we're all people trying to do this out here, and we're not all that different. I think it is an important time. Racially, socially, there have been things that have happened in my lifetime, but nothing like what we're experiencing right now. To have a platform like we both are fortunate to have, I think to *not* take advantage and try to help people, teach a little bit, and inform would be a little cowardly. I plan on being outspoken on things I know, and hopefully have guests that are gonna teach me things.

Etan: A few months ago the Kentucky players took a knee during the national anthem, and Kentucky as a whole didn't react very kindly. Laurel County sheriff and jailer John Root and Jamie Mosley, respectively, were burning Kentucky jerseys on TV, and pushing to move funding away from the basketball program. It was a big thing, not just that they didn't like it, but that they were trying to start a movement to punish the players. You publicly spoke out in support of the players and had very harsh words for the Kentucky fans who were criticizing them.

Chapman: It was straight racism, and I don't have any problem saying that. These young men were peacefully protesting, and we know what they were protesting. If I was on the team, I would've been doing the same thing. Wouldn't have even been a second thought. I'm trying to be an ally and I would've taken a knee with them. I'm trying to learn and help, and I'm exhausted. I can't imagine how you and my Black friends feel. Especially right now.

Etan: Were you surprised at much of Kentucky's reaction?

Chapman: You know, these young men who peacefully took a knee during the national anthem just got eviscerated back here by some "fans." Mind you, two days before this happened, "patriots" stormed the Capitol. The sheriff from Laurel County who you mentioned, that's where my mom's from. They're burning Kentucky jerseys because these players are peacefully protesting police brutality and social justice while literally a coup is staged to overthrow American democracy and government. But they weren't up in arms about *that*?

Etan: Yeah, you spoke out a lot about that as well. I still can't believe that actually happened.

Chapman: Tell me about it. And we're finding out they knew it was coming, everyone knew this attempted coup was coming. They actually pulled out the National Guard. My buddy is one of the biggest criminal attorneys here in the state. We lived together in Charlotte before he became a lawyer. Another young man was murdered by the National Guard while he was literally grilling a burger in his own house—David McAtee during the Breonna Taylor protests—and the National Guard was called out immediately. But when these dudes try to overtake the Capitol, the National Guard wasn't even on call? The fix was in. And you can't tell me if there had been five or ten thousand Black and Brown people storming the Capitol that there wouldn't have been bodies everywhere. We'd still be putting toe tags on people. But they're gonna be upset about some young Black Kentucky basketball players taking a knee? I think everyone should be speaking out about that hypocrisy.

Etan: I'm sure you get some backlash from other white people for talking like this.

Chapman: Oh boy, do I. But I don't pay attention to that because those aren't the people I'm trying to connect with. I know who they are, they've been showing me who they are for thirty or forty years. But at the same time, a big part of it makes me sad that we have to have white people speaking out in order for it to resonate with a lot of white America. It hurts my heart when I see my friends Steve Kerr, Steve Nash, Stan Van Gundy, Gregg Popovich picking their spots, because they're still in the NBA. I know the tightrope they do have to walk on some issues, but some of the stuff they've said, Black people have been saying for decades. I'm proud of them for saying it now. Proud to call them my friends. I'm proud to be of the group of white people who genuinely want to be allies in this fight.

Interview with Breanna Stewart

In the 2020 WNBA season, after battling back from an Achilles tear the previous year, Breanna Stewart won the WNBA Championship with the Seattle Storm, was the WNBA Finals MVP, All-WNBA first team, second team All-WNBA Defensive Team, and won *Sports Illustrated's* Sportsperson of the Year—a category that also included LeBron James, Naomi Osaka, and Patrick Mahomes. *Sports Illustrated* wrote, "When the moment came for Stewart to take a stand, the WNBA superstar didn't hesitate. Her support of Black Lives Matter never wavered, from the season's opening tip to the Storm's title celebration."

Etan: What led to your full support for Black Lives Matter? Sometimes people tiptoe in, but you went all in—what was the spark for that?

Stewart: First, I'm not a toe-dipper, and the fact that we were able to see all of the social injustices happening this past year especially, and I think it was magnified because we were all at home because of COVID, and the power of social media, and we kept seeing everything that was going on all summer, whether it was with Breonna Taylor, Ahmaud Arbery, George Floyd, and so many more—it was really a no-brainer for me. Our league is a league of over 144 women, and the majority of those women are Black. We knew when we started the season that we had to be bigger than basketball, so that was our focus.

Etan: The entire league was focused on this to the point that it felt like it became more important than basketball.

Stewart: Obviously I'm happy that we won the championship, but knowing that we had the power and ability to keep uplifting Black Lives Matter and bring light to these horrific cases and call for justice . . . this wasn't a one-time thing for us. A lot happened this particular season with our stance for Black Lives Matter, but we have been fighting for equality and social justice for years as a league. And we're going to continue fighting for years to come.

Etan: You mentioned Breonna Taylor, and I want to go a little deeper into that particular case and how it struck a nerve for you personally.

Stewart: Well, the first thing I asked: would this have happened if she was white? My answer is, probably not. The fact is, we see everything happening with Black Lives Matter, but for some reason everything happening with Black women is not in the spotlight the way it should be. That's why we wanted to really promote SayHerName this season. Before every game this season, we were able to have a video montage of who we were recognizing that day, whether it was Breonna Taylor or Sandra Bland or Michelle Cusseaux, and continue to educate ourselves and educate others, because our country is not equal and everyone is not treated the same. There was just a video released last week of a nine-year-old Black girl getting pepper-sprayed and handcuffed by police in Rochester. I'm from Syracuse, Rochester is two hours away. To see that happen, you have to think, would this have happened if she was a nine-year-old white girl? Probably not.

Etan: It's amazing to see society go into these debates after *every* police incident.

Stewart: It's so frustrating to see. The debate turns into, "Not all police are bad," and I'm like, "Nobody is saying that. Look at what is happening in *this* example and *this* example and *this* example. Something is not right. There are no excuses. Wrong is wrong, period."

Etan: I read a story about something that happened while you were in college—you were driving with an ex-boyfriend who was Black and you were stopped by the police?

Stewart: I was with my now-ex and he was driving and there was another Black guy in the backseat who was his teammate, and we were on the New Jersey Turnpike. We got pulled over. We weren't doing anything wrong. The officer asked for the two guys' licenses but not mine and asked me, "Is everything okay?" And I was like, "Yeah, what did we do?" He said we followed the car in front of us too closely. Which is impossible because that highway near New York City, there are so many people and so many cars. The reality is, he saw two Black guys and me, a white girl, and wanted to see what's going on here.

Etan: So he asked you if everything was okay, like, "Are you safe? Are you here against your will?"

Stewart: Yeah, exactly, and I was so shocked, like, "What are you talking about?"

Etan: It's crazy. That's a story you expect to hear from the fifties or sixties traveling through the South, but that was the New Jersey Turnpike in 2013, 2014, when you were winning everything with UConn.

Stewart: Crazy, right? We talked about it a lot after that. They talked about how they have been treated as Black men their entire lives. Those are experiences I don't have as a white person. I don't have to live with that. That's what white privilege is. The simple fact that white people are viewed differently than the same exact situation involving a Black person. That is white privilege. White people are able to get away with more. The US Capitol riots, a domestic terrorist attack on our country, actually just happened, and yes, the situation would've been way different if those were Black people. That's just undeniable.

So to tie it all back in, the special part about being able to play basketball with and against people who come from all different races and backgrounds is to be able to hear their experiences and learn from them and continue to use that to educate myself and educate my circle and my family, because yes, my family is white. And my fans, the people who are fans of me on the court, to be able to take a stand and tell everyone what's acceptable and what is not.

Etan: Other white people hear it differently coming from you—would you agree?

Stewart: Unfortunately, you're right. As a white person, I do have a different reach and a different platform. For me, it seems super simple, like, "Why can't we all be treated equally?" But something so simple is so difficult to achieve and get everybody on board with. So I wouldn't feel right if I didn't do everything I could to push for that. How could I possibly not care? But it's also important for me to pass the mic so the people in my reach can hear directly from Black women about their experiences and their fight that they've been fighting for an extremely long time.

Etan: You have been playing in the Olympics since you were very young. You once said, "It's not easy reconciling the way I feel about playing for Team USA, that pride, with the shame I feel about racism that contributes to my own privilege and the oppression of Black people." That's a strong statement.

Stewart: When you think of the United States, for me, I'm on the podium, we just won, the anthem is being played, and of course there was a tremendous amount of pride every time we won for our country in the Olympics. But to be representing everything else that's happening in our country, the racism, it's sickening. I'm not proud of the racial injustices and the horrific racism that is happening everywhere in our country on a daily basis. How could I feel pride in that? That's the dichotomy. But I can use that moment of athletic achievement to call attention to that, so I did.

Interview with Stan Van Gundy

Stan Van Gundy has been coaching in the NBA since 1981, and is currently an analyst for TNT. He is not afraid to use his platform to call out racism, police brutality, and white supremacy. He and I spoke together at an event for an organization called the Professional Association of Athlete Development Specialists. I heard Coach Van Gundy talk about activism, players' rights, and his support of activism. I also remember how he spoke out after Trayvon Martin and Eric Garner were killed.

Etan: Where did you get this level of awareness, this level of courage to speak up? It's not something that happens a lot with many white NBA coaches. You, Gregg Popovich, Steve Kerr—that's about it.

Van Gundy: Well, I think you grow up. My dad coached for forty-some years at the high school and college level. I grew up around the game. You work closely with predominantly people of color. You coach them, you work with them on the staff. These are the people you get to know and like. They're your friends and you start to hear their stories—their stories of how they grew up and how they're living now; stories of what they have to prepare their kids for. And it's so different than my experience. I say to people, "I'm a poster boy for white privilege." I didn't grow up rich, but I never had any real needs. And if I got pulled over by the police, number one, I was probably in the wrong. Number two, I never had to worry about what was going to happen to me in that circumstance. I started hearing these stories, and these are people you care about, and you're just saying, "Wow, this is screwed up. This is a mess."

It motivates you to learn and talk to more people and figure out what's going on. I think the simple part is, that's not the kind of country I want to live in. These are people I work with, care about. I don't want them treated that way. This has got to stop. You have more experiences, and it just piles up and piles up. But there's still a big difference . . . I speak out a lot, but I'll admit that every once in a while, I just want a day where I don't want to deal with this right now. I don't want to read another story. I don't want to send out another tweet. I want a break from activism or whatever.

Etan: It's exhausting, right?

Van Gundy: Yes!!! I'm aware that's white privilege too, because *you* never have that choice. You can't opt out of racial issues. It hits you in the face as a Black man in America every single day. I'm acutely aware of that because of the people I'm around. I want things to change, and I want life to be better. I want our country to be better.

Etan: I mean, speaking of that, not being able to take a break, just yesterday, my daughter Baby Sierra said, "Did you hear about what happened with that family and Aurora police?" And I was like, "Well, what do you mean?" She said, "They had a little girl who was like my age. She had on her princess tiara. She was facedown on the pavement. They thought that the family did something wrong, and they didn't even do *anything* wrong." Those are the things our children are coming to us about, hearing these things and getting scared.

Van Gundy: That's terrible.

Etan: Often, when people hear "white privilege," they get offended. They say, "Well, I didn't grow up with money." But it doesn't have anything to do with money. It's that you have a different set of experiences and concerns than your Black counterparts. But coaching Black players isn't enough for many coaches to see that and make that connection. A lot of coaches can say that they have been around Black players for decades. So there is a difference with you.

Van Gundy: I think it's starting to change. I really do. I look at the NBA coaches now. After George Floyd, Lloyd Pierce from Atlanta got everything started. He brought together every head coach in the league. They were kind enough to include myself and Dave Fizdale and some other recently fired guys. First thing they did: educate themselves. Lloyd set up group calls, they had Rashad Robinson from Color of Change one week. They had people from the Obama Foundation one week. They had Bryan Stevenson from the Equal Justice Initiative. Every single head coach in this league now is working with grassroots groups in their own city, Etan. It's amazing. I've never seen the coaches come together on anything, let alone something like this, and be actively involved. I mean, I know Erik Spoelstra well. I worked with him. He and Steve Clifford, two guys that I've worked with, and are right here in Florida. They're going to community meetings and meetings with the leaders about police accountability. And so it's changing. I think that people are getting to the point . . . maybe they knew it was going on, but maybe it didn't really touch them. I don't know. But now, everybody's basically saying, "Enough! This has to change, and we want to be part of the solution." It's been inspiring for me to watch everybody come together and do what they're doing.

Etan: I was listening to you when one of the teams took a knee during the national anthem. You made the point to say, "Okay, these men love their country. These men want their country to be better. These men are not anti-American." And you said that on the mic. What are your thoughts on why you have to say that? I looked at the Washington Wizards's site, when all the Wizards took a knee and people were pissed. *I'll never watch them again. See, that's why they should stand. They're anti-American.* You see those comments. Honestly, after their reaction to Kaepernick, I expect it from NFL fans, not so much from NBA fans.

Van Gundy: First of all, I don't understand why standing for the anthem or anything like that is a prerequisite for playing basketball anyway. I don't even understand why we tie the two together. But it seems to me, if what we're supposed to do is let our country do whatever they want, let our government officials do whatever they want, and we just go along, that we wouldn't be a country to begin with. If the people who came over here didn't fight the Revolutionary War . . . Well, if we didn't want protesters and people willing to fight, we'd still be citizens of Great Britain.

Etan: Great point.

Van Gundy: So I don't know what they're talking about, to begin with. Maybe I just know the best of the military people, but I've had several of them to say to me, "That's exactly what I fought for. I fought for our freedoms so that people could do this." I honestly believe if you love something, you want it to be better. I mean, you were just talking about your daughter. As a parent, yes, you're going to love your kid no matter what, but you don't just let them do whatever the heck they want to do and not say anything or do anything. Because if you really love your kids, you want them to be the best that they can be. When they're not doing that, you want to try to correct their course. That's what these people are doing. They're not saying, "I don't want to live here," or, "I hate America." They're saying, "Look, I want it to be the best that it can be." And right now, we have a significant part of our population that we have oppressed for four hundred years here in this country. And right now, we're not even going in the right direction, let alone getting to where we need to go. This needs to change. What could be more patriotic than that?

Etan: You wrote a great article in *Time* magazine a few years ago. I want to read a little bit of it, because you addressed the people directly who have an issue with kneeling. You said, "Honoring America has to mean much, much more than standing at attention for a song (one which, by the way, contains racist language in later verses). One of the most important freedoms that our military has fought for over two-plus centuries is the freedom of speech. When these professional athletes protest during the anthem, they are exercising one of the very freedoms for which our military men and women fought so valiantly, thus honoring our highest values and, in turn, those who have fought for them."

That really stuck out to me because my grandfather fought in the Korean conflict. He was proud that he fought for this country. Before he passed, he would say, "I fought so that you can have the right to speak out against the war in Iraq"—that's what was going on at that time. He would say, "So it's not where you have to just follow along with everything that the country says. You have the right to speak out." A lot of people villainize the athletes for using what our veterans actually fought and died for. And they don't make that connection.

Van Gundy: The other thing that has always sort of struck me about this whole thing is friends of mine, other white people, who say, "Yeah, I know some things have not been great, but this is the greatest country on earth." They need to see the United States as the greatest country on earth. My point would be, "Well, maybe it has been for you." It probably has been for the majority of white people, a great country. Can you at least understand that the experience of Black people in America is not your experience? It certainly is not the best country on earth for people of color. They came in bondage, went on to Jim Crow and mass lynchings, and now mass incarceration and police killings of unarmed people. And if that had happened to your family, would you still be saying, "This is the greatest country on earth"? Of course you wouldn't.

Etan: You break it all the way down for them.

Van Gundy: You have to, because things need to change. And this idea that just because it says in our founding documents, the Declaration of Independence and the Constitution, that we're about equality and freedom and all of that—we've never lived up to that. I mean, those are words on paper. When they wrote them, they were enslaving people. So this idea that, "Oh, this isn't who we are" . . . It's *exactly* who we are. This is what we've done the entire time we've been here. I mean, we committed genocide on the native people. Then we enslaved Black people. Bryan Stevenson brought this up when he was talking to the coaches, and it really hit home, Etan. One of the reasons we haven't been able to make progress on racial issues is a lack of education. I don't even think people really know what was going on. And one of the things the Equal Justice Initiative does, they put up commemorative plaques where people were lynched. Because I think a lot of us, we don't understand. And if we can't face up to what we've done and are still doing, we can't solve the problem.

I look at it the same as in basketball. If you're a 50 percent free-throw shooter, and you don't even acknowledge that as a problem, you're certainly not going to work on it and get better. The first step to improving anything is facing facts, facing the truth, and saying, "This is the reality." That's step one, and we haven't gotten to step one yet. I'll have people argue, "Oh, it really hasn't been that bad for Blacks in this country." I say, "First of all, as a white person, you can't make that statement. This is not up to you. You don't know what it's like. I don't know what it's like." I try to educate myself by listening to people like you, but even listening, I know that I'll never know what it's really like because I haven't experienced it. And so for somebody who looks like me to say, "Oh, it's not that bad. And 95 percent of the police are fine, and all of this, it's no big deal." I mean, that's easy to say when you look like I do.

Etan: A lot of times, the waters start to be muddied on purpose. People start to not be clear on what the actual issue is. It's not saying that all police are bad. Nobody's saying that. Nobody's saying that we want to get rid of the entire police system as a whole and not have police. But there needs to be checks and balances. There needs to be a system of holding someone accountable. I don't understand why that's so hard for so many to grasp. Everything has to have a system. For instance, my wife and I have three children. If we were to tell them, "You can do whatever you want to do, then you can investigate yourself and come back and tell us what you did wrong"—no parent would ever do that, that's ridiculous to even think about. But that's the system that we have with so many police departments. *They* tell us if *they* did something wrong. They give us the report, and that's what we go by. That's not a logical system.

Van Gundy: Okay, I may have to use that example. That's actually a really good analogy. People try to make it an either/or. If I'm against police brutality, I'm against the police. If I'm for racial justice, and I stand up against acts of racial injustice, I don't love our country. If I love my country, I can't point out the bad things. We all know that's not the way it works. But that's how people want to draw the lines in this whole battle. Are you for your country or are you for racial justice? I can't be for both?

Etan: Right. Exactly.

Van Gundy: I mean, it's nonsensical what we try to do. But that's . . . again, when you don't want to face the issue, you make distractions. So players kneeling—if you don't want to deal with police killings of unarmed Black people, if you don't want to face that reality, then you turn it around to make the issue about respecting the flag and respecting the country, because you don't want to deal with the unpleasant truths of what's going on in our country.

Interview with Mark Cuban

Mark Cuban and I have history. I was the first player he drafted after he bought the Dallas Mavericks in 2000. Following the murder of Jacob Blake, I wrote an article in the *Guardian* titled, "Words Aren't Enough: Sports Team CEOs Must Use Their Influence to Effect Change." In the piece I was calling on CEOs like Cuban—I don't call them "owners" for obvious reasons—Clay Bennett in Oklahoma, Steve Ballmer and Jeanie Buss in LA, James Dolan in New York, and Micky Arison in Miami, to use their collective power to push harder for change. I was seeing statements about Black Lives Matter and that was great, but after George Floyd's death, there were still more cases of police terrorism. So I was like, okay, change isn't happening fast enough. Mark Cuban didn't take it personally, he didn't get offended by my article. In fact, he messaged me and we started talking about it.

Etan: 2020 was an eventful summer. NBA players went on strike after Jacob Blake was shot seven times. We watched George Floyd get murdered by Officer Derek Chauvin, who knelt on his neck for over nine minutes. We watched Ahmaud Arbery get hunted down. I want to know first of all, how did all of this affect you personally? What was your response at seeing Breonna Taylor, seeing all the different cases that happened?

Cuban: George Floyd had the biggest impact, because that was just straight-out murder with everybody watching. It was just incredible to see a man die on a video camera while people watch, while there were police officers around, while there were people taping it. And it just hurt. It didn't make any sense to me at all. But it did contribute to the understanding, because when lots of people come out and say, "Well, it's not as big of a problem as they're making out," and then there's just one time, after another time, after another time, where just African American men, and women now, it just seems like they're being hunted. George Floyd really hit me hard, and it just made me a lot more aware and a lot more sensitive to the issue, and a lot more wanting to have an impact, and wanting to try to help where I could.

Etan: And what did you think of the NBA's response? A lot of the players have been using their platforms to really speak out and bring light to this issue.

Cuban: I think that's great. Look, every generation or every couple of generations has moments in time that are defining elements, defining actions of those generations. We look back at Martin Luther King, and the marches and speeches that really were defining acts, that really led to a lot of change with civil rights. And then here we are, almost sixty years later, and a lot has changed, but not enough. And so, this really felt like it was a chance to have an impact, and leave a lasting impression, and most importantly start to move toward change.

This was bigger than basketball. We have players with the biggest platform of any athletes in the country, and in many cases the world. It made perfect sense to use those platforms to try to change something that really needs to be changed. To really have an impact on racism, and police reform. I was proud of them, I'm very supportive. And recognizing there's still a lot of work that needs to be done.

Etan: Let's talk about your response to my article.

Cuban: I don't think we have as much influence as you think we do. I wish we did. I wish we could go to our politicians and just say, "Look, this is wrong, let's do A, B, or C." When the reality is, I don't have that influence. If I did, there's a hundred things I would try to impact, and a hundred things I would try to change. In addition to racism, in addition to police reform, there's so many . . . housing, and food shortages, and kids not getting educations. There's a thousand things that need change.

Etan: Let me read what I wrote: "Sentiments of support and solidarity were a good start, but it's time for billionaires in control of sports teams to wield their power to bring about tangible changes in their communities." This is what I suggested: "What if NBA CEOs took proactive roles in their respective cities, and pressured police departments to move toward specific reforms, and more police accountability?" I also wrote, "It's not as if men such as Mark Cuban or Micky Arison in Miami are lacking in clout in the cities where their teams play. They are billionaires, not millionaires like the players who have been doing an amazing job protesting, but billionaires with a B, which is a whole different level of influence."

I then said, "So what if the NBA and team CEOs use their influence to pressure cities to threaten to cut the funding of police departments, if they didn't adopt tangible police reform and police accountability measures?" And then, "I bet you would see results as immediate as what you saw in Washington, with the now Washington Football Team." Dan Snyder was not going to change the name regardless, he made it very clear. But then FedEx said, "Well, if you don't change the name, you're going to lose us as a sponsor." Then he saw the light. I also relate that to Donald Sterling. Donald Sterling was Donald Sterling for a very long time.

Cuban: Long time, yeah.

Etan: It was very well known who he was. He had the record for the most discrimination cases against him in the NBA, and that's for a decade. But then you saw sponsors pulling out, after that tape came out—

Cuban: You're saying it's the other way, right? You're saying you can influence the owners more than we can influence the politicians, whether they're local or national?

Etan: No, no, no. I'm saying, you in Dallas, Clay Bennett in Oklahoma, the places where the teams are located, where you go to events and have different dealings with this certain level of circles. To use your influence to be able to convince the city, to say, "Okay, you have to have this police reform, or some type of measure of police before, or you will lose this amount of funding or resources or check to the policeman's ball donation from the Dallas Mavericks.

Cuban: I see. Well, I'll tell you exactly what I did. I met with the Dallas chief of police, and I've got a great relationship with the police. After July 7, 2016, where the five officers in Dallas were killed, we worked very closely. I paid for overtime, for officers to add services in Oaklawn. Particularly after the Pulse shooting in Orlando, there was a lot of activity and violence in and around Oaklawn to the LGBT community, so I paid for overtime there.

After Chief Brown left, we hired him at the Mavericks. I hired him to work on programs, to try to connect kids to have better relationships with officers. He left last year to take on another job. But that gave me the relationship to talk to Chief Hall, the chief of police, and we had some conversations. Now, "defund police" can mean a lot of different things. I'm a big believer in *disrupt* police, because I think the challenge is not so much police funding, even though that's part of it. The challenge is that we have all these different stakeholders trying to have an impact on community, and it's all disorganized. And the police try to do too much. They have community programs which on the surface sound great. Let's get to know kids better, connect them with police. Well, hospitals have community programs, churches, synagogues and mosques have community programs, schools have community programs, the city and the county have community programs, charities have community programs.

So, you have these twenty different constituencies trying to all do the same thing to make communities safer, to make the communities healthier, and better educated, but they don't work together. So, I said to the chief of police, "We need to get you connected with all these other organizations, so that you can take that money out of your budget, because you're being asked to do things that you're not really great at, which is operating these community services. And have that money go toward organizing all of these other groups, so they work as one unit, so that we can really have an impact."

Etan: Well, that's what defunding the police is.

Cuban: I hear you, but I've also heard other definitions. Because the whole goal is to make these communities even more safe by improving their education, by improving their health care, by improving the housing circumstances, by making it so that they don't go hungry, and kids get fed, and there's day care.

That all ties back to the issues with the police department. No organization can be great at everything, none. Police are trying to do too many things, when they need to focus on the two or three things that the community needs from them, that they can be good at, and get good at that. And then when you talk to them about that, and then you start saying, "Okay, well, what's the next step?" then they start talking about the politics of it. Nobody wants to see their budget reduced, right?

Etan: Yeah, that's typically when the pushback comes.

Cuban: Right, but I had this conversation with [Chief Hall], and they said they were going to take a look at it. Never heard back really in any depth, other than they're looking at it. But at the same time, I also had the conversation, I'm like, "Look. On a basketball team, we know who the knuckleheads are, and you try to limit the knuckleheads." You've had teammates that you knew were crazy. And I said, "In your police department, do you know who the knuckleheads are?" And he's like, "Of course." I'm like, "Well, why can't you get rid of them?" And he goes, "You already know the answer." The unions, or in Dallas it's not so much a union, there's associations that do everything possible to protect them. And then they've got these immunity issues where they're not as much at risk.

There's all these different elements that make it a very in-depth and difficult issue to address. And that's not meant to make excuses, but those are the conversations I'm having. When I talk to them—and it looks like we're going to get a new police chief in Dallas because Chief Hall is resigning, I think in November—then we'll have the conversations again. You and I have talked a lot about how sometimes the narrative changes everything. People end up believing one narrative versus another, and that makes it difficult to get things done. I think part of the challenge is, while "defund the police" sounds really good, "disrupt the police" is what's really needed. You need to change the game, so that communities can be made safer in a way that communities want to be policed, as opposed to just saying, "You know what? Let's just cut it out and reformulate it from ground up."

Etan: The problem is with people who are dedicated to misrepresenting what the message really is. People know the difference between the words "defund" and "abolish." They're not synonyms. They're two very different words.

Cuban: You're right. People do know the difference, but that's the narrative, and that's the challenge. That's what you face when you try to get things done.

Etan: I'll use myself as an example. I don't have the clout that you have in

Dallas, but I have a relationship with Syracuse. So, a lot of things happened in Syracuse last semester, a lot of bad things, racially. We had incident after incident happen on campus. I had a meeting with the Department of Public Safety (DPS) chief, Bobby Maldanado. I'm going to have a town hall with him, but then I'm going to have other conversations where I make suggestions. I talk about the police hiring, police accountability, what they are actually doing if they find a bad apple. How they're protected, how we can better implement different things, so that there can be trust within the students. Because right now, the Black and Brown students do not trust DPS, and they have very good reasons not to. So, making that correlation right now for the Dallas police, after Botham Jean was killed, and then Atatiana Jefferson, a lot of the people in the community in Dallas don't trust the Dallas Police Department. People need to know what measures are being taken for police accountability, for the bad apples that you referenced.

Cuban: Let me jump in, because as a business guy, I put on my business hat, and I say, "Okay, let me get to the bottom of the problem." I've had organizations that have had problems, and how do you get to the bottom of it? More often than not, it starts with culture, and then you look to see what the issues are within that culture that are creating challenges and problems, and people that aren't doing what's in the employee handbook, aren't living up to the ideals. I think there's three thousand people in the Dallas Police Department—that's hard to manage. And within those three thousand police, I don't know how many active duty officers there are at different levels, but just the nature of that business is hard.

And the reason I bring this up is not to make an excuse for anybody. The idea is that when you're looking for change on the outside, and trying to ask the questions that drive change on the inside, you need to ask the right questions. Because it's not that what you're saying isn't right, of course it is. The problem is, and what we've seen time and time again over decades, is that they already know how to answer those questions just to buy time. As opposed to saying, "Here are the action items that I am going to commit to, that create change." Because they can train more, but who's doing the training? They can hire better, with better qualifications, but if the people that are still managing and training aren't doing it the right way, it's not going to change.

And even bigger, if you bring in those newly hired people who have better backgrounds, have been better trained, and they come into a culture where it's a macho culture, guys are about violence as a cure-all, you clean up the streets through violence and through intimidation, like some police departments, you're just bringing these newly better educated and better trained officers into an environment that is going to swallow them.

Think of it this way. We talk about the bad apples in every police department, and let's just say it's 1 percent or 2 percent. There's a reason why the other 98 percent aren't standing up and demanding change, undoing things. And to me, that's the harder question to answer: what is it that's preventing the 98 percent from taking action to stop the only 2 percent? And you saw it as sports teams too, right? You know this dude's a knucklehead, and you know he's messing things up for all of us, but nobody really says anything or does anything for whatever reason. And so I'll ask you: how do you get that 98 percent to change, to have the weight over the 2 percent, the 1 or 2 percent?

Etan: Correct me if I'm wrong, but in every championship-level, quality team, they have leaders on the team that hold everybody else accountable. Aside from the coach, aside from the GM, as you go up in the ranks.

Cuban: Hopefully. You're right, that's what makes a championship team, but there's twenty-nine other teams all tied for last, right?

Etan: Everybody still has to be able to act accordingly under the guidelines and rules that, say, somebody like Adam Silver set for everyone. So, whether they're knuckleheads or not, if they fall out of line, then they're punished. What we're looking at when we're talking about police, it seems like they're going unpunished and have a license to do whatever they want to do.

Cuban: I agree with you. We're agreeing that it's a problem, and they're going unpunished. The question becomes, how do you get that culture, how do you get that person in charge, and how do you get it so they have the authority? The police chiefs have the responsibility to keep everybody in line, and have everybody moving forward and doing things the right way. But they don't always have the authority to be able to get rid of those knuckleheads if they step out of line. And a lot of that has to do with the unions and associations. And that's the challenge that really is underpinning a lot of these issues, because I think 98 percent of people want to do it the right way, and their heart's in the right place, but they just don't have the authority to make those changes.

When I talked to the chief of police now and before, they're like, "Mark, we would change it in a heartbeat if we could." They don't want to deal with this mess. They don't want to face this. So how do we as influencers in one way or the other try to get them to change? I don't have that answer right now. I can talk until I'm blue in the face, and that's what I've done. I can say, "Here's who you should vote for, here's who you shouldn't vote for," and that has a big influence as well. You know the history of police forces in this country, and how they tie back to slavery, and then in the early 1900s they were immigrants that were put on the case. There's a long period of ingrained challenges, cultural challenges that need to be overcome, particularly in urban police forces, that have been very, very difficult.

And so, when we walk into this, I think we can't just say, "Okay, here's the questions, what are your answers?" And expect to get results. We need to find a better way to dislodge . . . Because I'm not a union expert, a police union or association expert, but a lot of this points back to the fact that it's very difficult to fire the people that aren't following the rules. And I don't know how we change that, but that's I think part of what we need to address. And I think a part of that is the George Floyd law that's being proposed, and there's things built around part of that. But those are the conversations that when you talk to them, like when I talk, it's like, "How do we change that?" Because it's the things that they haven't been able to change that need changing the most, that have the big impacts.

Etan: We're running into that same issue at Syracuse with the DPS and the unions, it's very similar. We started a group called the Black Oranges, and they're former Syracuse athletes, so we're trying to use our collective power and influence to be able to help push for accountability.

I think that you're right as far as the unions part—defining what the issue is, then working with them, and making suggestions as far as how they can improve relations and improve accountability. Because it's not just relations. A lot of times the police departments, they say, "Okay, let's go into the schools and talk, and be Officer Friendly," and all that stuff. That's all cool. But what people really want to be able to see is that if a police officer kills someone, they will be held accountable.

Cuban: Of course what you want is they don't kill or hurt anybody in the first place. But if the unfortunate happens, and this tragedy happens again, and you know it will, then yeah, you can't have the immunity levels that officers have. It's just not the way it should work, there shouldn't be an automatic protection of them. They should have every right afforded every American citizen, right to a fair trial, etc., but they shouldn't have *more* rights.

Etan: Yeah, they shouldn't be above the law.

Cuban: Definitely shouldn't be above the law. I just don't know how to change that. And I'm open to all suggestions, because if you guys figure it out or anybody figures it out, let's share it and get it done. I just don't know.

Etan: I definitely commend you for that. You always start off by saying, "Look, I don't have as much power as you think I do," and I hear you on that, but you do have power, and you do have influence, and you are definitely an influencer. You asked me, "Who should people look to as the leaders?" and I thought that was a really good question.

Cuban: You mean when I was asking who are the leaders of Black Lives Matter?

Etan: Right. Explain to me why that was important.

Cuban: What I hear from white people, particularly from those who are in the Fox News bubble, is that they used to go to Blacklivesmatter.com. And they would say, "Well, if you look at the leaders of Black Lives Matter, they're Marxists, and they want to destroy the nuclear family." They were smart, they just changed the Blacklivesmatter.com website so it doesn't reflect those things anymore. But they would use that as a way to try to influence the narrative, and really just reinforce that they don't want to deal with this problem within that little filter bubble that they're in.

What was always brought up to me is that the people who invented the hashtag, who ran Blacklivesmatter.com, must be the leaders. If they're self-proclaimed Marxists, like they say in interviews and on that website, then the Black Lives Matter movement must be a Marxist movement. If they say they don't support the traditional nuclear family, then the Black Lives Matter movement must be a bunch of Marxists that support ending the nuclear family. And I'm like, "That's crazy." You and I know it's crazy, anybody who's supportive of the movement knows it's crazy, but it enables this filter bubble to dismiss Black Lives Matter's movement.

So I ask the question, who's the leader? Because there's nobody speaking up for BLM, to talk about the movement. There's nobody going into that filter bubble to say that you're wrong, so that we get more support for the movement. Even if that support is recognizing that, okay, it's not a Marxist movement led by three people who created the hashtag.

Etan: My response to people who say that is, "When we say 'Black Lives Matter,' we're not talking about the organization, we're actually talking about our lives." I'll give you an example. Last night my wife was braiding my daughter's hair and we watched the Breonna Taylor story on Hulu. Afterwards, Imani's asking me questions like, "Okay, so what's going to stop this from happening again?" And, "Why doesn't her life matter enough for it to be valued?"

These are questions that Imani is asking us, about that officer not being held accountable for murdering Breonna Taylor. So we explained what the police officer was charged with, and that it was wanton endangerment.

Cuban: I still can't believe that was the verdict.

Etan: Right? So Imani was like, "Wait a minute, how could that be . . . ?" And she was like, "That just tells us that our lives don't matter." So that's what we're saying when we say Black Lives Matter.

The people I look at as the leaders, and who I want to elevate and keep pushing for as the leaders that I've been doing work with, are the family members of the victims of police brutality. I've been working with Emerald Garner, who is Eric Garner's daughter; Tiffany Crutcher, who is Terence Crutcher's sister; and Allysza Castile and Valerie Castile, who are Philando Castile's mother and daughter. Even the Fultons, Trayvon Martin's family.

And now, Lora Dene King, Rodney King's daughter; Alissa Findley, Botham Jean's sister; Atatiana Jefferson's sisters; Sean Monterrosa's sisters; Kori McCoy's brother; and Chikesia Clemons. I am working with all of them.

They all are pushing for legislative changes, all of them in their respective cities. They're not pushing for sensitivity training. Specifically legislative changes. I want to push them as the leaders, as the people who have been affected most by all of this. They actually lost a loved one. Immediately when something happens, the cameras go to them and then all the cameras go away, but they're left to really be pushing for justice for their loved ones. And so, I really want to push them as the leaders.

Cuban: To me, I can't be the one who decides that, but I'll be supportive of anybody. Because in this day and age with social media, and just general media the way it works, people consume information in short sound bites, little short videos. There's so much volume of those things, you need somebody there speaking all the time in all the places where conversations are being held. And in particular, it's not like *you* need to see them, it's not like *I* need to see them. It's the people who truly don't understand what's going on—that's who needs to see them. You need people who are going on Fox News, you need them going onto Breitbart or wherever some of these places are, and really conveying what's at stake and why this is important.

And I hear exactly what you're saying; and all the people you mentioned that are relatives of those who have been killed, they deserve a voice, because this is a nonstop issue that's not going to go away. And you don't want it to start to fade off, because you go through a period of time where someone doesn't get killed. You don't want people to say, "Well, see, it hasn't been a problem for six months," or, "It happened less this year than last year," because the underlying issues are the two big issues that aren't going away anytime soon, and that's racism and police brutality.

And so, you need somebody there to continuously hammer on these things, and make the points and be the spokesperson, and provide the information. Otherwise, you're not going to communicate with the people that really need to hear it.

Etan: There are people dedicated to misrepresenting and drowning the issues out, so that's a huge problem as well.

Cuban: Yeah, that's what they do. It's like, "I'm not going to watch the NBA because you've got a Marxist organization represented on your basketball court." I'm like, "Dude, if this is about the website, you'd see a dot-com there. You'd see Blacklivesmatter.com, stupid. If this was about the people who started the hashtag, they'd be in every ad, they'd be on every game talking. That's not what's happening." So, we know it's disingenuous, we know it's just a deflection because they don't want to deal with the underlying issue of racism. The reality is white people don't talk about racism, and don't want to talk about racism. They don't want to talk about white privilege, because no one wants to think that they're privileged. Black people have no problem talking about racism, white people do. It's just very difficult.

And so, you get this deflection within those filter bubbles, and you need somebody, or some people, that go into those bubbles and say, "No, you're wrong. And here's why you're wrong." You're not going to convince most people, because they're just going to turn a blind eye to it. But if you get 5 percent or 10 percent, and their kids don't receive the hate that they otherwise would, or aren't educated hatefully, that's part of progress. But you need leaders. I mean, when we look back in history—John Lewis, Martin Luther King, or whatever—we talk about leaders who have stood up and taken a position, and taken on the risk to really move things forward. In twenty years, who are we going to look back at for BLM and say, "You know what? They stood up for everybody, when everybody needed someone to stand up for then"?

Etan: And that's why I think, just seeing the work that the family members have been doing, *they* can become those leaders.

Cuban: I hope so. I'll do anything I can to help you and support you there, but it's got to happen. It's got to happen.

Etan: I agree. And I appreciate your willingness to be helpful.

Sisters of the Movement

Institutions work this way. A son is murdered by the police, and nothing is done. The institutions send the victim's family on a merry-go-round, going from one agency to another, until they wear out and give up. This is a very effective way to beat down poor and oppressed people, who do not have the time to prosecute their cases. Time is money to poor people. To go to Sacramento means loss of a day's pay—often a loss of job. If this is a democracy, obviously it is a bourgeois democracy limited to the middle and upper classes. Only they can afford to participate in it.

—Huey P. Newton

In my previous book, *We Matter: Athletes and Activism,* along with interviewing athletes, I interviewed family members of victims of police brutality. I interviewed Emerald Garner (daughter of Eric Garner), Valerie and Allysza Castile (mother and sister of Philando Castile), Tiffany Crutcher (sister of Terence Crutcher), and Jahvaris Fulton (brother of Trayvon Martin). These were the most difficult interviews I have ever conducted. The emotions were overwhelming. I have been committed to helping them with foundations, advocating for their causes, speaking at fundraisers, and trying to help in any way I can.

Last year, Tiffany Crutcher introduced me to a group of powerful women called Sisters of the Movement. I am so impressed with these amazing women who all share a common bond of having a sibling taken away from them by police terrorism. They are organizing together, channeling their grief through advocacy. The group is dedicated to lobbying for federal police reform in an effort to help prevent other Black and Brown people from being killed by the police without accountability.

They created a five-point proposal for federal legislation and met with lawmakers. They sat down with Donald Trump when he was president; US Senator Tim Scott, who led the police reform platform proposed by Senate Republicans; as well as President Joe Biden and other senators.

The sisters are demanding a "zero tolerance" policy that would disarm any police officer who receives an infraction for excessive use of force; mandatory independent investigations when police use of force results in death; an end to qualified immunity for police; increased oversight of federal funds that go to state and local police departments; and mandatory, independent psychological evaluations and background checks for police department applicants.

They are also independently fighting for local laws in their own cities and states, because each city and state presents a unique set of challenges and issues. In addition, each police department operates differently. So they attack the issues from federal, state, and local levels collectively.

When they met with Trump at the White House, he promised federal investigations of all of their cases, but unsurprisingly, he didn't follow through. Overall, they didn't get the support they hoped for from Trump or Scott, who is the Senate's lone Black Republican. Unfortunately, it appeared that those men were more interested in playing politics and shifting the blame to the Democrats for inaction. Nonetheless, the Sisters of the Movement remained fully committed to their goals. They brought their plan to Joe Biden and the Democrats once he took the reins. Cofounder Alissa Findley told me, "I don't think [the Republicans] see an issue. I think they see it as Black people complaining again."

Meanwhile, Findley said that Biden's campaign has expressed a willingness to work with the sisters on police reform. Their conversations are ongoing.

As I told Mark Cuban, these are who the leaders of the movement should be. No disrespect to any of the other organizations who do great work, but some of them have received support from around the world, from companies, organizations, businesses, etc.—while the family members struggle to find support to fight for their loved ones.

These impacted family members and their efforts should receive *all* of the support. Many people aren't aware of the work they do, but they should be. They have turned their tragedies to purpose. While they are still grieving the losses of their loved ones, they are fighting to make sure laws are in place to ensure that nobody else has to go through the same pain. While many in the country are frustrated, angered, saddened, and disgusted by the daily police terrorism and murder of Black and Brown people, imagine how the family feels. They deserve all of the support possible.

Interview with Alissa Findley
(Sister of Botham Jean)

On September 6, 2018, off-duty Dallas Police Department patrol officer Amber Guyger entered the apartment of twenty-six-year-old accountant Botham Jean and fatally shot him. Guyger said she had walked into the apartment believing it was her own and she shot Jean believing he was a burglar. Guyger was not arrested for several days, then only charged with manslaughter, thereby creating mistrust in the process and outrage over the killing of an unarmed Black citizen. This resulted in protests and accusations of racial bias. Two months later, the charge was upgraded to murder. Over a year later, on October 1, 2019, Guyger was found guilty of murder. The next day, she received a sentence of ten years in prison.

I sat with Botham Jean's sister, Alissa Findley, who is cofounder of Sisters of the Movement, to discuss her experiences and hear about her passion for justice.

Etan: How are you doing right now?

Findley: Well, we just found out two days ago that Amber Guyger's appeal is scheduled for April 27. Right now I am angry that we have to now go through an appeal after we went through this emotional trial. Now we have to gear up for an appeal. So yes, I am angry, drained emotionally but I am ready for this fight.

Etan: Whenever the police kill someone, there are multiple story lines floating around. I can't imagine what new ones will arise with this appeal. Can we briefly revisit the facts of what happened to your brother?

Findley: With so many of these police brutality cases, there is video of what happened. But in the case of Botham, there was no video. So we can only go by the word of Amber Guyger and try to pick out the truth from what she says. Amber Guyger said she was on the wrong floor of South Side Flats, she got to the wrong door, she heard movement, went in, thought he was an intruder, shot him. That's her word. But when Botham was shot, the bullet went in just above his left nipple and it went straight down. That can only happen if he was lying down in the process of sitting up, for the bullet to take that trajectory. What she says is she opened the door and he was pacing back and forth. We know that's a lie based on the journey of the bullet. So things like that make it difficult to believe her. We know she's not remorseful because we are going through this appeal.

Etan: I remember Amber Guyger on the stand, shedding her white tears. I immediately got upset because I knew what she was doing. It's a tactic that white women have historically used to gain sympathy, and it works. What was your take on her tears?

Findley: I saw it immediately. In fact, one of the officers told me to keep it down or he was going to put me out. I was so upset. She sat up there, gave her little account, then the tears started flowing. The prosecutor asked her questions and more tears started. It was really upsetting. I feel myself getting upset all over just talking about it.

Etan: Do you think white America had sympathy for her when they saw her tears?

Findley: I think a lot of white America did feel sympathy for her because I actually got letters to my home chastising me, saying things like, *She is remorseful, it was an accident, why are you doing this to her*, etc. It was really unbelievable, but yes, she definitely gained sympathy.

Etan: Another thing that troubled me was the judge coddling her, then handing her the Bible. What was going on with that?

Findley: Well, sentencing was done. The prosecutor asked the family if we wanted to have final words. I said no because I was still upset from the sentencing. My mom said no, Dad said no, Brandt was the only one who said yes. Which was surprising to me because before, when they asked him to write, he kept saying, "No, I don't want to say anything." So it surprised us all when he said he wanted to say something. So he went up there and said he forgave her and asked to give her a hug . . . I was blown away, to be honest. When Brandt first started walking, I was looking for the quickest path to him because I thought he would get up there and be angry or lunge for her, because the walls of the courtroom were all lined with armed police, so I was thinking, *I need to protect my brother.* So the judge came down to the family. First she told me I was strong—she said something to all of us, then she went to Amber Guyger. She asked the judge for a hug and the judge said she needed to turn to God, and she said she didn't have a Bible, so the judge gave her a Bible.

Etan: The media really ran with it. This is something that bothers me: people are in the middle of grieving, and the media shoves the camera in their faces to exploit their emotions and pain. I don't know if that's the time to speak to any family members. How do you feel about that?

Findley: Well, I saw it firsthand. Immediately social media blew up saying, *We supported you through this whole process, how could you do this to us?* I posted about the appeal, and multiple people said things like, *I stopped following your family after this hug,* and, *What did you expect after you forgave her?* and, *Why are Black people always so forgiving?*

Let me make this clear: We, the family, didn't forgive Amber Guyger. Brandt, my brother, a teenager, forgave Amber Guyger. A few months prior to the trial he was robbed at gunpoint. He lost his brother, his best friend. Brandt was so angry he was about to implode, and he just turned silent. After we told him about Botham, he stopped speaking. We didn't know what he was thinking for a whole year. I'm happy he got to the point of forgiveness, because for someone his age to go through life with all this anger and rage, it wasn't good for him.

Etan: When people get invested in a case, they really feel like they are experiencing what the actual family is experiencing, and they're not. They can't judge how a family member should react. In contrast, after Eric Garner's case, his wife Esaw said the opposite. She was very angry, said, "No, I don't forgive him. I will never forgive him." People were mad at that. But you can't judge how she feels; there's no playbook of how you're supposed to react when your loved one is murdered by the police. Support shouldn't be conditional.

Findley: It's like the support comes at a cost. I'm happy we got support from the community across the world. But at the same time, I lost my brother, my mother lost her son. People have no idea how that feels. They couldn't even imagine. The anxiety, the PTSD, the nightmares. I needed a babysitter at my own home. I was having panic attacks whenever my husband would go to work. I couldn't be in the house by myself. So my father-in-law was on a schedule to babysit me. I received the phone call from the hospital, I was listed as his next of kin and I got the call that Botham was shot through his heart and he died, so every time the phone rang . . .

Etan: So while grieving, and fighting PTSD, you take on this plight to fight for justice for not only your loved one but impacted family members all across the country. Walk me through that process, because honestly, I don't know how you have the strength and the courage to do that.

Findley: I started the Botham Jean Foundation mainly because I really needed a distraction. I spoke with Botham every single day. Up to his last day on earth. He called me on his drive home like he always did, and we spoke until he got up to the apartment. We were talking about the first NFL game of the season—his friends invited him to go to a sports bar to watch it. He didn't really feel like going and I felt good, *He's gonna stay home and get rest.* Then I get this call that turned my entire world upside down that he had been shot.

I needed to occupy my mind and thoughts with something to honor him. I started connecting with other impacted family members who were all going through the same thing I was. The mothers had their thing, which was great, but I was talking to all of these sisters of police brutality victims, and if I needed to scream or vent or just ask questions, that's where all the sisters came in. We all had this one common goal, which is to fight for justice for our loved one. If I was having a bad day I could call Ashley Carr, sister of Atatiana Jefferson, or Tiffany Crutcher, sister of Terence Crutcher, or any one of the sisters, and we can support each other.

Etan: I wanted to connect y'all with Emerald Garner. I know how important that support network is.

Findley: Sisters of the Movement is so important because a lot of people think they can tell our stories better than us. They use our loved ones' names to further their organizations. You have so many people who donate to these big names and hashtags, but they don't give to the families to help push along what we are trying to do or to help us, and we are the family. We want to fight wholeheartedly, and sometimes we can't because funding goes to these big organizations who are fighting on behalf of us, but it doesn't go to us.

Etan: I know that's a real challenge. Tiffany Crutcher has expressed the pain and frustration of feeling exploited on one end, and left out of the funding on the other end, while fighting to get laws changed in Oklahoma so that what happened to her brother doesn't keep happening. Let me ask you: what is the best way for people to support Sisters of the Movement and the individual foundations run by family members?

Findley: The best way to support is to go directly. Sisters of the Movement's website is SistersOfTheMovement.org and you can donate right on the website. BothamJeanFoundation.org, you can also donate right on the website. Same for TerenceCrutcherFoundation.org and AtatianaProject.org. I would say if you really want to support the family, you can go to their foundation directly rather than some of these national organizations, because I will say firsthand, it does not trickle down to the families.

Etan: Let's go into a little detail about the efforts of Sisters of the Movement to change legislation.

Findley: One thing we've been doing is attacking policies on a federal level, because it will blanket the various states rather than going state to state. I've been working with the Monterrosa sisters along with the Grassroots Law Project, which is Shaun King's organization, where we meet with congressmen and -women and urge them to push various policies. One in particular that is dear to my heart is to have the Department of Justice be the mandatory organization investigating all police brutality situations. Botham was killed on Thursday evening; I got the call early, like 12:29 a.m. Friday, because New York is an hour ahead; I was in Texas on Friday and we met with the Texas Rangers, who are supposed to be the independent party investigating Botham's case. We met with Ranger Armstrong and every question we asked, his response was, "We cannot answer that." But he volunteered to tell us this was just an accident, no one is at fault here, she is very remorseful. Then he got on the stand a year later and repeated the same thing he told to us—it was just an accident. So from that experience, I don't trust the police to investigate themselves.

Etan: The Texas Rangers were the independent investigators appointed by the chief of police?

Findley: Yes, that's exactly right, and that didn't sound right to us either. He even took possession of Botham's car to see if there was anything there. So they really investigated this entire case to get Amber Guyger off. That's why I feel it is so important to have the DOJ be the organization to investigate all of these police brutality incidents. Right now it is optional for the chief of police to invite them, but when the police kill someone, I think it should be mandatory. If the DOJ finds the police officer was in fact in the wrong, they have the power to decertify that police officer. Once that officer is decertified on a federal level, they can no longer go to another state or another county and get rehired. So we've been working on that.

Etan: Which congresspeople have you spoken to?

Findley: Tiffany Crutcher and I had a call with Senator Tim Scott from South Carolina to urge him to add more substance to his police reform bill, and it was a roadblock. The first thing he said was, "This is a dead issue, but I'll listen to you."

Etan: The Monterrosa sisters told me about some congresspeople who wanted to help and others who didn't. They said Nancy Pelosi wanted to help them.

Findley: Yes, Congresswomen Cori Bush has been very supportive. For those who haven't been supportive, I would have to create a list, because there are so many. I remember Congresswoman Eleanor Holmes Norton (DC) immediately told us if we are not her constituents, why would she speak with us, and she had a lot to do. She was so dismissive. I didn't want to be disrespectful but she did not want to hear us because we were not from DC. That's what she actually said out of her mouth to us while we were on the phone with her.

Etan: I think you need to call all of them out. You mentioned Shaun King and his Grassroots Law Project—how has he supported what you are doing?

Findley: Shaun King has been very supportive from day one with my brother's case. The Grassroots Law Project highlights cases like this, they try to help by running campaigns or pressuring a case to be reopened. For instance, they are working with DJ Henry's parents—he was killed ten years ago and his parents and sister, who is part of Sisters of the Movement, have been trying to get that case reopened. The Grassroots Law Project applies pressure, petitions, and has people calling the DA's office to urge them to reopen the case. They help give voices to the voiceless and help push policies to fight police brutality.

Interview with Amber and Ashley Carr
(Sisters of Atatiana Jefferson)

Twenty-eight-year-old Atatiana Jefferson was shot to death in her home by a police officer in Fort Worth, Texas, in the early morning of October 12, 2019. Police arrived when a neighbor called a non-emergency number, stating that Jefferson's front door was open. Police body camera footage shows officers walking outside the home with flashlights for a few minutes before one of them yells, "Put your hands up! Show me your hands!" and discharges his weapon through a window. Police stated they found a handgun near Jefferson's body, which, according to her eight-year-old nephew, she was pointing toward the window before being shot. On October 14, 2019, Officer Aaron Dean, the shooter, resigned from the Fort Worth Police Department and was arrested on a murder charge. On December 20, 2019, Dean was indicted for murder. Jefferson was Black and the officer who shot her is white, prompting news outlets to compare this shooting to the murder of Botham Jean in nearby Dallas.

Etan: Paint the picture of your sister Atatiana.

Ashley: She was the youngest of four. Our mother called us the A-team because all of our names start with A. She was determined and feared no obstacle. She went off to school out of state to Xavier and graduated. When she had a plan, she was going to execute it. She was a fun person to be around, a big jokester. She played video games in the wee hours. Those were the times you could call her and have long conversations and she would be there for you. She would listen to you complain, then say, "Now let's figure this out and execute this plan." It was crazy because I was the big sister but she would counsel all of us. She was so much to us. She was the glue that held us together. Gave us tough love when we needed it, supported us with anything, and always looked out for all of us. We really miss her.

Etan: It really hurts my heart to hear that. I watched an interview with the neighbor, James Smith. He explained how he was just trying to be neighborly, check on his neighbor. He called the police department's non-emergency line for a wellness check. He saw the door that was partially opened, which people do in the South—keep the door open to catch the breeze. I watched how devastated and guilty he felt for calling the police. He has so much regret. Correct me if I'm wrong, but the blame lies on officer Aaron Dean and his mishandling of the situation once he arrived, right?

Ashley: I don't think Mr. James was making a call for my sister to die. He even called a non-emergency line, which says, *We don't need any guns, we just want you to check on someone.* And to know that your act of kindness led to your neighbor losing their life, that's a heavy thing to bear. But I don't blame him at all, this was not his fault. This was the fault solely of the police.

Etan: So walk me through what happened once Officer Dean arrived. I saw the Dallas–Fort Worth police put out a picture of a gun afterwards to try to justify everything, as if Texas isn't an open-carry state that prides itself on gun support.

Ashley: Well, let's start with my mom's house. It has no back door, just windows and a front door. He showed up ready for a big showdown. He went inside the back gate where Atatiana's room is, and behind the back is a vacant building. There's nothing back there and no reason to hear any noise back there. He comes inside the back gate, said he perceived a threat from my sister looking out the window. And he shot her. Without giving any commands, he never announced himself, it was as if that was the plan for when he would arrive there. My sister wasn't a criminal, she was a graduate. She wasn't a threat to him, she was in the house minding her business.

Etan: Is it correct that there is still no trial date?

Ashley: No, there isn't. As I'm sitting here with you, we still don't have a trial date. Indicted him on December 19 of 2019, but there's no trial date set. There are cases in other cities and they have actual dates to look toward and hold out hope for a day of judgment—we have nothing. I don't know if the goal is to simmer it down as much as possible, but it's simmered. A lot of people don't even talk about my sister anymore. She's like a pass-over and she shouldn't be. They act like we are bothering them when we call and try to figure out what's going on. They give us the runaround and shift the blame around.

Etan: Officer Aaron Dean was a rookie. That's no excuse—he should've known how to follow the right protocol, but he never announced himself as a police officer? This is what happened with Breonna Taylor's case. He yelled something and shot three seconds later, like Tamir Rice. He never announced himself or gave your sister time to comply with whatever he was trying to tell her to do. Why was his weapon drawn in the first place for a wellness call?

Ashley: There are so many issues with this. And they placed a gag order on our case, so nothing has been exposed to the public or even outside of the same things you've seen and read. Any extra information that's told to us or our lawyers, we can't publicly discuss.

Etan: According to the Dallas–Fort Worth training record, this officer has been through sensitivity and cultural diversity training, but obviously it didn't work. Is it even possible to train fear out of white officers of Black and Brown people or going into Black and Brown neighborhoods? They don't act like that when they encounter white people and go into white neighborhoods. How do you train that?

Ashley: I think that's a learned skill. I think it's part of your environment. If everyone around you thinks like that, it becomes your ideology. So we have to infiltrate those places and make them understand that there's nothing to fear about us. We're regular people and want the best for our families and our loved ones, just like you do.

Etan: It's interesting when people get stuck on the phrase "defund the police." There should be a whole different department and level of training for wellness checks. I would see it differently if the police were called for an armed situation, or someone was being held hostage. For a wellness check, there's just no need for the police.

Amber: Definitely. Since my sister's murder, I've met so many other families who have experienced their loved ones being killed by the police after a wellness check. There should be a whole different department sent. If that were the case, my sister would still be alive.

Ashley: When people hear "defund the police," they think we don't want the police to have any money. It has nothing to do with that. When me and Amber had the opportunity to go to Louisville for a protest about Breonna Taylor, the police had tanks out there for peaceful protesters. All we had was water and signs, and they were ready to go to war. That shouldn't be in the budget. If you're policing the community, why do you need all that? That money could have gone to fund a department for the non-emergency services. We're not saying that we don't want the police to have any money. We're saying they should redistribute the funds they have to service our community the correct way. Why would you give someone the responsibility of something they're not trained for? As my aunt would say, that's not their ministry. And it's sad that we have so many people who can't see that.

Etan: The police chief, Ed Kraus, said that after he reviewed the video of the body cam, he felt the officer violated police protocol about use of force police, etc., so he would've fired him if he didn't quit first. Is there anything to keep that officer from being rehired by another police department, especially if he quit?

Ashley: That's one thing that a lot of families are currently fighting for, because there is nothing stopping another department from hiring him. There's no criminal background, no nothing, so he can be rehired like nothing happened. Or if he is charged but not indicted, there's no criminal record of anything. So in essence, they announced that he was charged just to cool everybody down, because there is an uproar and this happens all over the country. That's why the alliance we've formed with Sisters of the Movement is trying to get legislation passed, so we don't have no-knock warrants and we can have a non-emergency department.

Etan: Tell me about the Atatiana Project, the foundation that you and your sister formed.

Ashley: We're focused on the youth. We want to expose youth to STEM and gaming centers and build a lot of Atatianas. We keep her legacy alive by transferring her passions to the younger generation. She was so brilliant, intelligent, and gifted, and we believe that with the right motivation and the right resources, all young people could be that too. But we have to pour into them.

Etan: One of the things I am always concerned with is how the nephew is doing. He was right there and witnessed everything that happened.

Amber: Zion is my son and he is a typical nine-year-old, but mentally he's different. He's been robbed of his innocence and it's hard for me to be honest. He understands what is happening and he gets it. He can't help but hear the interviews and see the videos. We've tried to keep him away from everything as much as possible and protect him, and haven't done interviews with him. He definitely has his moments and he's overcome with emotion, but he's nine, and it's just too much for any nine-year-old to deal with at times, to be honest.

Etan: I do a lot of work with Emerald Garner, and one of the things she always stresses is the need for mental health and therapy after someone loses their loved one. She always uses the example of Tamir Rice's sister, who missed like a hundred days of school and there was nothing in place to help her, and they just moved to the next case. How important is it for the impacted family members to get mental health assistance?

Amber: I can't even come up with the words of how important it is. For us, Zion—and I have a younger son, Zayden—for all three of us, when it comes to them, therapy is a process. Zion wants to be around people at times and he needs so much. He lost his aunt in front of him and blamed himself for the situation, for not protecting his aunt. He was eight at the time. He has nightmares. Talks about the moments leading up to everything that took place that night. His emotions are all over the place. We'll be watching TV or playing video games and it will just hit him. He needs a lot of help and I'm worried about him. He's smart, intelligent, and so great. I call him my superstar, but he shouldn't have to deal with all of this at age nine. He should be able to be a regular kid. But we are going to make it. I guarantee you that. A lot of people don't understand what the impacted family goes through, which is why I want to continue to highlight the efforts of the family members. Like Ashley said, people skip over it and go on to the next case, trending topic, or issue, and they forget the family is still dealing with trying to put the pieces together. A lot of people don't know that they still don't have a court trial date right now. That needs to be known. People need to still be up in arms, just like they were when this first happened. It's like they are trying to dupe the public into cooling off when they don't have any intention of doing anything about the issue. That's what I see. I love the fact that they are all connecting with each other and what they are doing with Sisters of the Movement. They don't need activists to speak for them, they can speak for themselves, but what I want to do is just help them with a platform to get their message out. The families are the people who the focus should be on. They didn't ask to be activists. They were thrown in the middle of all of this because their loved one was taken away from them. Outside people have in their minds of how impacted family members should conduct themselves. How they should feel. And I believe that is ridiculous. There is no script.

Interview with Michelle and Ashley Monterrosa
(Sisters of Sean Monterrosa)

Sean Monterrosa was unarmed and kneeling with his hands raised when Vallejo police officer Jarrett Tonn fatally shot him through the windshield of a moving police vehicle in a Walgreens parking lot during the early morning hours of June 2, 2020.

The family couldn't get any answers from the police that night. It took a day and a half for the police department to admit an officer had killed someone. The police union filed a temporary restraining order to prevent the release of the names of the officers involved. Later it was discovered that vital evidence—the windshield from the police car—had been destroyed, prompting an investigation by the California Department of Justice.

Sean was shot less than an hour from when he sent his last text message to his sisters. Officer Jarrett Tonn has been involved in multiple shootings in recent years. The Vallejo Police Department is currently under investigation for the alleged practice of bending their badges to commemorate fatal shootings, first reported by Open Vallejo. The Vallejo Police Department is also the third-most-murderous police department in California.

Etan: Can you tell me who your brother was?

Michelle: He was a loving and caring brother, he was our protector . . . We also all shared a bedroom, so we were all really close.

Ashley: It felt like we were triplets, honestly, but he was a great big brother and really took me under his wing and schooled me on what to look out for, what to do, what not to do. We were like a team. I was the younger sister, but it was like I was Robin and Sean was Batman. I was always with him. He was always on the driver's seat. I was always on the passenger seat and we were just always together. I was his protector just as much as he was my protector. We just all had each other's back.

Etan: It's important to humanize people and not speak about them as just a hashtag or just part of the details of a case. If you don't mind, Michelle, can you tell me a little more about your brother's personality?

Michelle: You can ask every single one of his teachers, they all loved him. A lot of teachers say we're not supposed to favor students, but seriously, all of his teachers said that he was one of their favorites. And not like a teacher's pet, they just all fell in love with his personality, his commitment to learning. He was happy and eager to learn. He had a thirst for knowledge and always wanted to know more and go deeper. For example, he read fifty books in one semester, and you know high school, it's hard to motivate students to read three books sometimes.

Ashley: He was hungry for knowledge. Always. And he was reading deep books. He was reading *The 48 Laws of Power*, the Malcolm X autobiography, Assata Shakur. He was really passionate about social justice, empowering himself and people in the community, but also educating himself on history that we're not taught.

Michelle: He always spoke for the voiceless. He didn't like when people were being taken advantage of and not valued and respected like everyone else. It bothered him.

Ashley: Also, Sean would always take off his shirt to give to the next person and give his very last dime to help the other person.

Michelle: Fighting for the little man was his purpose. It's what drove him. He was always up for the fight. No matter how big or how small. He wanted to fight for what was right. For himself and his community. Being a young Latino man, there are a lot of adversities you are always up against. But Sean was ready to take each one head-on. That's who our brother was.

Ashley: Yeah, I really miss him.

Michelle: He was just an amazing person all around. Like, I looked up to him although I am older than him. I really admired him.

Etan: He sounds like an amazing person. Walk me through what happened.

Michelle: We got a text message from him at 11:49 to sign a petition on June 1, to fight for justice for George Floyd. And of course we both signed it. We supported any cause my brother wanted us to support. He didn't respond, and we started to get worried. It was late so we were about to go to bed, but it didn't feel right not hearing a reply. A girl my brother had just recently met and was hanging out with calls us saying Sean was dead, hysterically crying. As soon as she said that, I immediately got on my knees and started praying.

Ashley: There was a curfew at the time so we weren't allowed to go out after eight p.m. But we were like, "Forget them rules, this is my brother, my Batman," and we went to Vallejo.

Michelle: So we're driving and not really talking, but we were both feeling sick to our stomachs. We both felt that something wasn't right. I actually felt like I was going to throw up the entire night and was struggling to keep it together.

Ashley: And for me, I had some of the worst stomach pains I have ever had in life, the pain was almost unbearable. And at the same time, I'm completely nervous because I have no idea what we are about to find once we get to Vallejo. All types of terrible scenarios were going through my head.

Michelle: When we finally got there, we didn't get any of our questions answered. We knew that the police murdered Sean. We didn't know why or how. We didn't know anything.

Ashley: And we know our brother. I know you always hear people say that, but we really know him and we know what he's into and what he's not into. And we couldn't imagine what justification they could possibly come up with for doing what they did. He didn't even have a gun.

Michelle: He didn't even have a gun. What could possibly have gone so terribly wrong that they felt they needed to do what Jarrett Tonn did to him?

Ashley: He was shot in the neck and out the head. Then they flipped him over and handcuffed him, kept my brother in handcuffs until the paramedics came. I mean, what kind of human beings would do that?

Michelle: And it just goes to show how fearful these cops are with unarmed Black and Brown men. Even when they're dead, you're still scared of them? Terrified to the point that you have to . . . [*begins to cry*]. I'm sorry.

Etan: Please don't apologize to me. We can stop and take a break if you need.

Ashley: I'll jump in. This is what we do, we help each other when the emotions become too much. But my sister was saying, you're so scared of Black and Brown men that you still have to turn them over and handcuff them knowing that you already have . . . [*deep breath*]. The way the entry wound went into my brother, you know that he is no longer alive. Nobody can survive that. And the car didn't even stop. Jarrett Tonn was in the backseat. So my brother was not a threat to anyone. My brother is laying there dead but you still "feared for your life"?

Michelle: At the end of the day, Jarrett Tonn cannot be the executioner, the judge, and the jury. He can't be the one to decide that my brother doesn't deserve to live anymore. Whatever our brother was doing, it's not punishable by death. It just hurts. But I promise, I promise to never stop fighting for Sean and the other voiceless in Vallejo.

Ashley: You know, Sean's a martyr now, and martyrs never die. He had his sisters who will always be fighting for him.

Michelle: It just goes to show at the end of the day that my brother will not die in vain. I feel like my brother, with his last text message, it was a message to us to continue to fight.

Etan: I am sure Sean is looking down at you all from heaven right now, proud of his sisters for honoring him. Tell me how you are fighting for him. I saw that you all were meeting with some senators and congresspeople about getting the laws changed.

Michelle: Yes, Speaker of the House Nancy Pelosi has been great. Not only did she talk with us, but she released a whole statement of support. It reads, "I join Sean's family, Vallejo city officials, and community members in calling for an FBI investigation into Sean's murder, including into the destruction of essential evidence in this homicide case. We must insist on justice and accountability to honor Sean's life and the lives of all killed by police brutality in America."

Etan: That's a strong statement.

Ashley: Unlike the governor, who got us arrested for protesting at his house.

Etan: Wait, what . . . ?

Michelle: That's a long story.

Etan: I got time.

Michelle: Things weren't moving fast enough for us after our brother was killed. So we went to Governor Newsom's house. There were maybe twenty of us and we protested in front of his house demanding that he appoint a special prosecutor to investigate the case.

Ashley: Nothing was happening. There was no criminal investigation into Sean's death. They were just giving us the runaround. Then the Solano County district attorney, Krishna Abrams, recused herself from investigating the case, and Attorney General Xavier Becerra hadn't said that they were going to do any investigating. They were literally acting like nothing happened.

The police weren't just *not* doing anything, they were trying to cover everything up. Chief Williams confirmed the windshield Jarrett Tonn shot through was not preserved as evidence. Why would they do that if they weren't trying to cover it all up? They keep everything as evidence always. That's like their policy. But all of a sudden, with Sean, they don't preserve the windshield? They didn't even want to release Jarrett Tonn's name. Local media did that. So they are protecting the officer who killed our brother and they want us to just accept that? We weren't going to let them do that.

Etan: What happened while you were at his house? Did he stand with y'all? Because Newsom presents as if he is so liberal and for the people.

Michelle: Well, I don't know about all that, but I do know he had us arrested. He did not stand with us or support us at all. They charged us with trespassing, unlawful assembly, failure to disperse, failure to disperse at a public disturbance, and conspiring to commit a crime against the governor.

Ashley: They acted like we were going to harm the governor, like we were the people who stormed the US Capitol. We were girls with signs. We weren't doing anything violent. We were being extra civil, actually. We just wanted to have a conversation with Newsom and we told them that. All we wanted was for him to make a statement to appoint a special prosecutor, and fire and arrest Jarrett Tonn for murdering our brother. They were the ones being aggressive and saying, "Leave, or else."

Michelle: They arrested all of us, and we have yet to sit down with California Governor Gavin Newsom or Attorney General Xavier Becerra, who now has a cabinet position in the Biden administration. They act like they did us a favor by dropping the ridiculous charges that shouldn't have been made in the first place. But we want justice for our brother and we're going to keep fighting for justice for our brother.

Etan: How have some senators and congresspeople supported you?

Michelle: Some have, and you would expect the people of color to definitely support you, right? But that doesn't always happen.

Etan: Interesting. Who in particular?

Ashley: I'll name them. The lady from DC, Eleanor Holmes Norton, she told us if this wasn't in her district, it wasn't really her concern.

Etan: She told y'all that?

Ashley: Yes, she acted like we were bothering her or something. And Tim Scott in South Carolina, he acted like we were the bad guys and tried to lecture us on how valuable the police are in society. Cory Booker was good and Cori Bush was great. So we have had some good experiences too.

Etan: That's good, but it's important to put some of these politicians on blast, because they act liberal and present as if they are for the people, and you are just asking for them to do their jobs and push for language to be put in bills that would actually have an effect on police brutality and police accountability. So the fact that Eleanor Holmes Norton here in DC said that to y'all, people need to know that.

Michelle: But we have had a lot of support from so many activists and organizers—that part has been great. So many have shown up for us, like Jamilia Land, who introduced us. Like Gathering for Justice and Justice League CA. We have also met the family members of several other police brutality victims who have welcomed us into the club no one wants to join. Through and in community with them, we have become even more committed to creating a system of public safety that doesn't leave sisters and mothers and fathers and grandparents and uncles and cousins dealing with this same pain.

Etan: I should connect you with Sisters of the Movement.

Michelle: We're already connected with them. I love the work they're doing. We have already been on calls with senators pushing for laws to be changed. Alissa, Tiffany, Ashley, and Amber are all great.

Ashley: I'm definitely glad we connected with them. Let me also say that we wouldn't have been able to make it without our mother. It's crazy because two years ago, our mother actually prophesied that we would have this huge platform and be doing all of this amazing work for so many people, and honestly, I just brushed it off.

Michelle: I did too, honestly.

Ashley: That just isn't our personality. Not before all of this. That's what Sean was into. I just wanted to be a regular teenager. But now, this has become my life mission. I sleep and eat justice. This is all I care about. Nothing else matters.

Michelle: We understand and accept the call on our lives to advocate for those no longer here to do so themselves. We also understand that there is trauma in mourning a loved one. So many family members are bleeding, with no relief or healing. That's why it's been so great to connect with networks like Sisters of the Movement, so we can help each other grieve and fight and advocate for change together.

With our mom as the spiritual center and heartbeat of everything we do, we are committed to keep pushing for justice, change, and the removal of all officers involved in the shooting, as well as an impartial special prosecutor to investigate Sean's case and the entire department's violent policing practices. No family should suffer in silence or beg for crumbs of justice. No family should have to operate like a machine when what we truly need is grief support and transparency. We, too, deserve peace, joy, care, and empathy. We deserve to be listened to.

Ashley: So we don't have a problem showing up on an elected official's lawn, if that's what it takes to make sure our voices are heard and not ignored. They are the ones who swore an oath to protect and serve us, not terrorize us and murder our loved ones with no accountability.

 *Afterword*

A war is being waged upon us . . . You cannot keep having reactionary responses.

> —Chairman Fred Hampton Jr.

Chairman Fred Hampton Jr. is the son of assassinated Black Panther deputy chairman Fred Hampton Sr. and Comrade Mother Akua Njeri. He is the founder of the Prisoners of Conscience Committee and the Black Panther Party Cubs. Hampton is an active community organizer dedicated to fighting for justice, and has picked up the torch left by his father.

Interview with Chairman Fred Hampton Jr.

Etan: I want to open up with the movie *Judas and the Black Messiah*. What was your reaction to it? Was it traumatizing? Did it bring up a lot of anger?

Hampton Jr.: The actual release? To this day I have not watched it from a viewer's perspective. We were on the set, myself and my mother, Comrade Akua Njeri, in the capacity of cultural experts and consultants. There were a lot of battles on the set even for things like credits, because *everything* is political: words, terms, even the soundtrack. The release of the trailer, the type of discussions that were happening, for example, people acknowledging that it was Chairman Fred who authored the Rainbow Coalition. In essence, to answer your question, amongst other feelings, it was and it has been therapeutic.

Etan: Explain the therapeutic part. Was it therapeutic or was it retraumatizing, because that's your history, your life? Like toward the end, when the police came in and they put the gun to Fred Hampton's wife's stomach, that was *you* in there.

Hampton Jr.: We have a saying, the Black Panther Cubs, we say, *The people's pain reflects*. And actually it's our story. Even though the United States government had assassinated and taken my father, in a graphic depiction it reflects on what the system does to all of our fathers and mothers in one way or another by shooting them down, stringing them out, locking them up, breaking them. Taking them from us in one way or another. My situation is a microcosm of what happens to our people in one form or another.

The mantra of the Alcoholics Anonymous is the first step in addressing the problem is in recognizing we have a problem. This has been a discussion, it's been an issue with regard to revolutionaries and what happened to revolutionaries. If people have the conversation, they have it in a "coded" sort of way, like a southern secret. We know it but don't know it. I just had a discussion with a brother who said, "Chairman, a lot of people don't know." I said, "Nah, I beg to differ. They *do* know." That's the reason why people are hesitant about interviewing us and about having this conversation. We are just told not to acknowledge it. So this climate, to have the conversation, to acknowledge it, you know what I'm saying? Again, it's been therapeutic.

Etan: What was your reaction to the film's portrayal of the government's infiltration of the Panthers?

Hampton Jr.: We acknowledge these contradictions. Reality is the counterinsurgency. In other words, the war that has been waged on Black people in particular and other colonized communities in general, it's been consistent. There is an attempt to have a romanticism or to simplify what the Portuguese, Spaniards, English, and other colonizers did, and how they just kidnapped our people from Africa and the whole breaking process. They would take Africans and spread them throughout the Diaspora. The breaking-up of the families and the communities. Taking away the communication, the strategy of making the drum illegal in North America. These are parts of the counterintelligence and it's important to acknowledge.

The role that the schools, infiltration, and the media all play, all of these different dynamics must be included in the conversation. I recall the struggle. That's the other thing, objectivity. J. Edgar Hoover, in particular, was not just depicted as simply some racist white person. Once you start coming to some subjective points of view, it offsets the ecosystem. He was a representative of a machine that's ongoing. COINTELPRO, there's a science to it, it studies our contradictions and it exploits them.

Fast-forward to the Black Panther Party, the different chapters in the Black Panther Party. Similar to what I said earlier in regards to the assassination of my father, Chairman Fred Hampton: it's a blatant example of what happens to some degree in *all* the communities. The COINTELPRO, the counterinsurgency, it happens in our community, in the hip-hop arena, the streets, the music industry, all this, but the Black Panther Party heightened the contradictions. That was the term you heard, even in the movie, throughout our sit-downs and our political education we had with Daniel Kaluuya and others. That's something he remembers, that I always pushed in the script about heightening the contradictions. One of our initial concerns was the fact that the narrative would be coming from the perspective of William O'Neal, one of the agent provocateurs that was placed inside of the Black Panther Party.

Etan: *One* of them, right.

Hampton Jr.: One. When we were on the campaign, we said, "Hashtag, William O'Neal was not the only one." You cannot come through the movie industry and say you want to do a movie on Chairman Fred Hampton. Before it gets to the boardroom, it's gonna be stopped. And this is something people have to acknowledge because in many cases people tend to romanticize revolution. You want to look at the leather jackets, the berets, and say how great this is. But we deal with situations with the politics of the Black Panther Party, acknowledging the good, the bad, and the ugly. But if you're not familiar with who Fred Hampton was . . . In fact, Daniel Kaluuya said when there was criticism about actor/musician LaKeith Stanfield, he said, "You have to see who Chairman Fred Hampton was *not*, to see and appreciate who he was."

Minister Huey P. Newton said the contradictions are the ruling principle of the universe. Many organizations and individuals, whether race privilege or class privilege, can afford to just look at the nice, to just cherry-pick. A lot of people just say, and this is a quote from Chairman Fred Hampton Jr., "a lot of people option to be Black when it's beneficial. Play Panther when it's profitable. Connect to Cubs when it's comfortable." But this is a 24/7 situation for us.

So much misinformation, from revisions of history, bogus unauthorized books. People who may have been in the Black Panther Party—now mind you, we distinguish a person from being a Black Panther from those who were in the Black Panther Party. It's the difference between being a noun and an adjective. It's that dynamic of distinguishing the authentic, being the Black Panther Party even when it's not fashionable.

The continuous counterinsurgency, the situations that Tupac talked about with his mother, couldn't get employment. My mother going through those situations, also never could obtain steady employment. And in the face of watching other people benefit off the blood, sweat, and tears of Chairman Fred and Mark Clark.

Etan: In continuing your father's work, how do you not only honor his legacy but honor the legacy of his work?

Hampton Jr.: We say, your legacy is more important than your life because with life, we are going to be forced inside this physical shell for only a certain amount of time. Legacy serves as a template or a prototype. We utilize the philosophical tool, dialectical materialism, which amongst other things lays out to us that nothing stays exactly the same. What happened two minutes ago is history. We respect it as that. It's ever-developing. The legacy of the Black Panther Party, the politics of the Black Panther Party. They have something to do with the race and the class contradiction.

The core of capitalism, it may use different euphemisms in regards to where they are located. May have ups and downs throughout periods of history. But the deal is, what kept me alive, what kept my sanity amongst other things, is the ideology of the Black Panther Party. We're wedded with theory and practice. So our thing is, even if it does not sound fashionable, is to continuously wed theory and practice.

In other words, if you become a member of the Black Panther Party Cubs, you gotta put some skin in the game. You gotta get some dirt up under them claws. You can't just get up on no, do what Chairman Fred called "intellectual masturbation." You got to get out there into the community. You got to engage in the triple C's, children, community, and Cubs, which obviously is the Black Panther Party's free breakfast program. You have to go out there for the program, serving the people, engaging in the conditions, making the mistakes. Right now we're in the process of getting our forces together, to go down for this annual trip, every Father's Day, to Chairman Fred's tombstone, which law enforcement still shoots up every year like clockwork, they have not forgotten.

The world should see what this government goes to, to this day, annually shooting up the tombstone of Chairman Fred Hampton. Other people in our community say, "That was a long time ago." They do not forget. In fact, the colonialists, the slave masters, would raise their children for generations by telling them, "If you don't be good, the ghost of Nat Turner gonna come and get you." They know, they study our history.

Etan: Tell me about the Rainbow Coalition.

Hampton Jr.: A lot of people thought Jesse Jackson did it. A lot of people believe the public schools authored the first free lunch programs. Forgetting that the Black Panther Party started the first breakfast program. A lot of people will say, "Jesse Jackson of the Rainbow Coalition." It's a different dynamic. It's important context of the narrative, of the birthplace where they come from. Chairman Fred authored the Rainbow Coalition, and mind you, in a city that for all practical purpose remains one of the top segregated cities in the country. This is important to point out. The race contradiction in Chicago is a different dynamic.

So I just want to set what we're dealing with. Chairman Fred put his ear to the ground, he's a realist. Lot of people would say, "Well, we shouldn't be talking to these gang members," 'cause mind you, not only the race contradiction, but also the class contradiction. There has to be, at some point, a clash of the titans.

Cook County, at one time, was the largest county of Black people per capita, and housed the headquarters of every Black organization in the country. The Rainbow Coalition with Chairman Fred: who he took to which meetings, how he studied, which forces he touched down, when. The timing of the dialogue with Cha Cha Jiménez and leadership of the Young Lords.

The Young Patriots who were so reactionary at a time when they were wearing Confederate flags on their jackets. One thing you see, when people talk about coalitions, it's a lack of respect for self-determination. People say, "We come to help you." No, you come to *control* us, you come to run your agenda through us. Chairman Fred was a respected leader. He respected that precious entity of self-determination, how and when he moved, who he met with. All of this was taken into account.

Etan: The thing that would always fascinate me about Chairman Fred Hampton when you are setting the scene of what Chicago was at that time frame, organizing with the Young Patriots—that was something that was just unheard of. What Chairman Fred showed was that by unifying the have-nots, no matter what color they were, no matter where they were from, they could bond together and work against the haves. How can you apply that concept to today?

Hampton Jr.: Not how *can* we do it, how *are* we doing it? Let me tell you what we doing. When the twelve-year-old child from the Mexicano community was gunned down by the Chicago police, we was right there on the scene when it went down. The Black Panther Party Cubs, the Brown Berets, right there on 18th Street, we were right there on the streets. People waiting on the system to come tell us what's happening. This is happening *right now*. We have been doing this.

This must be inclusive in every conversation. A lot of people want reactionary. It's easy to say, "Okay, Black and white." We have to deal with some more detailed situations. We had to deal with December the fourth, 1969. Not just Hanrahan but James "Gloves" Davis, Del Howard, the other Negro pig that came along for the assassination. Our organization, the Black Panther Party Cubs, the amount of Negroes who they have used, agent provocateurs, they have sent at us. If we relate it to what Lenin said of the Russian Revolution, we define situations on how you view the state and how the state views you.

Etan: I remember watching the Rodney King beating. I remember hearing all the older folks saying, "That happens all the time." Talk to me about what went through your mind when you first saw the Rodney King verdict. Was it pretty much the same thing?

Hampton Jr.: Are you familiar with the case where I was sentenced to eighteen years in the penitentiary? The motive that the judge and the state's attorney gave was, that it was either a Mother's Day present for my mother or that it was in response to the Rodney King verdict.

They said I supposedly firebombed two Korean-owned stores right outside of Chicago. During a "trial," really it was actually a legal lynching, it was questionable if the store had even been firebombed. Sometimes we have a simplistic response, no slight on your grandparents and your elders, it's deeper than "this just happens."

You can go back on one of the largest drafts in United States history, July 1969, Los Angeles. They strategically did this draft to sweep up, because they smell potential uprisings happening. They know which locations, how big is the resistance, what's going to kick up, different penitentiaries and different individuals. The Black Panther Party, they knew who to target, who was serious and what plants. In sports, you are going to play basketball, let's say, we're gonna play the Nets. Who has an Achilles injury? Even down to the point of who is going through some issues *right now*? You study it. It's a structure with playing basketball, it's a respect for it. It's not just subjective, like this is my friend. How long has this person been with this team? How do they jive with each other?

With the location of Los Angeles when it went down, all those different dynamics, you have certain situations where you say, "That's it." With the conscious level of the people. Is it conducive? Can the people relate to something? There are conversations that I can have with people now that last year they couldn't hear it. There are certain moments in history where you say, "Whoa, wait a minute." The media says one of the biggest mistakes they made with Malcolm X was giving him access to the media. Certain individuals, even with the uprisings and the rebellions, you have to distinguish the time and the climate.

Ferguson, we call Mike Brown Town. The different responses you have. Go back and look at their responses, as opposed to the motus operandi years before that. Waited an eternity to come speak. The usual: same usual suspects come to be the spokesperson for the people. These are different dynamics. There is a different dynamic of coming up in a community where you made contact is just forbidden.

Etan: I spoke to Chikesia Clemons, who is from Alabama, and was beaten in a Waffle House, viciously. The police came in and beat her. Her top came up. She was exposed and they were trying to break her arm. All of that because she asked for some plastic utensils. Looking at the way our women are treated, looking at different cases, Breonna Taylor, Sandra Bland, and how the officers said that she was a threat because of her attitude and the fact that she raised her voice—talk to me about how important it is for us as a community to protect our women. That's something that the Panthers always had as a principle and I've heard you speak on many times.

Hampton Jr.: Put it in context: a war is being waged upon us. It puts it in context where, if you are engaging, you cannot keep having reactionary responses. We upped the ante. The war being waged on our people is because of the system. One week you hear about the boys, and the vicious gangs, then it's the women are engaging in crime now. It is a war on the people and it encompasses and it provides a protector, a safety net.

Everything is political. When I come speak, I hear, "Oh, here come Chairman Fred, he's going to blame the white man, or the government." I say, "Yes, and your point is what?" You all talk about Black-on-Black crime. Tell you what we have an issue with. It's a message sent to children, or to people, "I can do this to other Black people." It's a message, how we view our women. The policies, the politics, it puts it in context. It doesn't trivialize or reduce it. This is a war being waged on our people. How we deal with contradictions, because there are contradictions. We have issues in the community, when you call the police on each other. When you do certain damages. The impact of how we view ourselves, it's a war.

The state studies the DNA of the individual, lock you up during your reproductive period. You must look at this in regards to everything with our women. If you look at chattel slavery, the intent of it, they would rape the woman in front of the man. Even the system says rape is not sexual, they say there is a clinical and political analysis to it. Protecting our women and children but not in the bourgeois sense that relegates them to some sort of subjective, you the woman stand behind me. They are locking men, women, and children up, and the reality is all these forces have to be inclusive in this battle in defense of our people and our self-determination.

Etan: Donald Trump said something like, "I'm going to tell you all to put away your differences and unite over this enemy over here." He used racism as a tactic. Just thinking about how he approached things, it was like the evil form of what Chairman Fred Hampton did. Do you know the connection that I'm making?

Hampton Jr.: I hear you, but I think we sell ourselves short. Chairman Fred did not operate on an island of his own. William O'Neal did not operate on an island of his own. Long-held political prisoner Mumia Abu-Jamal told me on a visit years back, "Keep doing what you do, and you don't even have your daddy's team."

We're on the heels of some reactionary times. There have been so many counterfeit agendas about the Black Panther Party. This a time now, where people say, "Know what's what." You can't sell snake oil no more. People ain't going for it. You cannot talk about a different contradiction of the individual in a bubble.

The climate with Trump. Trump would say himself, the detainees, they been back here since Carter was around. This ain't nothing new. The president of France, they call him the Trump of France. So it's a climate. Contradictions that exist and the fact that people are not acknowledging. During the campaign, Trump—and let me preface with this, because I ain't pushing for no Trump—was acknowledging contradictions. Trump said, during the debate with Hillary Clinton, "The system is rigged." That's what he said. He said, "Black people, what do you have to lose?" The Democratic Party and all these other special interest groups wouldn't even say, "Black people." Won't even say the word "Black."

This climate, it can be correlated to the tenure of former president Richard Milhous Nixon. Coming off the heels of a class peace, from President John F. Kennedy. I know I'm gonna offend some people that got his picture up. We talking about the same President John F. Kennedy who authorized his brother, Attorney General Robert F. Kennedy, to wiretap Dr. King. Same President John F. Kennedy who authorized army tanks to be deployed throughout the South Side of Chicago and throughout Detroit, Michigan. Same President John F. Kennedy who had assassination attempt after assassination attempt of Comandante Fidel Castro, Bay of Pigs. But there was a class peace that existed when Nixon pulled the covers off. Campaign for "law and order." Not saying these contradictions did not exist, but an acknowledgment.

The dynamic is about, people can debate about how what's said or what's said, at certain times when people just acknowledge certain contradictions. It's a step up. The fact that people didn't even use terms like "postracial society" in America. People was going for that.

Etan: After President Obama, yeah, that was the term.

Hampton Jr.: In America! Race has been one of the top twos. The fact that this system is so Machiavellian that however you feel about it, that you would even say that term "postracial society." In America?

Etan: You're 100 percent correct. Looking at January 6, where the Trump supporters overran the US Capitol. We know there's things that white people can get away with that we can't get away with. We've seen the different footage and experiences of white people cussing out the police and nothing happening to them. White people spitting on the police, saying, "I'll have your badge number." We have to be angels, do everything right and don't make sudden movements. For that many people to be able to descend upon the US Capitol, climb the walls, walk up the stairs, walk past the guards into the building, walking through the offices, twirling around on the chairs, taking pictures, everything like that. And it not end up in a big slaughter? That was amazing to see even though we know white privilege exists. Would you agree?

Hampton Jr.: We don't know. We may think we know in a reactionary sort of way, in the edited version that they give us. A lot of time we get the end effect. Like Trump—lot of people are saying America is racist because of Trump. There's a whole process that's been going on. I would be cautious about even using the term "invasion." Everything down to even the transportation to get there. Could you imagine, just getting there without getting pulled over? The case in Wisconsin, the white teenager, just even riding with the gun with your mother into Wisconsin. The different dynamics must be inclusive in the conversation. "White people stick together, they were so brave, they invaded." No, you *encouraged*, you pulled up, they opening doors for you. There's something told to you. Imagine Black people saying, "Hey man, we're going to head down here." What? You going *where*? I remember we told some children to come down to City Hall, to see what was going on. They said, "Chairman, are you crazy?" This is Chicago City Hall. We want y'all to come see these politicians, the laws. "Man, I'm not going downtown, are you crazy?" They know about the tickets, the boots, the fines. We're told directly and indirectly what we can do.

When we say self-determination, our organizations and our music, we are told what to say. You want your stuff to play, all right. What the cat, Herbo, he had some song and said Fred Hampton as opposed to Donald Trump for president, he didn't get no airplay. He did the song "Chi-Raq" with Nicki Minaj, he comes back later with a song and says something about Obama. You're told what to say and what not to say. It's generationally passed down. On main street radio, up in the morning, they're told not only is it legal, this is the business. There's peer pressure for children and everybody else. You can be in your own subjective bubble. A sister told me, "I don't let my daughter listen to Nicki Minaj." While we're talking, her daughter is playing a video game with Nicki Minaj in the background.

Back to the movie, *Judas and the Black Messiah*, I had to raise this. Why is it the Black Panther Party is the only one with all these cigarettes? I'm not negating that they smoked, but in contrast you have a generation that has not seen people on TV or in the media smoking cigarettes. You don't have the feds smoking, or the Young Patriots. One person said, "You know, you're right, Chairman."

Etan: What is the best way, in your opinion, to achieve real police reform? Is it through each police department?

Hampton Jr.: Ain't no absolutes. We come in with the politics. When you talking about a family situation, organizations, I don't have this false illusion that everyone in the Black Panther Party was on the same agenda. We have been taught the narrative that the American Revolution was related to what Patrick Henry said. "Give me liberty or give me death." The reality is, what Thomas Jefferson said the American Revolution was: one-third was for it, one-third was against it, and one-third went whichever way the wind blew. That's the reality.

They had tried to raise some of my family members up, to try to go for the more palatable individual. Antoine Fuqua did a movie on my father but didn't talk to me, he went and got my uncle. I want the narrative to be written that we want self-determination. This has to be reassessed by situations, you have to take into context the climate. Don't draw the forgone conclusion that we all want the same thing. They have a policy and the lawyers tell a lot of the family members, "Don't even talk to Fred Hampton Jr. Stay far away from him."

Etan: Why is that?

Hampton Jr.: We heighten the contradictions. The whole system. A lot of times, they want to stage fights. They want to come in and say, "Okay, this is a bad policeman." Get a little payoff and keep on going. We say what Frantz Fanon said, "You can accept the concession, but never compromise our principles." They so Machiavellian, you gonna play like you chose them. You don't gotta do that. We was laughing recently—a brother said, about his wife, "Yeah, I remember I seen you," and she start laughing and said, "No, I seen *you*. You thought you chose me." The system knows how to make us think that it was some choice that we made.

America's definition of diplomacy is letting others have their way. Be careful of some of the demands because of the emotions and stuff. You get caught up with it and get what the state wants you to get anyway. I'm encouraged. We've been fortunate with some of the families. It hurts, but you have to be ready to get back on that battlefield. So many cases, you have been put back to the side, and told this is your spokesperson, because you don't have a degree. You don't need an amicus brief to fight for this. This case with Chairman Fred, even with this movie, Amy Goodman, *Democracy Now!*, they didn't talk to us. Go back and look at who they interviewed. I grew up with the climate of Black radio stations, they found people that's not even Black Panther Party. I'm like, damn, you have a woman that was in the room with him that covered down when they were shooting up the house. They didn't want her. It's not because she's a woman. It's political. I say, if you are there, if you are involved in it, you should have some role to be acknowledged. The role has to be respected.

Etan: Let's go back a little. You said that a lot of the lawyers tell the families not to really communicate with you. How do you advise the families to go about pushing for justice? What is it that the lawyers are afraid of with you?

Hampton Jr.: We gonna do what we do. We gonna heighten the contradictions.

Etan: Elaborate, if you could.

Hampton Jr.: Sure. Contradictions exist. Lot of people engage in liberalism—don't say that, you gonna hurt somebody feelings. It's right in your face, the disproportionate amount of Black children lost because of the infant mortality rate. Before George Floyd was murdered. When these police, excuse me, when these *pigs* walk up on that car, watch the video. "Yes, boss." What has happened, study the video before they murder him. If you came around a person, and you see a dog bow down, you'd say, "What have y'all been doing to this dog?" This is seen as the norm in our community. We just dismiss it. We say, "No, let's have this conversation." It's right there, you don't need to be no rocket scientist. The "relationship" that the police have with our community from its inception. This is how it goes down, and it's not just because there's videos out there now. It's 'cause the class peace is being shattered.

There are conversations now, on the streets, in regards to police terrorism. In the school system. This climate of the coronavirus is capitalism on steroids. They say we gotta go extra hard in the Black community about the vaccine because they don't trust it. Let's have the conversation about why not. People not waiting on you, we organizing. People are seeing the power of the people. Love it or hate it, but to be able to speak on your own terms.

The court system is a blatant example, you go through the whole process. The motions and everything, and you can't say nothing. I'm in the court one time standing there, the lawyers talking about, "Judge, I'm gonna be playing golf that week. How does August 5 look for you?" I'm listening, they running a whole false narrative about me, but I'm told, "Don't say nothing." It comes a time where people say, "I gotta speak, man. What I got to lose?" So we heighten the contradictions.

Police had a turn-your-gun-in campaign, you got people just emotional in Chicago. Which it's known, in Norfolk railroad dropping them guns, and automatic weapons in those babies' hands. It's known about the history of the Woodlawn experiment. People come back later on and it got exposed the guns that were planted on people came from the guns that other people turned in. People said, "Chairman Fred, you never did support that." I said, "I couldn't go against it, I couldn't fight your emotions." We gonna be consistent. Marcus Garvey said, "When all else fails to organize the people, conditions will."

Etan: So how do we hold the police accountable? Do we need to stop worrying about that part? Do we need to go back to self-policing our own communities and just keep them out?

Hampton Jr.: Heighten the contradictions. The police are some of the taxed apparatus of the system. Why do you think they have to put so much propaganda and resources into these programs that are here to help us? There's basic contradictions, such as why don't police live in our respective communities that police us? It's a consistent contradiction. The merchants in our stores and in our communities—if they were forced to eat the slop that they sell us in the hood, they wouldn't go along with this.

The police go through other communities. Go try and find out where sirens are played loud riding through your neighborhood? You don't even hear a siren. This is past the racist Derek Chauvin police. This is the policies. You don't turn your siren on, you don't flash your lights, you don't come through and disturb the community, because that traumatizes people. These are policies. I'm not copping no pleas for Derek Chauvin, you know what his defense should have been? All these police getting up there and testified that they don't know what's wrong with this dude, he doing this and that. At some point say, "You know what, wait a minute. Run the video footage of all his partners. Why wasn't there a look of shock and awe? So evidently, this is the modus operandi. Nobody said nothing, that that was an aberration. Heighten the contradictions. You be surprised what a little bit of pressure would do. You be surprised what the Sandinista said in Latin America: "The will of the people is greater than the man's technology." You seen the lieutenants in Derek Chauvin's trial, you seen all of them saying they ain't gonna snitch on him. Put a little pressure on, you'd be surprised. He was probably so shocked when they told him to go to the back room, he probably thought they was just playing. It's a different climate now.

Etan: After Trump, Biden was a breath of fresh air. The bar was extremely low.

Hampton Jr.: I still ain't breathing.

Etan: I hear you 100 percent. People seem to be relaxed a little bit now that Trump is out of office. They're not really paying attention to everything like they were before. Biden had the George Floyd family come up. They had a whole lot of things that were, in my opinion, for optics. He was hugging the girl, saying he was going to give her some ice cream, hugging the mom. But no bills being passed. I'm tired of the window dressing, of the smoke and mirrors. Symbolism and symbolic gestures. Is it time for our people to be tired of that as well?

Hampton Jr.: That was about it. So well articulated by Fannie Lou Hamer, Atlanta City, Georgia, when she spoke at the Democratic Convention. The position was they would give, and allow her, for Lawrence County, Alabama. You couldn't vote, but we'd give you two nonvoting seats. Image posturing. Fannie Lou Hamer said, we ain't march all the way down here for no two nonvoting seats. "We sick and tired of being sick and tired." And she left up outta there.

I tell people, I'm not into this for no attention. I been getting attention from the police my whole life, surveillance. People today can be specialists on the Black Panther Party. People say stuff about the Black Panther Party and Black people that they wouldn't say about or to a mechanic, athlete, or an entertainer. I went to the Hip-Hop Summit, they had the whole script written. They explained how Ludacris was going to speak for us. We said, "Wait up, hold on. Stop the car. We don't go up in the studio and write they lyrics. We speak for ourselves." But it was a forgone conclusion.

Where I struggle, it's a battle for self-determination and also we must acknowledge that everyone does not want the same thing. We have to be clear on that. Some people cool with just the image, to be popular. With our people, it's done so much with us, other people have variables and we have to say, "No disrespect but period." Even if it's the reaction to say we not going for this.

There are policies that say whatever police are going into our communities. When I say policy, people start, "I ain't got time to do all that reading." I tell people all the time, "Flip the script." What do it mean? Apply to your organization, your people, and see if it sound respectful or disrespectful. We had a situation with one of the gas stations in our community, the merchant was talking to the sister, we went up there. I said, "Flip the script." We come to your community and say that to the women, imagine us. He said, "Whoa." He said, "I never knew." I said, "You never been forced to look at it that way. That's all. I don't have to do a whole dialogue with you."

Imagine you go into your stores or your community, imagine turning on a white radio station with the stuff that's being said to our children. Imagine you come out, police killing your family, you gotta fight to reveal the name of who killed them. Imagine all the killings in *Chi-Raq*, people say, "I don't like the word." You don't like the word? How you feel about the situation? If all the killers in Chicago, today, I'm throwing a number out there: at least twenty people shot. Imagine reading that, and changing the narrative. Take the name of the Black people out of there and say, "Twenty white poodles shot today in Chicago." Could you imagine the response? Take the number and just say "poodles" or "dogs." You wouldn't have no conversation like, "This dog-on-dog crime is getting horrible." Somebody's gonna say, "There has to be some higher-ups involved in this. I just can't see simultaneously all us just dying."

Etan: How do you want to be remembered?

Hampton Jr.: Damn.

Etan: Take your time. We ain't in a hurry.

Hampton Jr.: I was somewhere yesterday. It was an event for this new media outlet called Our Black Truth, shout out to them, I'm studying it right now. I went in there and a lady said, "Frank Sinatra? When I hear the *Chairman*, I think of Frank Sinatra." We made a joke and said, "Nah, he said he did it his way. We doing it *our* way. This for the people. We are the service of the people." There is an old African proverb, *What is good for the family may not be good for the community. What's good for the community is good for the family and the community.* I am honored and humbled to be a servant of the people.

Etan: That was perfect. Much respect to you, sir.

What do you see when you look at me?
BY MALCOLM THOMAS

What do you see when you look at me?
A threat, a menace, or a human being?
Could you turn on your TV screen and see the police beat me like a dog
    and not feel a thing?
Would you ask what did I do to deserve them beating me like Rodney King?
Or would you say let's wait until the facts come out like Tucker Carlson or
    Sean Hannity?
Would you Fox News me?
Pull up every indiscretion throughout my entire life for the world to see?
Would you go back to middle school or elementary?
Find a picture of me posing or scowling in a selfie?
To convince white America to not feel so bad about what the police just
    did to me?

Would you treat me like the Central Park Five?
Assassinate my character like Trump and Giuliani did to five innocent
    teenagers?
And even to this day have yet to apologize
or they use creative tricks to justify what the police did to terrorize me and
    believe every word that came out of their mouths.

Would they itemize trumped-up charges against me like they did Chikesia
    Clemons after beating her in a Waffle House?

Lil Baby is my guy but is it really bigger than Black and white?
Because I don't see white people treated with the lack of humanity that
    Black and Brown people are every day and every night.

White people can:
Not obey commands
Cuss out the police
Actually possess weapons
Or be Mass murderers
And still won't be brutalized.

Dylann Roof murdering nine people in a Charleston church and the police
     bringing
him Burger King with soda and fries.
But you wanna answer our Black Lives
Matter with All Lives?
When in history have white lives ever not
mattered, but you've ignored our cries.

Trump supporters can storm the US Capitol and still escape with their lives.
But resource officers will body slam teenage girls on the concrete for rolling
     their eyes.
So yeah, it is a problem with their whole way of life.

You think George Floyd was the only case?
The police kill brothas every day, B, they're just not all caught on tape.
And if it weren't for seventeen-year-old Darnella Frazier whipping out her
     phone and pressing record, we would've never known anything about
     George Floyd's fate.
Their initial report before the video came out conveniently left out the part
     about Derek Chauvin having his knee on his neck for nine minutes.
And how the police took it upon themselves to be the judge, jury, and
     executioner to carry out his death penalty sentence.
And all of that for a suspected counterfeit twenty-dollar bill and alleged
     resistance.

But you want me to have faith in a system that
consistently carries out that type of injustice?
Man, listen!!!

My momma didn't raise no fool,
so stop trying to school me with your smoke and mirrors,
to make me think you're bringing me clearer or closer to justice.
I don't need a Steph Curry hesi to pause on your rusted premise.
You keep playing the white supremacy card.

Breonna Taylor, Botham Jean, Atatiana Jefferson, Willie McCoy, Sean
    Monterrosa, and so many more have left me feeling scarred.
Like trusting the system would make me look gullible in the eyes of God,
because He gave me enough wisdom to see through frauds.
We don't need symbolic gestures, we need real change.
No sensitivity training videos, just holding police accountable when they
    murder us in vain.

It's really that simple.
Checks and balances.
Don't tell me you're investigating yourself and you did nothing wrong.
Blue lips have sang that song for decades and many more.
Stop telling me it's just a few bad apples and not the whole system that's
    rotten to the core.

But you wanna trip on the word *defund* as if budget cuts don't happen
    literally every fiscal year.

It's great that attorney Ben Crump gets the families paid, but no amount of
    money can replace the loss of your loved one being slain.
And to make matters worse,
there is literally nothing being done to actually stop it.

Why don't they take away the murdering cops' pensions?
Or make the settlements have to go through the cops' own individual in-
    surances so they no longer come out of the taxpayers' pockets.

But you're trying to rock me to sleep with lullabies of having faith in the
    police?

You think I don't know that cops were originally created for slave-patrol
    duty?
Their jobs were to
locate and return my enslaved ancestors who had escaped,
crush potential uprisings,
make sure nobody was learning to read or going to school,
and punish any of my enslaved ancestors who violated any plantation rules.

Back then they hung us from trees.
Today they use Derek Chavin's knees.

The system is working exactly how it was originally designed to be.
This country wasn't founded on Christianity,
it was founded on white supremacy.

White evangelicals are so consumed with their so-called superiority that it's
    been impossible to even see a glimmer of Christ in thee.

Instead of actually doing God's work,
like the original Coptic church,
they intertwined their God complex, perverting what was meant for good
    and making it evil.
They actually used Christianity to justify enslaving an entire group of people,
and now they wanna whitewash their history with a nice red, white, and
    blue bow,
tie it neatly together with promises of freedom, justice, and equality at the
    end of the rainbow.
Instead of reparations for your crimes,
you wanna rid any trace of accuracy out of history books to keep the truth hid.
If you were truly sorry, you would at least teach the truth to your kids.
Then they could abandon your wicked ways instead of being unaware of
    the white privilege in which they live,
so if they ever did see me being beaten by the police, they would actually
    look at me like a human being,
and their first thought wouldn't be, *What did he do to deserve what the police
    officers just did?*

Resources

Lora Dene King
I Am a King scholarship

Raymond Santana
parkmadisonnyc.com
innocenceproject.org
The Central Park Five documentary: pbs.org/kenburns/the-central-park-five/;
based on the book *The Central Park Five: The Untold Story Behind New York's Most Infamous Crime*, by Sarah Burns
Docudrama series *When They See Us*: netflix.com/title/80200549

Officer Carlton Berkley
100 Blacks in Law Enforcement Who Care: blacksnlaw.tripod.com
Email: Chucky438@optonline.net

Kori McCoy
The Willie McCoy Foundation: thewilliemccoyfoundation.com
The Secrets of the Rabbit Hole Media Network: thesecretsoftherabbithole.com

Officer Joe Ested
Police Brutality Matters: policebrutalitymatters.com

Chikesia Clemons
Follow Chikesia on Twitter to learn when she is running her community events: twitter.com/chikesiaclemons

Captain Sonia Pruitt
Black Police Experience: therealbpx.com

Sisters of the Movement
sistersofthemovement.org
Email: contactus@sistersofthemovement.org

Alissa Findley

The Botham Jean Foundation: bothamjeanfoundation.org

Ashley and Amber Carr

The Atatiana Project: linktr.ee/atatiana_project

Emerald Garner

WeCantBreathe.net

Related Foundations

georgefloydmemorialfoundation.org

justiceforbreonna.org

philandocastilefoundation.org

notreaching.com/why-not-reaching

trayvonmartinfoundation.org

garnerwayfoundation.org

terencecrutcherfoundation.org

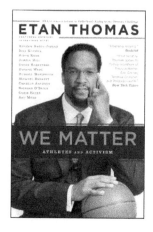